The European Union and British Politics

CONTEMPORARY POLITICAL STUDIES SERIES

Series Editor: John Benyon, University of Leicester

Published

DAVID BROUGHTON
Public Opinion and Political Polling in
Britain

MICHAEL CONNOLLY
Politics and Policy Making in
Northern Ireland

DAVID DENVER
Elections and Voters in Britain

JUSTIN FISHER
British Political Parties

ROBERT GARNER
Environmental Politics: Britain, Europe and
the Global Environment; 2nd edn

ANDREW GEDDES
The European Union and British Politics

WYN GRANT
Pressure Groups and British Politics

WYN GRANT
Economic Policy in Britain

DEREK HEATER and GEOFFREY BERRIDGE
Introduction to International Politics

DILYS M. HILL
Urban Policy and Politics in Britain

ROBERT LEACH
Political Ideology in Britain

ROBERT LEACH and JANIE PERCY-SMITH
Local Governance in Britain

PETER MADGWICK
British Government: The Central
Executive Territory

PHILIP NORTON
Does Parliament Matter?

MALCOLM PUNNETT
Selecting the Party Leader

ROBERT PYPER
The British Civil Service

Forthcoming

CLYDE CHITTY
Education Policy in Britain

RAYMOND KUHN
Politics and the Media in Britain

ANDREW MASSEY and ROBERT PYPER
The New Public Management and
Modernization in Britain

The European Union and British Politics

Andrew Geddes

First published 2004 by
PALGRAVE MACMILLAN
Houndmills, Basingstoke, Hampshire RG21 6XS and
175 Fifth Avenue, New York, N.Y. 10010
Companies and representatives throughout the world

PALGRAVE MACMILLAN is the global academic imprint of the Palgrave Macmillan division of St. Martin's Press, LLC and of Palgrave Macmillan Ltd. Macmillan® is a registered trademark in the United States, United Kingdom and other countries. Palgrave is a registered trademark in the European Union and other countries.

ISBN 0–333–98120–0 hardback
ISBN 0–333–98121–9 paperback

This book is printed on paper suitable for recycling and made from fully managed and sustained forest sources.

A catalogue record for this book is available from the British Library.

Library of Congress Cataloging-in-Publication Data
Geddes, Andrew, 1965–
      The European Union and British politics / Andrew Geddes.
         p. cm. – (Contemporary political studies)
      Includes bibliographical references and index.
      ISBN 0–333–98120–0 (hardback)
         1. European Union – Great Britain. 2. Great Britain – Politics and government – 1964–1979. 3. Great Britain – Politics and government – 1979–1997. 4. Great Britain – Politics and government – 1997–
      I. Title. II. Contemporary political studies (Palgrave Macmillan (Firm))

HC240.25.G7G44 2004
327.4104—dc22   2003053623

10 9 8 7 6 5 4 3 2 1
13 12 11 10 09 08 07 06 05 04

Printed and bound by Creative Print and Design (Wales) Ltd, Ebbw Vale.

Per Fede

Contents

List of Tables, Figures and Boxes

Tables

Figures

Boxes

Acknowledgements

I would like to thank John Corner, Neil Gavin, Steven Fielding, Robert Geyer, Richard Gillespie, Yvonne Noor Jannah Janvier, David Richards and Jonathan Tonge for help in the preparation of this book and Ian Holliday, whose idea it was in the first place. David Baker, Julie Firmstone, Andrew Gamble, Emily Gray and Andrew Russell were a great help during the preparation of the manuscript when they participated in a seminar series on Britain and Europe organized within the Europe in the World Centre at Liverpool University. I am also very grateful to Steven Kennedy at Palgrave Macmillan for his expert editorial advice.

The author and publishers would like to thank the Audit Bureau of Circulation for permission to reproduce national newspaper circulation data; HM Customs and Excise for permission to reproduce Table 7.1; the Office for the Official Publications of the European Union for permission to reproduce Tables 3.1, 3.2 and 10.1 and for the use of other data from their publications *Eurobarometer* and *European Economy*; the Office of the European Parliament in the UK for permission to reproduce Tables 6.7, 6.8 and 6.9 and for the use of other European elections data; HM Stationery Office for permission to reprouce Figures 7.1 and 7.2 and the use of other material from government publications and parliamentary debates under Click Licence C02W0003371; Taylor & Francis Publishers, Professor Martin Burch and Dr Ricardo Gomez for permission to use data from an article published in *Regional Studies*; Blackwell Publishers and Professor Ed Page for permission to reproduce Table 8.1 from an article published in *Public Administration*.

Every effort has been made to contact all copyright-holders, but if any have been inadvertently omitted the publishers rule be pleased to make the necessary arrangement at the earliest opportunity.

ANDREW GEDDES

List of Abbreviations

BCEM	British Council of the European Movement
BIE	Britain in Europe
BSE	Bovine Spongiform Encephalopathy
CAP	Common Agricultural Policy
CEC	Commission of the European Communities
CFSP	Common Foreign and Security Policy
CIE	Committee of Independent Experts
CMSC	Common Market Safeguards Campaign
COREPER	Council of Permanent Representatives
DEFRA	Department for the Environment, Food and Rural Affairs
DoE	Department of the Environment
DTI	Department of Trade and Industry
EC	European Community
ECHR	European Convention on Human Rights
ECJ	European Court of Justice
ECOFIN	Economic and Finance Council of Ministers
ECSC	European Coal and Steel Community
EDC	European Defence Community
EEC	European Economic Community
EFTA	European Free Trade Area
EMS	European Monetary System
EMU	Economic and Monetary Union
EP	European Parliament
EPC	European Political Co-operation
EQ	Economic Association Committee
ERM	Exchange Rate Mechanism
ESDP	European Security and Defence Policy
EU	European Union
EUF	European Union of Federalists
FCO	Foreign and Commonwealth Office
FRG	Federal Republic of Germany
FSG	Fresh Start Group
GDR	German Democratic Republic
GNP	Gross National Product

IGC	Intergovernmental Conference
JHA	Justice and Home Affairs
KBO	Keep Britain Out
MAFF	Ministry of Agriculture, Fisheries and Food
MEP	Member of the European Parliament
MP	Member of Parliament
NAFTA	North American Free Trade Area
NATO	North Atlantic Treaty Organisation
NRC	National Referendum Campaign
ODP (E)	Overseas and Defence Policy Committee
OEEC	Organisation for European Economic Co-operation
PR	Proportional Representation
QMV	Qualified Majority Voting
SDP	Social Democratic Party
SEA	Single European Act
SI	Statutory Instrument
UKIP	UK Independence Party
UKRep	UK Permanent Representation
VAT	Value Added Tax
WEU	West European Union
WTO	World Trade Organisation

1

The European Union and British Politics

Introduction

Why can't Britain be a little more European or Europe a little more British? Such have been the plaintive cries of many British politicians since Britain joined the European Community in 1973. While European politics have been transformed during the last 50 years by economic and political integration within the European Union (EU), Britain has been marginal to some key developments (Economic and Monetary Union – or EMU – and the Euro being the latest), failed to resolve basic tensions that have long characterized relations with the EU, and displayed levels of public support for European integration that tend to lag behind those in other member states. This is because European integration asks fundamental questions about Britain's place in the world, about national self-understanding and about its laws, economy, political system and policy priorities. Other member states have been asked similar questions too, but for various reasons most have been willing to accept or embrace the changes that European integration has brought with it. Britain has been less enthusiastic.

Analyses of Britain's role within the EU have tended to focus on 'reluctance', 'awkwardness' and 'semi-detachment' (George, 1992, 1998; Gowland and Turner, 2000). From this perspective the story reads as follows: Britain stood aside from the first steps towards European integration and has spent a good part of the time since accession in 1973 agonizing about the EU's shape, form, scope and direction. The result is that British vacillation has occurred from the sidelines rather than in 'the heart of Europe', and this is a shortcoming or failing that strikes at the heart of

British politics. A quick checklist of this 'awkwardness' could highlight the following:

- did not join the first supranational European organization, the European Coal and Steel Community (ECSC), when it was founded in 1951
- did not take seriously the Messina negotiations in 1955 that led to the Treaty of Rome
- made unsuccessful applications in 1961–3 and 1967
- experienced divisions within and between the main parties in the late 1960s and early 1970s on membership
- sought a renegotiation of the terms of accession soon after joining in 1973
- fought a divisive 1975 referendum on the renegotiated terms
- disputed its level of contributions to the EEC budget (this heated discussion intensified after the election of Margaret Thatcher as Prime Minister in 1979 and was not resolved until 1984)
- a civil war within the Labour Party over Britain's EC membership became a core bone of contention that led to the creation of the break-away Social Democratic Party comprising more pro-European figures
- Margaret Thatcher's Bruges speech in 1988 asserted a vision of a Europe of nation states and opposed key aspects of the plans for future European integration
- the resignation on European issues of six cabinet ministers during Margaret Thatcher's time as Prime Minister (Leon Brittan, Michael Heseltine, Nigel Lawson, Nicholas Ridley, Sir Geoffrey Howe and finally Thatcher herself)
- Thatcher's demise as Prime Minister in 1990 was linked to her increasingly vociferous Euroscepticism
- the Maastricht Treaty of 1992 and the subsequent civil war within the Conservative Party
- sterling's ejection in September 1992 from the Exchange Rate Mechanism (ERM)
- the ejection from the Parliamentary Conservative Party in November 1994 of the 'gang of eight' Eurosceptic Members of Parliament (MPs)
- John Major's 'put up or shut up' challenge in June 1995 to Conservative Eurosceptics. Major called a leadership election. John Redwood stood as a candidate of the Eurosceptic right against Major. Redwood lost, but the rebels did not shut up as Major had hoped they would
- the bovine spongiform encephalopathy (BSE) crisis in 1996 and the ensuing British beef ban by other EU member states that had highly damaging effects on British agriculture

- the 'war on terrorism' and the conflict in Iraq exposed once again tensions between UK Atlanticism and competing calls for closer relations with key EU states, particularly France and Germany
- the Labour government led by Tony Blair had by 2003 still to clearly resolve its attitude towards what had become the EU's defining project: the creation of EMU and the establishment of the single currency, the Euro.

This is a long list, although Britain has not uniquely been Europe's 'awkward partner'. Other member states can be 'awkward' or 'reluctant' too, while some European countries (such as Norway and Switzerland) have chosen not to become members. Moreover, Britain has engaged relatively enthusiastically with some forms of co-operation and integration with other European countries, such as defence and foreign policy co-operation through the North Atlantic Treaty Organisation (NATO), as well as single market integration within the EU. But crucially Britain has been on the sidelines for key steps in economic and political integration, both when the organization was founded in the 1950s and more recently with EMU and the Euro. Public opinion data show that British people declare less knowledge of, interest in, and confidence in the EU than citizens in other EU member states, whilst they are also more likely to construe the EU as a threat to national identity. To give two examples: in the spring of 2002, the Commission published its regular 'Eurobarometer' opinion poll gauging pan-EU public opinion. Figure 1.1 shows there was a majority in the UK in support of European integration,

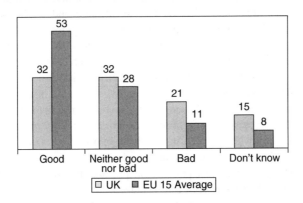

Figure 1.1   Support for European Union membership (%)
Source: Data from *Eurobarometer Standard Report* (Spring 2002).

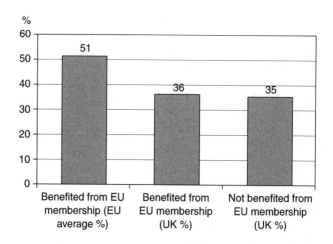

Figure 1.2   Benefit from European Union membership
Source: Data from *Eurobarometer Standard Report* (Spring 2002).

albeit at a level lower than in other member states. Figure 1.2 shows that when asked the question of whether they felt that Britain had benefited from EU membership, UK responses revealed only a small majority of 1 per cent who believed that membership had been beneficial.

Yet despite evidence of a relative lack of support for European integration, it is a political fact of life in contemporary British politics that Britain has become progressively more integrated with other EU member states in both economic and political terms. Why then, given that British political elites have at times been divided on the question and public opinion has been sceptical, has Britain become quite so engaged with European integration across such a wide range of issues? How does this tally with national self-understanding, with competing ties such as the alliance with the USA, and with the organization of British political, economic and social systems? This book attempts to unravel the extent of this engagement while also explaining the scepticism and reluctance. It explores these from a historical perspective in order to examine continuity and change in British relations with the EU, while also exploring the ways in which European integration has become absorbed within the organizational and conceptual logics of British politics; or, put another way, the extent to which British politics has been Europeanized.

To attain these objectives the book examines Britain's *conditional* and *differential* engagement with the EU. The engagement is conditional in the sense that identification with the EU seems not to be deep-seated and appears based on pragmatic calculations about costs and benefits rather than any attachment to European ideals. It is differential in the sense that some areas of British political life have clearly been more affected than others. It is argued that decisions made in the 1950s and 1960s about Britain's role and future and the extent of its engagement with nascent EU institutions had important structuring effects on the context within which later decisions about engagement with European integration were made after accession in 1973. To use the terminology of historical institutionalist theory, a 'path' of Euro-ambivalence was established in the 1950s from which it has subsequently been hard to deviate, with the attendant consequence that 'Europe' has not become deeply embedded within the preferences, identities and interests of either Britain's political elite or its population. At the same time the European context has changed with other actors (EU institutions, other member states, pressure groups, sub-national government) becoming more deeply involved in the decision-making process with the effect that national central governments have become one of many centres in an integrating Europe. Thus Britain's half-hearted, conditional and essentially defensive 'choice for Europe' has also been exposed to the dynamics of new forms of supranational political integration that challenge some of the core underlying premises of British politics.

Britain in Europe and Europe in Britain

The book's objectives can be broken down into two linked themes. The 'Britain in Europe' theme centres on analysis of British relations with the EU and the role of British governments in attempting to shape Europe's institutional architecture. The focus here is on inter-state relations and exploration of the UK's role within the EU and the attitudes of various UK governments to the development of European integration over the last 50 years. This shows the ways in which Britain has engaged (or not) with European integration since the 1950s and how Britain has sought to use its influence in the councils of Europe across the wide range of policy issues with which the EU is concerned. Britain's European policy has contained three central elements based on perceptions of the UK, its interests and its place in the world, as set out below:

1   A preference for intergovernmental structures that enshrine the central role and legitimate authority of national governments. This combines with a dislike for 'federal' solutions to European problems

and a self-consciously pragmatic attitude to discussions of grand projects and the EU's *finalité* (or final destination).

2   A strong emphasis on the Atlantic alliance as the core element of British foreign policy, which was an approach reaffirmed by Tony Blair in 2003 in a speech to UK ambassadors when he spoke of the UK as a bridge between Europe and the USA. The war in Iraq gave a practical demonstration of this central tenet of British foreign policy.

3   A preference in the realm of the international political economy for arrangements that promote global free trade, which over 20 years or so has become support for measures that promote market liberalization of the European economy.

The kinds of question raised by the Britain in Europe theme include the following. What factors have motivated British policy towards the EU? Have British governments possessed the capacity to turn preferences into EU priorities? Have British governments been particularly effective players of the EU game? How have British policies towards the EU changed over time, and what factors have contributed to these changes?

The second of the book's elements can be called the 'Europe in Britain' theme. This involves analysis of the extent to which European integration has been absorbed into the logic of British domestic politics. The kinds of question that are explored include the following. What impact has European integration had on the organization of the British political system (including decision-making in Whitehall, the organization of the British polity and the role of sub-national government)? To what extent do British policy priorities and the organization of the British economy and welfare state fit with those in other member states and with an emerging EU model? What impact has European integration had on debates within and between the main political parties? In what directions have public attitudes towards the EU developed and what part has the mass media played in shaping these views?

A key advantage of combining the 'Britain in Europe' theme with the 'Europe in Britain' theme is that it prevents the simplistic assumption that European integration simply 'happens' to the UK as though the EU were a supernatural phenomenon with its own mysterious powers, rather than a supranational organization of which Britain is a leading member. 'Europe' does not just happen when government ministers fly to Brussels, Luxembourg or Strasbourg to meet ministerial and official colleagues from other member states or deal with EU institutions located in those cities. If this were so then this would imply that decisions made at EU level would follow a simple and inexorable logic of integration driven by higher forces that render it both inevitable and detached from national politics. This is conspiracy theory, not serious analysis. It is more useful to identify the ways in which British governments have consciously chosen European integration, the reasons for and effects of these choices, and the ways in which economic and political integration have then become integrated as central concerns in British politics. European integration is not simply a foreign policy issue because it works its way into domestic decision-making structures. These structures refract rather than simply absorb European integration's effects. Analysis of the ways in which the British political system shapes or is shaped (and perhaps transformed) by European integration provides a key perspective on British relations with the EU and on other key changes in British politics, while also facilitating understanding of the 'Europeanization' of British politics without assuming that the nature of British political change is uni-directional and linked exclusively to the impact of European integration. Europe is but one potential source of British political change.

This can be better understood if the UK political system is seen as nested within a series of interlocking relationships that extends 'down' to the sub-national and 'up' to the supranational, as represented in Figure 1.3. The diagram is intended to illustrate the ways in which intensive links between levels of government leads to overlap in terms of authority and competence and to a sharing of power between the various levels of government with regard to some of their key functions. The key circle remains the 'national' circle, although both devolved power to Britain's

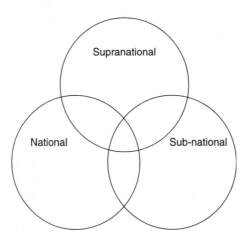

Figure 1.3   The European Union's multi-level system

sub-state nations as well as integration within the EU have weakened this national circle. Furthermore, the ways in which sub-national, national and supranational government are enmeshed indicates the extent to which British politics and policy become Europeanized, understood as the impacts of European integration on laws, institutions, policies and collective identities in Britain (Radaelli, 2000).

Organization of the book

This book aims to assess Britain's role in the EU and the EU's impacts on British politics. This introductory chapter has sketched some fundamental themes:

- Chapter 2 extends the analysis to explore explanations for British 'awkwardness' and contends that the ways in which domestic institutional structures refract the impacts of European integration need to be central to analysis of the EU and British politics.
- One of the more baffling and off-putting aspects of the EU is the terminology and jargon. The survey of 'Eurospeak' in Chapter 3 seeks to clarify some of the terms and concepts that are used when analysing the EU.
- Britain's relations with emerging structures of European economic and political integration as well as the influences of competing calls from the USA and the Commonwealth are considered in Chapter 4. Central to this are the positions of British governments at the time of the Treaty of Paris (1951), the Treaty of Rome (1957) and the failed membership applications of 1961–3 and 1967.
- Chapter 5 assesses Britain's role within the EU since accession on 1 January 1973. This chapter also begins to develop the Britain in Europe theme through evaluation of the stances of successive British governments on key issues such as the Single European Act (1986), the Maastricht Treaty (1992), the Amsterdam Treaty (1997) and the Nice Treaty (2000). The pace of European integration has quickened considerably since the mid-1980s as the profusion of Treaties since the Single European Act indicates. As the pace has quickened, so has the capacity of European integration to strike at the heart of British politics.
- Chapter 6 analyses the role of the EU's main institutions (the Council of Ministers, the European Council, the European Commission, the European Parliament, and the European Court of Justice) and explores the attitudes of British governments to these institutions, as well as the ways in which the development of law-making capacity

at supranational level affects some of the fundamental precepts of British politics.

- Chapter 7 assesses key EU policies. A particular concern in this chapter is to illustrate the 'fit' between EU socio-economic priorities and those pursued in the UK. The chapter examines agricultural policy, competition and industrial policy, environmental policy, social policy, economic and monetary policies, foreign and security policies, and internal security policies.

- Chapter 8 looks at the 'fit' between the organization of the British polity and EU structures. This chapter explores the ways in which the organization of the British state has affected the ability to deal with the EU. The chapter also explores the changes in the national 'circle' of British politics marked by devolved power to Scotland and Wales, as well as other trends in British patterns of governance (such as privatization and other instances of changed patterns of governance) which have been seen to 'hollow out' the British state.

- Chapter 9 examines the impact of European integration on British party politics. The stances of the main political parties on European integration are outlined and the debates within and between the parties on European integration are evaluated. The most vigorous and divisive debates have often occurred *within* rather than *between* the parties as the civil wars of the Labour Party (in the 1980s) and the Conservative Party (since the 1990s) demonstrate.

- Chapter 10 then assesses British public attitudes towards European integration and assesses the impact of media outlets on debates about and understandings of the EU. What are the views of British people on key EU questions? How do they compare with the views in other member states? From where do people get their information on the EU? To what extent are people's outlooks on the EU shaped by what they see, hear and read?

The book concludes with an assessment of the influence of these factors and some reflections on Britain's place in this transformed EU. The overall aim is to assess the conditional and differential engagement with the EU. As has already been noted, it is usual to encounter analyses of Britain's role within the EU that highlight UK's inability to come to terms with key aspects of European integration. This is an important question and one that this book addresses. But it is equally pertinent to ask why – given evident scepticism at both elite and popular level about 'the European project' – Britain has become quite so engaged with the EU; where are these points of engagement and how can the differential nature of this engagement be explained?

2

Britain on the Edge of Europe

Introduction

This chapter sketches some background on the EU and provides information on its key features, as well as its historical and political developments. It then suggests a series of factors that could explain British attitudes towards European integration. Various possible explanations are put forward for 'awkwardness', 'reluctance' and 'semi-detachment', such as Britain's geographical position and its distinct history, before it is argued that the ways in which the domestic political context refracts the impacts of European integration needs to be central to the analysis. The insight that domestic politics 'matter' and the ways in which domestic political structures both shape and are shaped by British relations with the EU is not something that is unique to the UK. All member states adapt to European integration in ways that accord with domestic political logics (Bulmer, 1983). Moreover, European integration can strengthen rather than weaken European states (Moravcsik, 1994). Thus we could hypothesize that the organization of the British political system refracts rather than simply reflects European integration effects and that in those areas that tally with domestic political preferences there may well be British support for European integration if the attainment of domestic political objectives will be made more likely. Similarly, if EU objectives do not accord with British preferences then reluctance or awkwardness could be anticipated.

What are we talking about?

While the EU casts an increasingly long shadow over many of the key issues in contemporary British politics it is important to remember that some key political concerns that have been central to recent general elections such as health care, education and law and order remain essentially national concerns. Even so, Britain's economy is closely tied to that of other EU member states while hot-tempered disputes over European integration and the divisions they caused were central to the electoral obliteration of the Conservative Party at the 1997 and 2001 general elections. But while politicians and newspapers have at times seemed obsessed by the European issue and its implications for, among other things, the slippery concept of 'national sovereignty', the British people remained distinctly underwhelmed and far less interested in the EU than the political elites because the EU can seem remote from people's day-to-day concerns about employment, health care, education and so on.

A key element of EU is that it is supranational: this means that in certain areas, such as trade and agriculture, the member states have ceded power, or sovereignty, to Union-level institutions to make decisions which are legally binding on them. This supranationalism is both a central and a controversial aspect of the EU. Its implications for Britain are a key aspect of this book.

One puzzling aspect of analysing European integration is the plethora of terms used to describe it: the EU, the European Economic Community (EEC), the European Community (EC), the Common Market, the Union and the Community, to name six. It may be even more puzzling that basically all refer to the same organization. The key point is that the Maastricht Treaty (1992) created the European Union and, since the Treaty was finally ratified in November 1993, it has become usual to see references to the EU. This is the term most frequently employed throughout this book. At various points, however, readers are likely to encounter other terms or acronyms such as the Common Market, the EEC or EC. All these terms have historical, legal or political importance. To highlight their significance and explain the development of European integration, terms other than the EU will be used when appropriate. These situations will be clearly explained and the relation between these terms and acronyms and what we now know as the EU will become evident. When analysing events before the Maastricht Treaty that created the EU, it is accurate to refer to the EEC, EC or Community, as will often be done in the book's earlier chapters. Also, it should be noted that when terms such as 'Britain' and 'the British government' are used they are shorthand terms that refer to the far more complex workings of the British political and administrative systems. Even at times when the great ship of state has appeared to be proceeding serenely, there has been furious activity in the engine rooms below.

EU facts and figures

The total EU population in 2002 was just over 380 million (see Table 2.1), the largest member country being the reunified Germany created in 1991 following the collapse of the German Democratic Republic (GDR). For comparison, the USA has a population of 288 million, and Japan a population of 126 million. The population of an enlarged EU is likely to rise to close to 500 million people during the first decade of the twenty-first century.

The web of interdependence created by ever-stronger trading links means that the economic health of individual member states depends increasingly on the prosperity of their Union partners. Consequently prosperity becomes a collective endeavour. Unfortunately for Britain it joined the EC in 1973 at the very moment when EC economies entered the recession that followed the increase in oil prices. European integration moved into a period of stagnation. Moreover, British membership in 1973 was not the mark of a wholehearted conversion to European integration. Economic recession then raised further doubts about the benefits of membership. Recession and the Exchange Rate Mechanism (ERM) crisis in the early 1990s prompted similar misgivings. As the EU becomes central to

Table 2.1   Population of the EU and its 15 member states in 2002

Country	Population ('000)
Austria	8,159
Belgium	10,344
Denmark	5,377
Finland	5,210
France	61,826
Germany	82,464
Greece	11,005
Ireland	4,012
Italy	58,227
Luxembourg	454.0
Netherlands	16,133
Portugal	10,330
Spain	41,051
Sweden	8,989
UK	60,447
EU15	382,091

Source: Data from *European Economy*, Commission of the European Communities (2002a), accessed October 2003.

member state economies so economic problems tend to be laid at the door of the Union. Support for integration dwindles during hard times, yet there is no doubt that EU membership has also at times been linked with high growth rates. Whether there are relationships of cause and effect here is of course disputable.

Table 2.2 shows gross domestic product per capita as a percentage of their average for the 15 countries that were EU member states as of 2002. The relative economic decline and recovery of Britain is striking. By this measure, the UK was the fourth richest EU member state in 2002 having languished in twelfth place in the mid-1990s, although the strength of sterling did contribute to this resurgence. Britain has become a more confident EU member state based on this improved economic performance. Debates about membership in the 1960s and 1970s were set against a picture of apparent national decline. Arguments about the Euro since the 1990s can often rest on a more confident understanding of the national position. These improvements are often attributed to market-based economic and social reforms that were instigated during the Thatcher era and that have continued since, but which do not always find favour in other member states. Indeed, this preference for market liberalization is a key element of Britain's EU policy.

The EU is both an economic and a political entity, and seeks integration at both levels. The precise link between these two processes is, however,

Table 2.2 Gross domestic product per capita at current market prices (EU15 = 100), 1960–2002

	1960	*1970*	*1980*	*1990*	*2000*	*2002*
Austria	85.1	84.8	104.3	109.3	113.1	111.2
Belgium	115	112.8	122.5	103.4	107.0	106.0
Denmark	123.3	140.3	132.4	135.7	144.3	145.5
Finland	108.2	102.5	108.7	143.4	112.3	112.4
France	124.1	120.3	122.7	109.2	103.6	103.0
Germany	120.6	129.2	130.4	124.0	109.4	107.2
Greece	41.4	54.3	49.8	43.2	51.7	53.5
Ireland	63.2	61.2	61.3	70.4	120.0	133.8
Italy	73.5	85.0	78.8	101.5	89.3	90.5
Luxembourg	177.1	148.8	142.0	151.7	208.9	203.6
Netherlands	99.1	114.5	124.7	102.9	112.0	116.0
Portugal	30.7	35.7	30.0	37.3	49.8	52.7
Spain	36.5	49.4	58.4	68.6	67.6	71.3
Sweden	179.2	182.6	153.6	145.4	124.1	116.0
UK	127.4	94.4	94.2	90.0	115.6	114.8

Source: Data from *European Economy*, Commission of the European Communities (2002a), accessed October 2003.

a matter of great contention. Some argue that economic integration should be separated from political, while others maintain that no such separation is possible. Underlying this debate is an undeniable drive towards economic integration in Europe accompanied by the development of a political-institutional framework to back up economic objectives. All statistics show that the EU is increasingly becoming a single economic area. More than 50 per cent of British trade is with other EU member states. The EU has also assumed an increased role in social and regional policies. Since 1993, all citizens of member states have become citizens of the Union. On January 2002 a single European currency, the Euro, entered circulation with national currencies in the 12 participating states phased out. Since the 1990s the EU has also tentatively entered the domain of 'high politics' that impinge far more directly on state sovereignty with increased responsibilities for foreign policy, defence co-operation, policing and border controls. As the EU becomes more concerned with such issues then questions of national authority and national identity come to the fore because foreign, defence, immigration, asylum and monetary policies impinge squarely on collective identities that have tended to be focused on nation states rather than international organizations.

There are currently 15 members of the EU, although this number will rise to as many as 28 when the next wave of accessions from central, eastern and southern Europe occur in the first decade of the twenty-first century. The EU's founders were France, West Germany, Italy, Belgium, the Netherlands and Luxembourg. In 1951 these six countries signed

Table 2.3   European Union members and dates of accession

The EC6 (1951 and 1957)	First enlargement (1973)	Second enlargement (1986)	Third enlargement (1986)	Fourth enlargement (1995)	Projected Fifth enlargement* (May 2004)
Belgium	Denmark	Greece	Portugal	Austria	Cyprus
France	Ireland		Spain	Finland	Czech Rep.
Italy	UK			Sweden	Estonia
Luxembourg					Hungary
Netherlands					Latvia
West					Lithuania
Germany					Malta
					Poland
					Slovakia
					Slovenia

* Candidates for inclusion as of Summer 2003.

Table 2.4   European Union treaty landmarks

Date	Event
1951	Treaty of Paris establishes the ECSC
1957	Treaties of Rome establish the EEC and the EAEA*
1965	The Merger Treaty creates a common institutional framework for the three 'European communities'
1970	A Treaty establishes a financing and budget system
1986	The Single European Act launches the single market programme
1992	The Maastricht Treaty puts forward a plan for EMU and closer co-operation between member states in areas of 'high politics' such as foreign policy, defence and immigration
1997	The Amsterdam Treaty denotes the EU as an area of freedom, security and justice with increased responsibility for internal security
2000	The Nice Treaty seeks the institutional reforms necessary for the absorption of up to 13 new member states

* EAEA = European Atomic Energy Authority, also known as Euratom.

the Treaty of Paris, which established the European Coal and Steel Community (ECSC). In 1957 they signed the Treaties of Rome creating the European Economic Community (or Common Market as it was known in Britain) and the European Atomic Energy Community (Euratom). The Treaty of Paris establishing the ECSC expired in July 2003 after 50 years in force. In 1973 Britain, Ireland and Denmark joined, to be followed in 1981 by Greece and in 1986 by Portugal and Spain (see Table 2.3). One effect of the 1980s enlargements was to tilt the EC's geographical axis southwards and prompt increased attention to the issues of regional development and social cohesion.

The European Union is a Treaty-bound organization in the sense that it is based on a series of Treaties negotiated between the member states that then through legislative, executive and judicial processes at European level are turned into a set of laws and rules which bind the member states (see Table 2.4).

This law-making capacity and the binding nature of these laws is a distinct and unique feature of the EU as a *supranational* organization, a term which will be analysed more fully in the next chapter. At this stage, it is important to note that this supranationalism involves the capacity of EU political and legal processes to turn treaties agreed in international law between participating states into laws that bind those states, as represented in Figure 2.1.

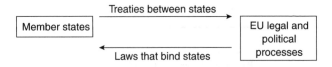

Figure 2.1   Basic features of the European Union supranational system

Until the 1980s, even though European integration's implications were important, it had tended to be rather uncontroversial because it dealt with rather technical issues associated with economic integration. European integration thus tended to centre on matters of low politics such as trade, where interdependencies were evident, rather than matters of high politics that impinged more squarely on the political identities of the member states (Hoffmann, 1966). This changed in the 1990s and the first decade of the twenty-first century as the pace of integration quickened. The highly significant and controversial Maastricht Treaty, negotiated in December 1991, signed in February 1992 and finally ratified in November 1993, marked a progressive extension of the idea of European unification. The words 'federal vocation' had been mooted during the negotiation of the Treaty, but were not included in the final version. Even so, a far more engaged discussion about the European project's *finalité* was initiated, which is often a source of anxiety for the self-consciously 'pragmatic' British.

The Maastricht Treaty created a European Union with citizens of the 12 member states becoming citizens of this Union. The Treaty's centrepiece was the plan for EMU and its final stage, the creation of a single currency (from which Britain opted out). The British Conservative government also refused to sign Maastricht's 'Social Chapter' covering aspects of social policy. This meant that the other member states were forced to append it to the Treaty as an agreement of the 11 excluding the UK (the Labour government elected in 1997 opted back into the Social Chapter). Maastricht also created intergovernmental pillars dealing with common foreign and security policy (CFSP) and justice and home affairs (JHA). The idea was that these sensitive issues would be included within the framework of the EU, but would not be subject to the usual Community decision-making procedures within the 'Community pillar', with powers for the Commission, European Court of Justice (ECJ) and Parliament. Rather, these pillars would be based on intergovernmental co-operation with unanimity as the foundation for decision-making. To understand this rather complicated institutional architecture an allusion can be made to a Greek temple with three pillars supporting the roof ('the Union'), as shown in Figure 2.2.

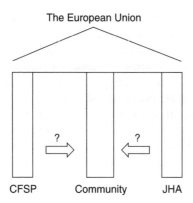

Figure 2.2   Maastricht's European Union

The allusion is to classical symmetry with a central Community pillar
within which supranational integration was well established and that
covered the core commercial and economic concerns of the Union (the
single market, EMU, the Common Agricultural Policy (CAP), regional
development policies and social regulations that had developed within
the Treaties prior to Maastricht). Alongside these would be the flanking
pillars covering sensitive matters of high politics that would be dealt
with separately, would depend on unanimity amongst participating
states and for which the policy-making process would marginalize
supranational institutions such as the Commission, the European Court
of Justice and the European Parliament. The key point was that such
intergovernmental co-operation in the flanking pillars would strengthen
the hands of national governments and their officials and effectively
shield them from scrutiny and accountability at either national or
European level, or so it was thought. This kind of institutional architecture also meshed with a long-standing UK preference for intergovernmental co-operation, and it was heralded by the UK Prime Minister,
John Major, as a great victory for such a vision.

If this was such a 'victory' then the basic question was as follows:
would these separate 'pillars' remain a permanent state of affairs or
would they be drawn closer to the 'Community' where the usual
'Community' decision-making rules and methods applied (as the arrows
in Figure 2.2 suggest)? For John Major, the Maastricht Treaty and the
intergovernmental pillars were a triumph for a British vision of Europe
within which intergovernmental co-operation consolidated the powers of
the member states in sensitive areas of high politics without empowering

supranational institutions. This vision was not widely shared by other member states. For most other member states, the pillars were a rather untidy compromise that had secured British agreement at the Maastricht negotiations, but which would not remain a permanent state of affairs. Even so, the EU's decision-making rules meant that the EU 'convoy' was bound to proceed at the pace of the slowest ship.

This did not mean that the more reluctant or recalcitrant member states such as Britain could control the scope, pace and direction of European integration; they, too, would have to compromise on some issues. What it did mean was that their lack of enthusiasm could have a constraining effect on the range of possible outcomes. This particular problem has led to an increased emphasis on what is known in EU jargon as 'flexibility' in the sense that measures were put in place by the Amsterdam Treaty that allowed for 'closer co-operation' between like-minded states. This raises the possibility of a multi-speed Europe with a 'fast lane' comprising the more integration-minded member states, and a 'slow lane' comprising those who are unable or unwilling to partici-pate in deeper integration. The advantage for integration-minded mem-ber states is that they can proceed more quickly without being slowed by states unable or unwilling to adapt to higher levels of integration. The disadvantage is that the European legal and political orders can become more confused as groups of 'ins' and 'outs' are created on key policy issues with less clear decision-making and some grey legal areas.

EMU is an area in which a two-speed Europe can be seen with 12 mem-ber states signing up to the Euro and (in 2003) the UK, Sweden and Denmark remaining outside the Euro-zone. Free movement of people is another area where there is evidence of a two-speed approach. Here too Britain has opted for the slow lane. The British government has objected to common EU measures that would reduce the ability of the UK author-ities to control the country's external frontiers. This preference was accommodated within Maastricht's intergovernmental pillar. However, the Amsterdam Treaty moved immigration and asylum from the inter-governmental pillar to the Community pillar with the UK, Ireland and Denmark opting out of certain provisions (Geddes, 2000). One cost of this multi-speed approach is a more complicated decision-making structure and increased legal uncertainty.

In 1995, membership expanded to 15 when Austria, Finland and Sweden joined. The Norwegians rejected membership in a referendum, just as they had done in 1972. In 1996 and 1997 the functioning of the Union was reviewed with the resultant Treaty of Amsterdam intended as the equivalent of a car maintenance service on policies and institutions.

Amsterdam's centrepiece was the creation of 'an area of freedom, justice and security' within which citizens of EU member states would be able to move freely and the EU could assume responsibility for aspects of immigration and asylum policy. Britain (as well as Ireland and Denmark) optedout of provisions contained in Amsterdam's Title IV covering free movement of people, immigration and asylum because it wanted to maintain its own border controls.

The Treaty of Nice (agreed in June 2000 and ratified following a second Irish referendum in October 2002 after rejection in a first referendum in June 2001) was designed to look towards this next enlargement and lay the institutional and policy foundations for a much larger EU. The number of seats in the European Parliament was capped, as was the size of the Commission, with the bigger nations giving up their second Commissioner in return for a re-weighting of the votes in their favour in the EU's main legislative body, the Council of Ministers. The effect was a 'triple lock' on qualified majority voting (QMV) within the Council: any decision will need to receive a specified number of votes (71.3 per cent of those cast rising to 74 per cent when membership hits 27 states); any qualified majority will have to be supported by at least half the member states; and any member states will be able to request verification that the QMV represents at least 62 per cent of the EU population. If this 'demographic cushion' is not met then the proposal will fall.

The future of Europe and an EU constitution were the subjects of the Convention on the Future of Europe chaired by ex-French President Valéry Giscard d'Estaing (due to report by 2003). Within this convention the British government's initial opposition to an EU constitution has softened, but a long-standing preference for an emphasis on the central role of the member states and national governments, combined with a suspicion of grand plans and discussion of the EU's *finalité*, remain clear in the attitudes of the UK Labour government elected in 1997. What has changed is that the Labour government appears more confident that it can make and win arguments in the councils of Europe that reflect UK preferences, although whether this is the case remains to be seen.

Britain in the European Union

British governments distrusted the supranational aspirations of the nascent European Community in the 1950s and 1960s and, since it joined the EC on 1 January 1973, Britain has acquired the reputation of being a reluctant 'European'. Other countries have been awkward too, so whether this reputation is justified can only be determined by looking both at the development of British policy towards the EU and at how EU membership has affected Britain. Indeed, as has already been suggested, over the last 30 years or so Britain has become closely engaged with the EU across a range of policy areas with important implications for British policy and politics. This suggests that 'reluctance' is not the whole story. Indeed in some areas such as the development of the European single market, British governments have been positively enthusiastic. As already noted, there are some areas where European integration may connect with state policy preferences and be seen as both in the interests of that state and as potentially strengthening it by increasing the likelihood of key objectives, such as those in the realm of market liberalization, being attained.

EU membership has had an extensive impact on British politics, economy and society. Responsibility for important policy sectors has been transferred to common decision-making structures in collaboration with other member states and EU institutions. Good examples of this are agriculture and fisheries where national policies have almost ceased to exist; measures are instead decided collectively within common policy frameworks. The decisions within these EU institutions can over-ride national law. As these powers have been ceded to the Union so other aspects of political activity have also been refocused. Government ministers meet frequently with colleagues from other member states in EU decision-making forums. British government officials lugging heavy bags full of EU-related documents and background papers can be seen boarding Brussels-bound planes on most weekday mornings at London airports. Interest groups will look to both Whitehall and Brussels because they follow the basic law of pressure group politics: follow the power and seek to exert influence on it. For instance, in the 1980s the British trade unions that had at one time been staunch opponents of European integration became much more favourably disposed to the EC as it offered them a route to influence denied to them by the Conservative governments. Political parties from across the EU have also come together in Europe-wide confederations, although the foundations of party politics still remain largely national.

These kinds of development indicate that it is important to understand the workings of EU institutions and the role of UK governments and other actors within them rather than simply regard the EU as a 'foreign policy' issue detached from domestic issues. The EU's remit clearly stretches to a wide range of domestic activities and we have to consider the ways in which the UK has sought to 'upload' its priorities and preferences (and also think about what these are and how they have developed and changed) as well as the impacts of EU rules and laws being 'downloaded' on the British political system. Yet, at the same time, it is important not to exaggerate the EU's effects and to leap to the assumption that the EU alone has driven key changes in British politics. Many aspects of policy – such as health, education, taxation and law and order – remain largely beyond the EU's remit, while the organization of the British economy, labour market and welfare state remain quite distinct and could be seen to bear more relation to the USA in their enthusiasm for market liberalization than they do to other EU member states.

There are also strong elements of continuity in the British approach to European integration. UK governments have long displayed a preference for a vision of Europe and an associated institutional architecture that enshrines the centrality of member states and national governments. Moreover, Britain's European relations have been set against a continued preference for maintenance of strong transatlantic ties with the USA. These preferences can actually connect British governments in the 1970s with those of governments in the first decade of the twenty-first century and remove some of the lustre of 'newness' from the mantle of 'New Labour'.

For these and other reasons Britain has often been peripheral to the economic and political integration that has characterized EU history. Having been the leading European nation at the end of the Second World War, Britain chose not to participate in the development of supranational European integration and has often been marginal since. Hence was born the 'awkwardness' thesis, although there are some risks of hindsight here because, as Wolfram Kaiser (1996: xvi) remarks, it is much easier for contemporary observers to condemn the decisions made by politicians and officials in the 1950s when Britain stood aside from the first steps towards European integration, but this 'is based on the normative assumption that the path taken by the six [EC founder member states] was not only successful but natural, and also morally preferable to the British preference for trade liberalization within intergovernmental structures'. There was undoubtedly scepticism among British ministers and officials in the 1950s about 'the European project'. Britain's interests were seen as lying elsewhere. With the advantage of hindsight we can say that they were mistaken (and there were those who argued at the time that they were), but this could not have been known for sure.

The facts are that Britain stood aside from the negotiations in the 1950s that gave birth to the EC, endured failed applications for membership in 1961–3 and 1967 and finally joined the club on 1 January 1973. Since then there have been periodic outbursts of Euroscepticism, most notably in 1974–6 while Labour were in power and also in 1979–84, 1988–90 and – most intensely – 1992–7 under the Conservatives. By this reckoning, Britain has been at loggerheads with other EU member states for 14 years, or around 50 per cent of its time as an EU member.

Analysing awkwardness

We can now attempt to put some flesh on the bones of the metaphors of awkwardness and reluctance by analysing the historical, political and institutional dimensions of Britain's engagement with the EU. Has Britain been landed with the 'awkward' tag because of its geographical isolation? Perhaps a distinct history and national self-understanding sets it apart from other European countries? Maybe Britain has a different position in the global political economy from that of other member states? Do institutional compatibilities render the UK distinct from other EU member states? This section considers such explanations for British relations with the EU. It is argued that national history and self-understanding continue to have important effects on contemporary domestic political structures and the idea of 'Britain's place in the world'. The compatibilities between these domestic structures and the EU are central to analysis of the EU and British politics.

This institutional dimension of British politics has two components of particular relevance to understanding the EU and British politics. The first is historical and the second is social, although the two are inter-linked. First, drawing from the insights of historical institutionalism (Pierson, 1998) decisions made in the post-war period about Britain's relations with other European states (which themselves drew, of course, from deeper-rooted national self-understandings and ideas about Britain and its place in the world) have continued to affect attitudes towards European integration since. If the proposition that cause and effect are not necessarily contemporaneous is accepted then current political events can have longer-term causes whose origins lie in institutional arrangements that have become entrenched and which limit possibilities for future policy development. Attention is drawn to issues of timing and sequence so that formative moments or conjunctures can be distinguished. Thus 'it is not only a question of what happens but also of when it happens. Issues of temporality are at the heart of analysis' (Pierson, 2000: 251). Levi (1997: 28) likens the effects of this institutional entrenchment on policy choices to a tree: 'From the same trunk, there are many different branches and smaller branches. Although it is possible to turn around and clamber from one branch to the other – and essential if the chosen branch dies – the branch on which a climber begins is the one she tends to follow.' Institutional processes become reinforcing, with the result that the further one goes down the path then the harder it becomes to change course. It also implies potential path inefficiency: the longer-term outcomes may be less desirable than those that would have arisen if an alternative path had been chosen. The classic issue here is Britain's decision not to join the ECSC and EEC in the 1950s. Of course, policy-makers would not have been be able to anticipate path-dependent inefficiencies at the time decisions were made and act in advance to remedy long-term disadvantages.

Historical institutional analysis thus focuses on the ways in which institutions 'constrain and refract' politics and 'shape both the strategies and goals of political actors' (Fairbrass and Jordan, 2001: 7). Furthermore, as Pierson (1998: 30) argues, member states can play a key role in the key decisions that shape the EU, but can also agree to policies that then fundamentally alter their own positions in ways that could not have been anticipated at the time the original decisions were made. As European integration proceeds then a range of additional actors (sub-national government, EU institutions, other member states, EU pressure groups) impinge to greater or lesser extents on supranational decision-making processes and can limit the ability of the British state to influence outcomes decisively. Moreover, these outcomes can differ from those that were initially foreseen at the time when the original decision to cede sovereign authority was made. European integration's 'path' can have unanticipated consequences.

This historical dimension has important social effects on the capacity for European integration to become fully embedded over time as a central component of the interests and identities of British political actors. The extent to which political actors *learn* (or not) to become European is central to assessment of the EU's impacts on British politics. We can now explore some of the factors that might help explain Britain's conditional and differential engagement.

Does geography make a difference?

As an island on the north-west edge of Europe Britain does not share land borders with other EU member states. British people can speak of 'going to Europe' or travelling to 'the continent', which implies that Britain is physically detached from the rest of Europe. Because of this peripheral location Britain can also choose to opt in or out of engagement with European countries, or so the argument goes. There are three problems with this contention. Geographers would point out that Britain is part of Europe, which is understood to be the western extension of Eurasia. Moreover, if geographical peripherality shapes attitudes to Europe, then why has Ireland been a far more enthusiastic EU member state than Britain? Why has Greece, which shares no land border with another EU member state, been more enthusiastic? And why have attitudes to European integration within the UK and over time varied? Geographical location alone does not appear a particularly promising explanation.

Do patterns of functional interdependence make a difference?

Perhaps, then, the point is that Britain is not exclusively European. The argument here is that Britain is, as Churchill put it, 'with' but not 'of' Europe in the sense that Britain's European vocation remains contested by competing callings from the Commonwealth, from the 'special relationship' with the USA, and with political relations and trading patterns that are more global than strictly European. In a speech to the House of Commons in May 1951 Churchill asked:

> Where do we stand? We are not members of the European Defence Community, nor do we intend to be merged in a Federal European system. We feel we have a special relation to both, expressed by prepositions: by the preposition 'with' but not 'of' – we are with them, but not of them. We have our own Commonwealth and Empire.

The question still remains a perplexing one. Britain is a permanent member of the UN Security Council, has the world's fourth largest economy, is the closest ally of the USA in Europe (as the 'war on terrorism' and, very starkly, the war in Iraq demonstrated), and is a leading member of the Commonwealth. But the UK has become much more closely linked to the EU and its member states (Aspinwall, 2003). Indeed, despite talk of globalization, the UK economy has actually become more *regionally* focused on the EU over the last 30 years (Hay and Rosamond, 2002). While in the 1950s and 1960s Britain traded extensively with non-EU member states, since accession British trade has become ever more closely linked to the EU. This is a point also made by Andrew Gamble (1998), who discusses the relation between Europe and the global economy and argues that European integration is often seen as resulting from underlying shifts in the European and global economies that generate increased interdependence and drive closer economic and political integration in Europe. 'On this view', Gamble (1998: 25) goes on to argue, 'it is the trends towards regionalization of the European economic space through trade and investment flows which is the central reality of the past fifty years'. Hirst and Thompson (1996) identify the emergence of three powerful trading blocs (US/Americas, Europe and the Pacific Basin) and contend that the British economy is still dominated by British domestic capital and that the international operations of British companies are strongly focused on the European region.

This then raises the issue of the relation between national economies, regional trading blocs and the global economy/globalization. Globalization has been seen as centred on 'a world no longer based on geographic expanse but on a temporal distance constantly being decreased by our transportation, transmission and tele-action possibilities' (Virilio, 2001: 71). Yet a regionally focused EU economy based on the single market and EMU co-exists with the global economy as partly a reaction to it and partly a defence against it. Moreover, as the unrest on the streets of Seattle and Genoa indicates, the notion and practices of globalization are deeply contested, and not only by anti-globalization activists who identify the huge iniquities associated with global capital, but also by some EU member states which see unconstrained 'globalization' as a threat to their economic and social models. This idea of globalization as a threat has not been particularly evident in the discourse and actions of UK governments since the 1980s, which have sought a 'pro-business' EU and the continued rolling back of the frontiers of the state through liberalization and deregulation of the British and European economy. This ties in with a longer-standing UK preference for global free trade and is another example of the ways in which historically embedded choices (this time in the realm of international political economy) have important effects on contemporary political dilemmas regarding Britain and Europe. In such circumstances 'globalization' is a movable feast that can be constructed by some as an inexorable force that requires certain fundamental realignments of the relationships between states and markets in both a European and global context to which 'there is no alternative', as Margaret Thatcher used to say (Rosamond, 2003). Yet this is not the only understanding that is available: for instance, Bauman (2002: 13) argues that globalization also presents an ethical challenge that draws into view the links between the richer and poorer parts of the world and the ways in which global capital could and should be harnessed.

What effects does this regionalization then have on economic and political integration? There is a school of thought particularly associated with 'transactionalism' that sees the increased intensity of interaction as a driving force for integration and as bringing with it greater identification with other European countries and their peoples. The effects of Europe can hit different groups within society in different ways so that, for instance, big business may be more in favour than smaller businesses, or younger people more supportive of European integration than older people. The general argument, however, is that as goods, capital, services and people move more freely within Europe, as people meet other Europeans, and as the symbols of images of a united Europe (the flag, the anthem, the currency) become more commonplace, then people will become more accepting of European unification and the demand for 'more Europe', with deeper integration, could also grow (Aspinwall, 2003).

However, while it is true that Britain is closely linked to the EU in trade and, of course, through economic and political integration, closer ties over the last 30 years have done little to inculcate deep-seated enthusiasm and demand for more Europe. Britain appears to retain a Churchillian 'with' but not 'of' Europe. This also suggests that political and social identities are not quite so malleable and so easily refocused on the EU as rather straightforward functional imperatives might suggest. A holiday in Tuscany or an appreciation of French wines does not necessarily translate into full-hearted enthusiasm for the Euro. In turn, this suggests a continued role for domestic political processes that refract rather than simply absorb European influences. It is to the domestic context that we now turn.

History and identity

The argument here is that Britain's history and traditions inculcate certain types of collective social identity that set it apart from its European neighbours. The immediate objection is to this notion of Britain. What does this mean? England? Scotland? Wales? Northern Ireland? At once we see that British national history is far from clear-cut and can be deeply contested. That said, many of the grand narratives of British history enshrine ideas about the nation and its people within an 'imagined' national community.

Thomas Risse (2001) compared British, French and German national identities and argued that since the 1950s 'Englishness' as a variant of British national identity has been constructed as distinct from Europe and as incompatible with federalism or supranationalism. Although this perspective tends to group 'the English' as irredentist Thatcherites and neglects the fact that there have also been strong pro-European voices, it does encourage us to think about the part played by collective social identities of which Risse (2001: 201) identifies four components, as shown below:

1   Ideas that individuals have about their membership in particular groups. These attachments are often based on emotional ties.
2   Membership of a particular group can lead to distinctions from other groups and to differences between in-groups and out-groups. It is a well-known aspect of national identity formation that these are formed in relation to 'the other'. The complex relationship with France formed an important part of British (or, to be more precise, English) national identity.
3   National identities within the 'imagined community' (*pace* Anderson, 1991), are closely linked to ideas about sovereignty and the state. Within these national identities there are also often ideas about what constitutes a just social order such as the French evocation of *liberté, égalité et fraternité*. There can also be ideas about what constitutes the good life: for example, John Major invoked a sentimental and reactionary vision of 'Englishness' as 'the country of long shadows on county [cricket] grounds, warm beer, invincible green suburbs, dog lovers and pools fillers, and as George Orwell said, old maids cycling to communion through the morning mist ... Britain will survive, unamendable in all essentials' (cited in Seldon, 1997: 370). Others have argued that it is possible to establish a more outward looking, progressive British national identity that is connected to Europe (Leonard, 2000).
4   Individuals hold multiple identities that are context-bound, which means that the real question is 'how much space is there for "Europe" in collective nation state identities' (Risse, 2001: 198). Risse argues that there is not much space for Europe in 'Englishness'. A reported observation made by Margaret Thatcher is worth recalling when she stated to the then Chairman of the Scottish Conservative Party, Michael Ancram, that 'I am an English nationalist and never you forget it' (cited in Naughtie, 2001: 21). For an English nationalist, European integration could rather straightforwardly be construed as a threat.

This 'Englishness' does need to be contrasted with Scottish, Welsh and (more problematically) Northern Irish identities. Scottish and Welsh identities in particular have been strongly influenced by Englishness in that they have been largely defined in opposition to it, and could thus have more space for 'Europe'.

There also exist competing interpretations of British historical relations with Europe such that 'England against Europe' is too sweeping. The 'Anglo-Saxons' may have all the best tunes, as William Wallace (1991) put it, but that does not mean that there are not pro-Europeans in Britain who have a different understanding of Britain's history, identity and place in the world. Moreover, if the UK's history is portrayed as in some way exceptional then it must be acknowledged that so too are those of other European countries. It would be absurd to claim that Britain alone has been influenced by a distinct sense of its own history and an idea of its place in Europe and the world. Historical exceptionalism is actually the European norm, not a peculiarly British trait. Moreover, many 'ancient traditions' that are invoked when historical claims are made are actually quite recent creations. The 'invention of tradition' was a key element of the forging of the British nation state during the nineteenth century (Hobsbawm and Ranger, 1983; Colley, 1992). Many, such as the grandeur of the state opening of Parliament, embody an attempt to bestow splendour on the constitutional monarch, and thus a particular notion of British history, society and politics.

Evidence suggests that British collective identities remain quite strongly focused on the British nations rather than Europe, although devolution since 1997 has brought fundamental political changes.

The practical consequence of this interaction between national interests and national identities was late accession in 1973 to the European Community which, as Helen Wallace (1997: 68) notes, had profound consequences in the sense that it was an 'equivocal and pragmatic' shift without 'a conversion to the symbolism of integration' and with the political parties failing 'to embed the discourse of integration as a positive virtue'.

Churchill famously saw Britain as at the centre of three circles of influence: the empire, the special relationship with the USA, and Europe (with Europe third on the list of priorities). While the original EC six concentrated during the 1950s on commercial economic policies, Britain sought to re-establish sterling as an international currency via sterling–dollar convertibility. As Alan Milward (1992: 390) wrote, 'the pound, once good as gold, would now be as good as dollars'. The forced devaluation of sterling in 1967 was a sign that this policy had failed and that Britain's global powers had faded. Rather than being a symbol of national regeneration, the EU was for the British an indication of relative decline to regional power status and a diminished role in world affairs. The cognitive readjustment to this role as a European regional power was a painful process as the UK lost an empire and tried to find a role for itself in world affairs. Contemporary commentators, such as *The Guardian* journalist, Hugo Young, argue that Britain needs to cast off its attachment to 'Anglo-Saxon' identity and its identification with the USA and, instead, embrace Europe far more enthusiastically (Young, 1999). Others, such as Mark Leonard (2000), maintain that there is a European lifestyle and European personalities to which British people do feel an attachment and that these positive foundations could be built upon to inculcate a deeper sense of belonging to a European community. British people could reflect on this point as they enjoy a cappuccino, sip a glass of Chianti, book a holiday to Spain, or cheer on the English or Scottish national football teams coached respectively at the time of writing by a Swede and a German. Yet these positive images of Europe can effortlessly be countered by the ubiquitous presence of American brands such as MTV, Starbucks, Nike and McDonalds. This prompts a fundamental ambiguity when the impact on attitudes to Europe of British history and national identity are examined. The result is that when the question 'Is Britain European?' is asked, then the answer must be 'Yes, but not only' (Garton Ash, 2001).

Does domestic politics make a difference?

The ways in which decisions made at earlier points of time have effects that can still be felt in contemporary politics is a key insight provided by historical institutional analysis. The next step is to identify where, how and why historical influences have shaped British attitudes to European integration without assuming either that Britain is exceptional or to take national myths for granted. Rather, if decision-making processes remain strongly grounded in national contexts then this suggests that we need to explore some key conceptual and organizational features of the British polity.

It is here that Stephen George's (1998) awkward partner thesis enters the equation. This focuses in particular on the domestic political influences on Britain's relations with other EU member states and the ways in which British governments have over time sought to pursue EU objectives. Parliament and the attitudes of the main political parties are central to this approach.

The party system and its effects on the British legislature were also the focus of Mark Aspinwall's (2000) analysis that takes seriously Margaret

Thatcher's injunction that 'No one will ever understand British politics who does not understand the House of Commons' (Thatcher, 1993: 858). Aspinwall identifies a 'structural bias' in the British decision-making process that explains the ease with which anti-European opinion can enter the political mainstream. The reason for this lies with a 'fundamentally anti-centrist' orientation caused by the first-past-the-post electoral system. This contrasts with the proportional representation and coalition systems in other member states that encourage coalescence around the centre and thus tend to be more pro-European. British 'anti-centrism' can thus give power to Eurosceptic groups within the main parties because party leaders must straddle pro- and anti-European factions. This characterization prompts Aspinwall to make two predictions:

1   Where the impact of EU policy on national authority is high then there is a greater need for balancing by party leaders between pro-EU and anti-EU wings of their parties.
2   When the size of the governing majority is small then there is more need for balancing. As one of the leading lights of the anti-Maastricht campaign put it: 'with a majority of 100 a rebellion was futile. But with a majority of 20 Conservatives, a group of MPs can change government policy' (Gorman, 1993: 36).

The government of John Major is a good example of this search for balance. By his own account, Major (1999) veered during his time in office from unbending man of principle to consensus-seeking party manager.

At the time of the Maastricht Treaty Major argues that his pursuit of British interests during the negotiations was based on principle: 'I genuinely stood apart from both sides', he wrote, 'and decided upon the policy I believed to be right; it was coincidental that it fell smack between the two' (Major, 1999: 273). Later in his memoirs, survival instincts and party management take precedence as EU tensions intensified. In the mid-1990s he wrote that: 'To have one wing of the Party up in arms was sufficient. Two would have been cataclysmic if I was to keep the Party in one piece. For me, the strain and frustration of trying to maintain a balance between the two sides was immense' (1999: 616).

Much of the 'balancing' of the European issue has been within the main political parties (this will be analysed in more detail in Chapter 9). Evidence suggests that European integration imparts novel nuances to British politics because it can cross-cut the traditional left–right continuum and render party management more akin to a game of multi-dimensional chess than a balancing act. This multi-dimensional balancing act, illustrated by Steve Ludlam's analysis of the Conservative Party during the 1990s when the European issue was highly salient, suggests that a four-dimensional model is needed if Conservative MPs' attitudes towards the EU are to be understood. This model has two strong sovereignty dimensions structured around 'absolutists' who see state sovereignty as inalienable and vested in the nation state, and 'poolers' who see it as something that can be shared. The other two dimensions are based on a more traditional left–right distinction centred on attitudes towards intervention in the economy. The outcome in terms of the structure of attitudes to European integration within the Conservative Party 'includes some complex distinctions between constitutional supremacy and policy interdependence, but also … remains entangled with the more traditional left–right dimension focused on the role of state intervention' (Ludlam, 1998: 50). Ludlam goes on to argue that sovereignty became the most important faultline within the Conservative Party by the mid-1990s.

Sovereignty is, however, a rather slippery concept (a point considered more fully in the next chapter). To illustrate this point, consider the attitudes of four prominent Conservative politicians to EMU. Margaret Thatcher (Prime Minister, 1979–90) opposed both the ERM and entry to the single currency. Nigel Lawson (Chancellor of the Exchequer, 1983–9) supported ERM membership but opposed the single currency. Geoffrey Howe (Chancellor of the Exchequer, 1979–83; Foreign Secretary 1983–9) supported both ERM membership and adoption of the single currency (Howe, 1995: 534). Kenneth Clarke (Chancellor of the Exchequer, 1993–7) supported the ERM and entry to the single currency, but opposed the creation of a European Central Bank. All could do so by invoking 'sovereignty' arguments. Even the arch-Eurosceptic and inveterate anti-Maastricht rebel, William Cash, MP, supported the use of QMV in the Council of Ministers if it was in support of free trade (Ludlam, 1998: 44). Perhaps this suggests that European issues are characterized by multiple points of equilibria that make the task of seeking balance within a political party more acute when the European issue inflames the party, as was the case with the Conservatives in the 1990s.

Analysis of the party system underlines the importance of considering domestic political factors that mediate the relationship between Britain and the EU. The parliamentary arena was indeed the key location for the Euro-turmoil that affected British politics in the 1990s. Forster (2002b) argues that since the Maastricht Treaty ratification saga of 1992–3 and the pledge to hold a referendum on Britain adopting the Euro there has been a broadening of the debate beyond the parliamentary arena to also include a wider public debate. One effect is some reduction in the ability of party leaders to control the terms of the debate and use party management techniques. Usherwood (2002: 228) points out that the development of extra-parliamentary groups can lead to a radicalization of anti-EU politics and can potentially instigate a pressure cooker effect as the distance increases between the pro- and anti-EU wings of British politics.

Focusing solely on Parliament and the main political parties gives important insight into the origins, development and effects of pro- and anti-EU sentiment in Britain, but can also mean that the analysis fires on just one cylinder. Other factors also mediate the relationship between Britain and the EU, such as the organization of the state (including the role of central, sub-national and local government), socio-economic priorities and their relation to EU priorities. Simon Hix (2000) observed the particular position of the UK economy in relation to those in other member states: 'Britain has lower levels of welfare spending, lower levels of social protection, generally lower wages, more liberal markets ... is more open to the global economy and is stronger in certain sectors such as financial services.' If we extend this analysis to other aspects of the organization of the British polity then Wilks (1996) observes that it is useful to consider the extent to which the UK is an 'awkward state' in terms of, for instance, the balance between centralized and decentralized political authority. Furthermore, an often neglected dimension is the way in which media representations of Europe may affect public attitudes towards the EU (B. Franklin, 1994; Anderson and Weymouth, 1998; Gavin, 2000, 2001). Chapter 10 shows that newspaper and television coverage can reinforce zero-sum ideas of national sovereignty with the British government often portrayed as seeking to advance its interests in competition with other member states. This is not fertile ground for the kinds of 'we-feeling' that could support the development of European identity in the UK.

Conclusion

This chapter has examined basic characteristics of the EU and some explanations for Britain's relations with the EU. It has been argued that the ways in which a series of historical choices have become embedded within the domestic political context is central to analysis of Britain's relations with the EU. Areas within which these effects can be analysed include the organization of the British state, key socio-economic priorities and party politics. Arguments about Europe often centre on terms such as supranationalism, intergovernmentalism and sovereignty. It is thus essential to acquire some understanding of these terms and of the ways in which they are used in debates about Europe.

3

Eurospeak

Introduction

European integration provokes both fervent support and deep mistrust, yet key terms used in debates about integration are often obscure or misunderstood, if not plain baffling. A key task in any discussion of Britain and the EU is therefore to acquire some understanding of the meaning of terms such as integration, supranationalism, sovereignty, federalism and Europeanization. Later chapters will show that Britain's preference has long been for intergovernmental forms of co-operation with opposition to federalism. As a result plans for supranational integration that could point in the direction of federation have tended to be viewed with wariness, but if we are to get to grips with these terms then a conceptual framework – a way of thinking – about European integration is needed. Otherwise any analysis is no more than a collection of dates and facts within which assumptions about the nature of the integrative process remain implicit and obscured, rather than explicit and explained.

What is economic and political integration?

This book is about European integration, but the very meaning of both the word Europe and the term integration need to be explored. The EC emerged during the Cold War and was composed of capitalist economies in Western Europe. In the 1990s, following the collapse of the Soviet bloc, it faced the challenge of responding to the 'new Europe'. This immediately makes the point that the EU and Europe is not one and the same thing. The two terms cannot be transposed. Within the wider Europe beyond the EU a complex web of interdependent states and markets co-operate in an array of organizations such as the Council of Europe and the North Atlantic Treaty Organisation (NATO). What is significant about the EU, and distinguishes it from other organizations, is that it is supranational. This term will itself be analysed later in this chapter.

Integration has been defined as 'a process for the creation of political communities' within which 'states cease to be wholly sovereign' (Haas, 1971). As such, integration leads to the creation and maintenance of patterns of interaction among participating states with both political and economic dimensions that can also have effects on non-participating, bordering states. Integration has both a formal dimension based on outcomes that result directly from political decisions, such as new laws, institutions and policies. It also has an informal dimension where processes such as trade and other cross-border transfers that have effective consequences develop, but were not dependent on formal, authoritative intervention (W. Wallace, 1990; see also Rosamond, 2000: 13).

In post-war Europe the main drive has been towards creation of structures to promote economic integration. Such integration can be divided into five levels (Laffan, 1992):

1 A free trade area within which tariffs and quotas are eliminated between member countries.
2 A customs union within which tariffs and quotas are removed and an external tariff is imposed on goods and services entering the union.
3 A common market within which people, goods, services, and capital can move freely.
4 An economic and monetary union involving a single currency and harmonization of some national economic policies.
5 Total economic integration whereby the same economic policies are pursued in all the member states.

In the 1950s Britain preferred to limit itself to the first of these five levels of integration. In July 1959 it established the European Free Trade Area (EFTA) with six other countries (Austria, Denmark, Norway, Portugal, Sweden and Switzerland). Britain, like many of its EFTA partners, was fearful of the implications for national sovereignty of the EC, which was a customs union and had supranational structures. In subsequent years, many of the EFTA countries nevertheless lodged applications to join. In 1986 the Single European Act (SEA) set the EC on course for the third level of economic integration – a single market – within which people, goods, services and capital should be able to move freely. The single European market officially came into being on 1 January 1993, though it has not yet been fully realized. In 1991 the Maastricht Treaty embodied plans for progress towards the fourth level, economic and monetary union. The single currency was introduced in 2002 and is accompanied by common economic and monetary policies and a European Central Bank that sets interest rates for the Euro-zone.

Economic integration and the interdependence it generates may create pressure for political integration. There are four aspects to this (Laffan, 1992):

1   Institutional integration, comprising the growth of collective decision-making structures with common institutions and formal rules.
2   Policy integration, whereby responsibility for particular policies is transferred to the supranational level.
3   Attitudinal integration, which involves growth of support amongst the peoples of the participating countries.
4   Security integration is founded on security communities within which the expectation of war between participating states was minimized.

There is clear evidence of institutional and policy integration in the EU with the development of common institutions such as the European Commission and the European Parliament, and common policies such as the Common Agricultural Policy (CAP). During the Cold War, west European security was defined by the presence of an ideological competitor to the east in the form of the Soviet Union and its satellite states and by the linkage between west European security and the USA within NATO. Since the end of the Cold War there has been the opportunity for peaceful relations to extend across the continent of Europe founded on co-operation and integration.

Despite there being a high level of support for the general objectives of European integration, the events of 1992 and 1993 when the Maastricht Treaty staggered through its ratification process suggested an 'uncorking' of popular opposition to European integration (Franklin, Marsh and Mcharen, 1994). The Danes rejected the Maastricht Treaty in a referendum in June 1992, when 51 per cent voted 'No' and 49 per cent 'Yes'. The people of France delivered no more than a *petit oui* to Maastricht in September 1992 when 51 per cent voted 'Yes' and 49 per cent 'No'. In September 2000, the Danes voted against the Treaty of Nice. The Danes have used two of the eight Euro-referendums to say 'no' to deeper European integration. In June 2001, with the second lowest turnout in the history of referendums in Ireland (35 per cent), there was a vote against the Treaty of Nice. At the second time of asking the Danes and Irish got the answer 'right' and voted 'yes' to Nice.

Part of the problem is that the process of European integration tends to be driven by political and economic elites. Despite the founding Treaties' aspiration to create 'an ever closer union of the peoples of Europe', EU institutions can seem distant from the people whose interests they are supposed to serve. There is talk of an EU 'democracy deficit' which includes an absence of shared interests, democracy and accountability that prevent it from acquiring the political legitimacy necessary to attitudinal integration. But to this can be added a wider democratic deficit that affects national as well as EU politics as demonstrated by falling turnout, declining membership of political parties and a lack of interest in the formal political process and mainstream political institutions. If there is a 'democratic deficit' then it is more than just an EU issue and is more accurately thought of as a gap between the people and politicians across Europe.

European security integration has possessed a strong Atlanticist element provided by the US-led NATO. The USA provided the security umbrella for the liberal democracies of Western Europe during the Cold War. In these years Atlanticism, rather than Europeanism, shaped the collective defence structures of Western Europe. There has been a strong attachment in Britain to Atlanticism evident in both Conservative and Labour governments.

What is supranationalism?

Britain chose not to participate in the creation of the EC in the 1950s. One reason for this was a dislike of the supranational aspirations of the founder member states. Supranationalism was seen as undesirable, idealistic and not in Britain's interests. Britain feared the implications of supranationalism for national sovereignty.

Supranationalism involves the establishment of formal structures of government above the nation state and possesses three key features:

- the institutions of the supranational government are independent from those of member states
- the organization can make rules that bind members and has the power to enforce those rules
- the institutions of the supranational government are part of a new legal system to which member states and individuals are subject (see Capotori, 1983).

EU law over-rides national law, and institutions exist at the supranational (EU) level that are independent of member states. Supranational government has clear implications for national sovereignty. In formal terms, national sovereignty means that a country has supreme authority within its territory. Any country that is bound by the rules of a supranational organization no longer has supreme authority and is therefore no longer fully sovereign.

Britain has long preferred intergovernmental co-operation to supranational government. Intergovernmentalism implies unanimity as the basis of decision-making, and allows a veto to be exercised to protect national interests. However, the founders of the EC – France, Germany, Italy and the Benelux countries – were suspicious of political systems based on the notion of a national veto, and sought to move away from intergovernmentalism. They pointed to the intergovernmental League of Nations which, in the inter-war period, was for a number of reasons unable to exert the authority necessary to prevent the drift towards the Second World War.

National sovereignty: myth or reality?

The Labour politician and ex-cabinet minister Tony Benn once said in the House of Commons: 'I don't know what sovereignty is ... We are talking about democracy.' This pithy observation highlights two points. Sovereignty can be a slippery concept that means different things to different people or can even evade ready comprehension. Second, when it comes down to it, the basic issues that people are most likely to grasp are 'who decides' and 'who decides who decides'.

A sovereign state can be said to be one that holds and exercises supreme authority within its territorial jurisdiction. This can be called the Westphalian model (after the Treaty of Westphalia of 1648) of territorially exclusive sovereign states with an internal monopoly of violence (the ability to make and enforce law and order), control over external security, a central administration with tax-raising powers and central institutions with policy-making powers (Caporaso, 1996).

For many years, the United Kingdom of Great Britain and Northern Ireland was formally a sovereign state, as constitutional lawyers would understand the term, although some would ask whether the 'golden age' of fully sovereign nation states actually ever existed. If we think of nation states as the defining feature of European political organization then we need to bear in mind that they only became widespread during the nineteenth century. Since then, nation states have come and gone while Europe's geo-political map has been redrawn on many occasions (the disappearance of Yugoslavia has been one of the most recent changes; what was left of Yugoslavia renamed itself Serbia-Montenegro in 2003). Nation states clearly are not immutable and unchanging presences. Moreover, since their creation they have encountered limits on their sovereign power such as the powers of large neighbours, or interdependencies such as those centred on trade.

Some would argue that these limitations on the sovereign authority of states have become even more evident and that the idea of the sovereign state is outmoded in the contemporary era of interdependence and globalization. European integration is seen as an important aspect of this challenge to the sovereign authority of states. Clearly any country that signs up to a supranational body of law is compromising its national sovereignty as defined in the terms used above because laws that are determined collectively over-ride those that it creates itself. But these are not the only changes that affect this understanding of sovereignty. For instance, there are those who argue that the British state has been 'hollowed out' with powers moving 'up' to Brussels and other forms of international organiza-tion, 'down' to sub-national level and 'out' to market and quasi-market organizations. All challenge a Westphalian sovereignty discourse.

In Britain the idea that sovereign authority is vested in Parliament can appear a quaint illusion when the concentration of power in the hands of the executive is considered, or the 'rolling back' of the frontiers of the state initiated by the Thatcher governments is borne in mind, and that is even before the transfers of power to the EU are factored in. But by ratifying the accession Treaty that took Britain into the EC then it is possible to say that the British Parliament self-limited its sovereign authority because in some areas supranational institutions such as the Council of Ministers and the Commission make laws. But the point is that the power and authority of the British Parliament have also been diminished in other ways too, such as the steady accretion of executive authority, the development of devolved government in Scotland and Wales, and the movement 'out' of government of tasks to quasi-governmental agencies and private sector organizations.

This provides a complex picture of re-ordered patterns of British governance in the EU and is one to which much Eurosceptic rhetoric – with its focus on 'Queen and Parliament' – has been slow to adapt. Opponents of the EU argue that loss of sovereignty to EU institutions in a democratic political system reduces the rights of citizens to exercise control over decision-making authority. The ultimate recourse of the British electorate is to 'kick the rascals out' by voting for a change of government at a general election. However, if the national government is no longer the sovereign authority in the strict sense of the term then national elections and policy preferences expressed in them may make little difference. This may be because they run counter to preferences agreed at EU level, but can also occur because of the other locations of power away from the traditional parliamentary locus.

The slipperiness of the sovereignty concept can also be seen in the way that pro-Europeans use the term to support European integration. They counter Eurosceptic claims by contending that sovereignty is not a static concept to be jealously guarded. Tony Blair, it has been argued, 'sees sovereignty as the capacity of a nation to promote its security and prosperity rather than as some precious and indivisible jewel. The national interest counts above Westminster's jealous guardianship of its prerogatives' (Stephens, 2001: 68). 'Sovereignty' is to be utilized to the greatest benefits of the citizens of a particular state. From this point of view, EU membership means that sovereignty is 'pooled' at supranational level in some policy areas, such as trade, where it can be utilized more effectively. To put it simply, 15 are stronger than one, and are far more likely to secure beneficial results for Union citizens than are the unilateral actions of one country.

In 1966 Edward Heath (1998: 357) provided a poolers' manifesto:

> Member countries of the Community have deliberately undertaken this to achieve their objectives, and, because they believe that the objectives are worth that degree of surrender of sovereignty, they have done it quite deliberately ... When we surrender some sovereignty, we shall have a share in the sovereignty of the Community as a whole, and of other members of it. It is not just, as is sometimes thought, an abandonment of sovereignty to other countries; it is a sharing of other people's sovereignty as well as a pooling of our own.

Yet it would seem that notions of pooling and conceptualizations of sovereignty as 'non-zero-sum' have not worked their way too extensively into the collective UK consciousness. Public opinion polling suggests the British tend to be 'absolutists' rather than 'poolers'. UK respondents to the EU-wide Eurobarometer opinion poll published in Spring 2002 showed reluctance to cede authority to the EU on a number of issues when compared to people in other member states, as Table 3.1 shows.

Table 3.1   Areas where the EU15 average (but not the United Kingdom) believe decisions should be made jointly within the European Union (%)

Issue	UK support	EU15 support
Defence	36	51
Currency	32	68
Fight against unemployment	36	50
Agriculture and fisheries	38	50

Source: Reproduced from *Eurobarometer Standard Report* (Spring 2002).

There were a number of areas where UK respondents did support EU decision-making, although even in these areas the support in the UK lagged behind the EU average, as Table 3.2 shows.

As well as this debate between 'absolutists' and 'poolers', a distinction can also be made between formal and informal sovereignty. William Wallace (1986: 367) argues that 'it has been the formal and visible transfer of sovereignty embodied in the issue of UK membership of the EC which has provided the main focus for public concern ... Successive British governments have taken a pragmatic, even a relaxed attitude to the informal processes of international interdependence, and the consequent erosion of national sovereignty.'

Focusing on formal aspects of sovereignty may neglect disguised informal transfers of sovereignty that heighten Britain's interdependence within the international economic and political order. Disguised informal transfers of sovereignty long pre-date Britain's EU membership. Formally, Britain was still a sovereign nation before it joined the EC in 1973, yet informally it was losing sovereignty on an annual basis because economic integration in an increasingly interdependent world reduced its ability to

Table 3.2   Areas where the EU15 average and the United Kingdom believe decisions should be made jointly within the European Union (%)

Issue	UK support	EU15 support
Protection of environment	49	61
Humanitarian aid	60	62
Fight against poverty	50	62
Information about EU policies	59	72
Foreign policy towards countries outside EU	54	71

Source: Reproduced from *Eurobarometer Standard Report* (Spring 2002).

control its own affairs. Indeed, the MacDonald government had found itself largely at the mercy of international financiers in 1931, and the Wilson government had been similarly embarrassed in 1967 when devaluation of the pound was forced. Even in 1973, then, it could hardly be argued that Britain was a 'sovereign' state in the Westphalian sense. In the years since then the point has been made ever more clearly. Ironically, Margaret Thatcher may have hastened processes of informal integration by seeking to roll back the frontiers of the state and embarking on a programme of liberalization and privatization after 1979 that removed potential powers over, for example, capital movements from the armoury of British government. Even after sterling's ejection from the Exchange Rate Mechanism (ERM) on 16 September 1992, Britain found that its economic policy continued to be greatly influenced by decisions taken by the German Bundesbank and then by the emerging structures of EMU. In addition to this, it is also worth noting that defence sovereignty has been 'pooled' for over 50 years within NATO and beneath the umbrella of American protection.

So what does this mean for British sovereignty and interdependence? When precisely was the British state wholly sovereign? Perhaps if sovereignty has long been constrained then the absolutist case is based on a 'golden age' of sovereign authority that never was, and interdependence has actually been the norm. Euro-enthusiasts take the interdependence point to argue that 'national sovereignty' loses much of its meaning. Indeed it can become, as David Baker (2002) puts it, 'outdated', 'largely symbolic' and 'emotive'. Yet, as Kenneth Waltz (1979: 95–6) pointed out: 'To be sovereign and to be dependent are not contradictory conditions. Sovereign states have seldom led free and easy lives.' If sovereignty and interdependence are mutually constitutive and necessary features of the international system then much of the debate between 'poolers' and 'absolutists' is beside the point because the universality of the particular condition of national sovereignty is a key feature of the international political order, and without this notions of independence and interdependence can lose their meaning.

This brings us back to the questions raised at the start of this section. Debates about British national sovereignty are closely linked to those about power and democracy. Tony Blair, in a speech to the Warsaw stock exchange, called for an EU that would be a superpower not a superstate. He argued that: 'Europe today is no longer just about peace. It is about projecting collective power' (cited in Stephens, 2001: 68). There remains a strong association in the UK between notions of power and democracy and the British state as the perceived legitimate basis for political decision-making. But changes in these states as powers move 'up', 'down' and 'out' challenge such a sovereignty discourse.

What is federalism?

Federalism is another tricky idea, or as Bulpitt (1996: 179) put it: 'a very convenient, increasingly popular, always ambiguous, and sometimes dangerous concept', and not least because there are many strands of federalist thought and different types of federal system in operation around the world (Forsyth, 1986; Bosco, 1991).

In *federal systems*, such as the USA and Germany, neither the central nor the regional level of government is supposed to be subordinate to the other. Federalism is seen as generating effective central power for handling common problems whilst preserving regional autonomy. Five main features of a federal system of government can be highlighted (Wheare, 1963):

- two levels of government, a general and a regional
- formal distribution of legislative and executive authority and sources of revenue between the two levels
- a written constitution
- a supreme or constitutional court to adjudicate in disputes between the two levels
- central institutions, including a bicameral legislature within which the upper chamber will usually embody territorial representation, as is the case with the US Senate and the German Bundesrat.

Federal ideas and European federation were strongly opposed by the Conservative government. When the Maastricht Treaty was negotiated John Major insisted successfully that the words 'federal vocation' be removed from the draft 'despite the known opposition of the Commission and every other head of government in the room' (Major, 1999: 280).

In earlier ages Britain, through plans drawn up for former colonies, was one of the world's great federalizers (Burgess, 1986). However, British governments have consistently seen federation as appropriate for others, not for the British. The Eurosceptic nightmare is a 'federal' (read centralized) European superstate with powers draining from the British state to a nascent United States of Europe.

In the EU there are some signs of federation, although these are limited. There is a multi-level system linking the sub-national, national and supranational. In addition, an established body of European law overrides national law. The European Court of Justice (ECJ) acts as umpire in disputes between supranational and national levels of government. But in terms of its budget and policy competencies, the EU is far from being a fully fledged federation as the term would normally be understood, and neither should it be assumed that it is necessarily locked in some trajectory that will lead inevitably towards federation. Bulmer and Wessels suggest that what is emerging is a system of 'co-operative federalism': the EU and national governments share responsibility for problem-solving in some areas because neither of them has the legal authority or policy competence to tackle the challenges that they face on their own (Bulmer and Wessels, 1987).

British opponents of EU federalism use the term in a way markedly different from the meaning given to it by most federalists. For its Eurosceptic opponents a 'federal Europe' means a European superstate with a huge centralized Brussels bureaucracy limiting the sovereign authority of member states. Advocates see federation as a way of combining the political virtues of unity and diversity. For them, federalism is a means of decentralizing power, not centralizing it. This decentralization was to be based on the notion of 'subsidiarity', another slippery bit of Eurospeak.

The search for subsidiarity

Never has a term been better placed to perplex and baffle than 'subsidiarity', which entered EU terminology in the 1990s, but before any clear meaning had been ascribed to it. The significance of the term and its political usefulness derives from the fact that any resolution of the dispute between federalists and anti-federalists will depend in large measure on questions of detail. The key is to decide which powers are to go to which level: supranational, national or sub-national?

In the late 1980s and the early 1990s the EU was keen to proceed on the basis of what is known as *subsidiarity*, maintaining that power should be exercised at what it calls 'the lowest appropriate level'. Subsidiarity is a rather nebulous notion and is one of the words used in debates on the European Union that baffles people as much as it informs them.

The word *subsidiarity* originates from the Latin *subsidium*, meaning reserve troops. It first appeared in Pope Leo XIII's 1891 encyclical. In 1931 Pope Pius XI used it to denote that political and social decisions should not be taken at a higher level than necessary. The EU's leaders seized on the principle as a way of bridging the gap between the people and the Union. Lawyers, though, warned of the dangers of taking a religious principle and converting it into a legal text. Unfortunately the EU deployed the word without giving it a clear meaning.

British governments have tended to view subsidiarity as implying a division of responsibility between the EU and member states, with member states and national governments holding the upper hand. Subsidiarity could also mean powers going to lower levels of government than the national state. This could mean a transfer of power to regions or to Britain's sub-state nations of Scotland and Wales. Germans tend to see subsidiarity as meaning a distribution of power between regions (the *Länder*), the national government and Brussels because this fits with the constitutional order of the *Bundesrepublik*. Smaller member states, such as the Netherlands, Belgium and Luxembourg, have often blocked reduction in the powers of the Commission, which they believe gives a voice to smaller member states. Since 1992 the Commission has been obliged to incorporate a subsidiarity justification in legislative proposals. This is not too hard to do. Given that the term is vague, it is not hard to think of a subsidiarity justification for most proposed measures.

Although their ardour seems to have diminished since their heyday at the end of the 1980s and in the early 1990s, regionalists seek a 'Europe of the regions' with nation states by-passed as powers move down to the local level and up to the EU (Jeffery, 2000). The Commission has been active in encouraging links between regions and the EU and between regions themselves, especially those that straddle borders. The European Parliament's 1988 Charter of the Regions is a further indication of the importance supranational institutions give to the fostering of regional identities within the Union. Just as corporatist styles of representation were fashionable in the 1950s and gave birth to the little-known Economic and Social Committee, the enthusiasm for regionalism brought with it the Committee of the Regions of representatives from local and regional government across the EU who meet in an advisory capacity. The Committee held its first plenary session in March 1994 and meets regularly, but rarely impinges on public consciousness.

Forms of European state

Now that the issue of the 'European superstate' has been broached we can reflect on discussion of the forms of state organization that could be emerging within the EU. This is particularly important in relation to debates about European integration because British governments have consistently advanced a minimalist state-centred vision of European integration. This tends to conceive of the EU as a union of sovereign states pursuing a series of core objectives centred on market integration.

Furthermore, since the 1980s, this British vision has possessed a distinct neo-liberal element centred on deregulation, liberalization and economic reform.

James Caporaso (1996) provided a useful guide to emerging forms of European state when distinguishing between three ideal types: the Westphalian, the regulatory and the post-modern. These are not mutually exclusive and European integration can display aspects of each. In Britain a tension can be identified between support for a minimal 'regulatory' European state emphasizing EU stewardship of a deregulated economy combined with a continued attachment to the nation state as the legitimate basis of international politics. The tension is between attachment to formal notions of state sovereignty while endorsing more disguised, informal transfers of sovereign authority.

The Westphalian model sees the EU assume tax-raising powers, a greater role for central EU institutions and more control over internal security policies (immigration, asylum, policing, judicial co-operation) and external security policies (foreign and defence policy, perhaps even with a European army). This vision of the EU as an organization that drains power from the member states and leads to some kind of United States of Europe is the stuff of Eurosceptic nightmares, but Caporaso shows that this is not the only vision. Koopmans (1992) takes this point further to contend that there is no a priori reason to assume that European integration is mimicking the processes of nation state creation in this kind of Westphalian manner and, actually, many good reasons to believe that it is not. This becomes more evident when we consider Caporaso's identification of two other tendencies in EU forms of state organization that he argues also cast light on the EU system.

The regulatory state could be seen to accord with the more minimalistic vision of British governments with a strong emphasis on the development of the single market. The regulatory state concerns itself with countering 'international externalities' that hinder trade and thus with enforcing the European single market so that an EU-wide level playing field can be created. EU institutions concentrate on regulation of the market rather than the redistributive (welfare provision) and substantive (fiscal, monetary and economic policies) concerns of the member states. The European Commission and Court of Justice devote themselves to eliminating international externalities in the form of unfair national rules that can frustrate competition (Majone, 1996).

Despite its intrinsic appeal to UK governments, a problem with this form of state is that regulatory structures and agencies at EU level are difficult to hold to account and are often not particularly transparent in their activities (although this too may be part of the appeal because it does not offer new sources of legitimate authority that challenge the nation state). The institutions of the regulatory state are hardly likely to inspire the trust, confidence and enthusiasm of EU citizens. If the EU lacks the 'magic' that Walter Bagehot ascribed to the British constitution, then a European food standards agency or other similar organizations are unlikely to help the cause. There is also a risk that powerful interests will capture agencies and that these agencies could then serve the concentrated concerns of a powerful few rather than the more diffuse interests of the majority. Despite the hopes of some on the left that European integration could open the door to an internationalization of labour that could confront international capital, the evidence so far is that footloose capital has been privileged by European integration compared to relatively immobile labour.

The post-modern state presents a plural and diverse view of Europe's future. The post-modern state involves a fundamental reappraisal of ideas about sovereignty in a direction that is more 'abstract, disjointed, increasingly fragmented, not based on stable and coherent coalitions of issues or constituencies, and lacking in clear public space within which competitive visions of the good life and pursuit of self-interested legislation are discussed and debated' (Caporaso, 1996: 45). The two main features are, first, a weak core that is not certain to grow and, second, the location of EU activity at many locations. The EU is thus a 'multi-level' polity, but also more than this because the term 'multi-level' could be seen as morphological in the sense that there are layers one on top of the other when instead the linkages run across, between and within levels in complex patterns of inter-connectedness and interaction.

One's views on this form of state are likely to be influenced by one's views on pluralism and diversity. European governments are distinctly Janus-headed on this issue. Debates about immigration and ethnic diversity illustrate this point (Geddes, 2003). European countries are multi-national and multi-cultural with many people seeing this as a positive and enriching development. On the other hand, European governments have shown an increased determination to protect themselves against some aspects of post-modern diversity and enforce some rather old-fashioned sovereign power when it comes to controlling immigration that their policies define as 'unwanted'. Also, going back to a point made in the previous section, who benefits from this post-modern diversity? European integration has thus far strengthened mobile capital at the expense of relatively immobile labour. How could a post-modern EU state with its multiple locations and weak central institutions correct this imbalance?

At the very least, it is important to acknowledge that a European superstate is but one possible form of European state and that there are also reasons to think that it is a least likely alternative because the conditions that gave birth to the modern European nation state no longer pertain in the twenty-first century (Tilly, 1975). It may be that the EU combines elements of all three visions: a stronger centre, but continued multi-site politics; a concentration on single market development, but with some compensating social policies; and a continued ambiguous relationship to 'post-modern' plurality and diversity.

For British governments, Westphalian, regulatory and post-modern forms of EU state raise their own problems, but there has been a long-standing preference for the rather minimalistic European regulatory state concentrating on enforcing single market rules and developing a more deregulated and 'flexible' European economy. This vision of a European state does little to recast the balance between capital and labour. As such it is antithetical to key elements of the social democratic project. The fact that New Labour seem happy with this indicates a distance between their economic project and conceptions of social democracy in other EU member states (Gamble and Kelly, 2000).

Neo-functionalism

If there are signs of federation in the EU, then what forces are driving this process? Why has integration occurred? What problems was it designed to solve? What methods have been employed? And what are the motive forces behind integration? This section considers one attempt to get to grips with these questions: neo-functional theory. This approach has had important effects on the study of European integration from the 1950s right through to the contemporary era, during which time it has also faced vigorous challenges (Haas, 1958; Sandholtz and Stone Sweet, 1998; and see also Hoffmann, 1966, for the beginning of the backlash). From the point of view of British Eurosceptics, this kind of neo-functional approach has some merit because it emphasizes a tendency that particularly worries them: the autonomous power of EU institutions to promote European integration and to over-ride individual state interests in pursuit of the greater European good.

In the wake of the devastation wrought by the Second World War the European Union of Federalists (EUF) was established. As Ben Rosamond (2000: 20) notes: 'For as long as there have been states, intelligent people have been trying to think of ways in which conflict between them might be averted.' This was particularly the case as intellectuals surveyed the ruins of Europe after the two world wars (Weigall and Stirk, 1992). Many members of the EUF had fought against the Nazis. The EUF did not think it too far-fetched to hope that a United States of Europe could emerge to shape post-war Europe. For them maintenance of a system of nation states would very probably continue to breed the nationalist politics that had been responsible for two world wars. However, advocates of constitutional federalism were to see their dreams overtaken by events. Nation states were soon restored to Europe, and advocates of closer integration sought an alternative approach.

The origins of just such an approach were found in the work of David Mitrany whose book, *A Working Peace System* (1943), proceeded from the question of what the essential functions of international society should be and then sought to prioritize welfare needs as opposed to 'the sanctity of the nation state' (Rosamond, 2000: 33; see also Taylor, 1994). If the emphasis was on the performance of key functions (hence *functionalism*) then international institutions (such as continent-wide railway systems or global aviation institutions, not a world government or world state) were to be preferred to the dogmas, exclusions and conflicts of nation states. Moreover, if tasks were performed effectively then popular loyalties would drain from nation states and be transferred to these new international institutions. Mitrany's profoundly anti-statist aspirations were not to find direct expression in the substantive plans for regional west European integration that developed in the late 1940s and early 1950s, but there were functionalist influences on the ideas that were put forward, such as the notion that a more substantive political form would follow the transfer of function and the key role to be played by technocrats in the integration process.

The Schuman Plan of 1950 exemplified an alternative, stealthier approach to integration than the creation of a United States of Europe. Robert Schuman was the French foreign minister in the early 1950s. His plan for sectoral integration was much influenced by a French official, Jean Monnet, whom many see as the founding father of European integration (Duchêne, 1994). The Schuman Plan led to creation of the ECSC in 1951 that established a common market in coal and steel, both key areas for industrial economies. However, Schuman planned far more than a mere coal and steel community. He saw the ECSC as a first step on the road to economic and political integration in Europe. Schuman hoped that successful integration in one area would create pressure for integration in other areas. A common market for coal and steel could create functional pressure for broader co-operation in energy policies and then more generally in industrial and economic policies. A small step would snowball with the result that national economies and political systems would become enmeshed. As functions were transferred then so too could be the loyalties of Europeans as they became focused on these new institutions. European interests would develop, consolidate and form the basis for political integration. An important point in relation to this view of step-by-step integration is that popular support was supposed to follow rather than drive European integration. The aim of the EC's founding fathers was to get key social interests (such as big business and the trade unions) on board and then, once this was done, assume that popular support would follow.

The Labour government in Britain between 1945 and 1951 was implacably opposed to such plans. There was some scepticism that such ambitious plans could work, as well as a hostility to supranational integration that had been apparent when the Council of Europe was created in 1948. What is more, the ECSC proposed common structures for the management of coal and steel at a time when in Britain these vital resources had just been nationalized.

Despite the initial small steps, the text of the Schuman declaration clearly indicates the more ambitious objectives:

> Europe will not be made all at once or according to a single plan. It will be built through concrete achievements which first create a *de facto* solidarity ... The setting up of this powerful productive unit, open to all countries willing to take part and bound ultimately to provide all the member countries with the basic elements of industrial production on the same terms, will lay a true foundation for their economic unification. (cited in Weigall and Stirk, 1992: 58–9)

Note the ambitions. Those in the UK who were later to argue that Britain joined a glorified free trade organization and that plans for deeper integration were a corruption of these original purposes had not paid close attention to the declarations of the member states when European economic and political integration was instigated in the 1950s.

Neo-functionalists describe the snowballing effect and expansive logic of integration in more theoretical terms as 'spillover effects', with co-operation in one area creating pressure for integration in others with the newly formed High Authority (later to become the European Commission) seen as the driving force or engine of integration. This seemingly inexorable logic is known as neo-functionalist spillover (Pentland, 1973). For neo-functionalists, however, spillover means something quite specific. It was expected that spillover effects would be generated at the supranational level with the Commission in the lead as the engine of integration. The role of the Commission would be to upgrade the common interests of member states and to seek European solutions to the problems that they collectively faced. As integration continued then functions linked to areas that had become subject to European integration would also encounter pressure to pass to the supranational level. 'Functional spillover' would also generate a 'political spillover' in the sense that there would be a re-focusing of activity by organized interests on increasingly important supranational institutions. European integration could develop a self-reinforcing dynamic with supranational institutions to the fore. This spillover could also take a geographical form as surrounding states and regions are drawn into the web of interdependence.

This provides us with what could be characterized as a supranational account of European integration that focuses on forces 'above' the nation state. An alternative explanation would contend that that ECSC was founded on a classic intergovernmental deal between France and Germany centred on essential elements of economic reconstruction. France sought peaceful relations with its neighbour and West Germany sought rehabilitation into civilized international society. The main coal and steel-producing areas in the Rhineland and Alsace Lorraine had also been sites of Franco-German conflict. As Rosamond (2000: 53) argues: 'From this perspective, the likes of Monnet were playing typical games of power politics, but employing the fashionable rhetoric of supranationalism and European unity.'

Neo-functional theorizing sounded plausible to the extent that it appeared to fit EC development in the 1950s and early 1960s; however, the theory no longer seemed applicable in the period from the mid-1960s to the mid-1980s. In 1965 the French President, de Gaulle, enforced national rights of veto in EC decision-making, thereby reducing the scope of supranational authority. During the 1970s, 'spillback' and 'Eurosclerosis' seemed better metaphors than spillover. During the 1970s the EC seemed incapable of acting during severe economic recession. On 20 March 1982 *The Economist*'s front cover showed a tombstone bearing an inscription for the EC. It read:

EEC
Born March 25, 1957
Moribund March 25, 1982
Capax imperii nisi imperasset
[it seemed capable of power until it tried to wield it]

At this time the momentum of the integrative process appeared to have dissipated. 'Eurosclerosis' was widely held to have set in. Not surprisingly, neo-functionalist theories fell into obsolescence.

The obsolescence of integration theory?

It has been argued that an erroneous 'end of ideology' assumption underpinned neo-functionalist theory which implied that economic growth would continue unabated, and that the main question facing Western societies was how to distribute the fruits of this wealth. Neo-functionalists thought that the best way was the appointment of experts – technocrats – at the supranational level who, because of their expertise, would arrive at decisions that were best for everybody. It did not quite work out like that. In the 1970s governments were faced with the problem of coping with both rising unemployment and increasing inflation. Supranational integration was not an option many appeared to consider.

Neo-functionalists were also criticized for trying to write nationalism out of the political equation. They thought that nationalist views would be consigned to the dustbin of history, overwhelmed by the logic of integration. Again this was not to be the case. In the 1960s the EC came into conflict with Gaullists in France and then, in the 1980s and 1990s, with Thatcherites in Britain. De Gaulle and Thatcher would not be swept along by the 'inexorable logic' of integration. Their resistance to European integration indicated a continued attachment to nation states as both organizational units and the repositories of the loyalties of their citizens.

How, then, do we explain the resurgence of integration since the mid-1980s? It could seem strange to try to breathe new life into neo-functionalist theory when it appears to have failed to explain events from 1965 until 1984, although there it has been argued that central neo-functionalist insights do still apply (for example, Sandholtz and Stone Sweet, 1998). Some analysts pointed instead to the importance of member states in the process of integration.

'Realist' views

In creating a spillover effect, what matters, 'realists' contend, are the interests of member states rather than the role of supranational institutions. If member states do not want to integrate then they will not do so, and there is not much the Commission can do about it. For realists, nation states were, are and probably will remain the basic units of international politics.

Stanley Hoffmann (1966) developed one of the most influential critiques of neo-functionalism. He contested the assumption that supranational sentiment would begin to override national loyalties because he thought that this view seriously underestimated the continued resonance of nation state identities. He also thought that integration could be possible in areas of 'low politics' that were primarily technocratic issues and that did not impinge too directly on state sovereignty, but when integration struck more squarely at national authority, identity and 'high politics' then there was likely to be stronger opposition. John Pinder (1968) developed this point by distinguishing between 'negative integration', which concerned itself with the removal of barriers and was easier to achieve, and 'positive integration', which was concerned with the creation of new structures. British governments have traditionally been far more supportive of negative integration in areas of low politics.

In opposition to neo-functionalists who identify an integrative dynamic at supranational level, intergovernmentalists focus on the impetus national governments give to the process. From an intergovernmentalist perspective 'successful spillover requires prior programmatic agreements among governments, expressed in an intergovernmental bargain' (Keohane and Hoffmann, 1991: 267).

This state-centred account could appear plausible because, as Rosamond (2000: 152) observes, 'it reflects the understanding of the political process *held by political actors*' (emphasis in original). If there is an assumption that sovereign states are the most important units in international politics then this strongly influences the assumptions made about European integration. But just because something is thought to be true does not mean that it is, and if analysis proceeds from the assumption that something is true then this might close our eyes to other forms of international development that challenge this 'sovereignty discourse' (Camilleri and Falk, 1992). Moreover, just because new and novel forms of international organization do not accord with state-based forms of political authority, this does not mean that nation states necessarily retain their pre-eminence. Ideas about the state and state authority can be confronted with new forms of transnational economic, social and political action and with alternative forms of state organization within the EU (such as the regulatory and post-modern versions discussed earlier).

The debate has so far tended to postulate an intergovernmental vision of the EU against a supranational representation. There are, though, a variety of possible outcomes between these two poles (Schmitter, 1996). The contest between these competing theoretical visions can neglect important developments within the EU political system. Jeremy Richardson (1996) writes of the nine-tenths of EU activity that are matters of 'low politics' and lie beneath the water line of the EU iceberg. We can now touch upon a core issue related to the EU iceberg, and that is the issue of Europeanization: what do we mean by it, how do we recognize it and where can we see its effects on the British political system?

What is Europeanization?

If European integration is understood as the establishment of new competencies and common structures at supranational level, then Europeanization can be taken to refer to the EU's impact on laws, politics, policies, institutions and collective identities in EU member states (Radaelli, 2000). One of the most comprehensive analyses to date of the EU's impact on domestic politics in the member states identifies 'domestic adaptation with national colours' in the sense that there has been a response to European integration that has been influenced by national institutions rather than a simple process of convergence (Green Cowles, Caporaso and Risse, 2000). It is also suggested that a key factor mediating the relationship between member states and the EU is institutional compatibility, or 'goodness of fit' as it is also called. The idea here is that the organization of domestic politics and institutions play crucial roles in determining 'fit' with EU priorities. If we want to understand why and how adaptation occurs then we need to explore these domestic structures quite closely, which is what this book proposes to do in the chapters that follow. If there is a 'good' fit then there are likely to be few adaptational pressures. If there is a poor fit then we are likely to find stronger adaptational pressures. It is also possible to make a distinction between policy convergence (which can be easier to attain) and deeper structural, institutional convergence, which can be more difficult to achieve because it involves deeper-seated changes (Green Cowles, Caporaso and Risse, 2000: 16). The UK has shown that adaptational pressures can be avoided (perhaps only temporarily) if opt-outs are possible. This 'variable geometry' can be one way in which (non-) adaptation to Europe continues to have 'national colours'.

Europeanization is increasingly widely used to refer to a wide array of EU activities with the result that its widespread application makes it more difficult to specify what the term actually means and to use it in a way that makes sense. Four aspects of this difficulty can be identified:

1 Europeanization varies across countries with adaptational pressures more evident on some member states (or prospective member states in central, eastern and southern Europe who have a fair amount of work to do to bring their domestic structures into line with those in the existing member states).
2 Europeanization varies within countries because some sectors have become more Europeanized than others. Agricultural policy, for instance, is more extensively Europeanized than transport policy.
3 Europeanization affects non-EU member states such as accession states, but also non-European countries such as North African states that are affected by the EU and thus to some extent Europeanized because of the EU's powerful profile and its links with surrounding states and regions.
4 Finally, when analysing Europeanization we have to be sure that changes ascribed to European integration were actually caused by European integration. This requires us attempting to disentangle national, European and international sources of political change.

In the chapters that follow, the Europeanization of British politics is assessed through exploration of the ways in which the territorial basis of British politics (national, sub-national and local government), the party system, key policy sectors and the media shape, and are shaped by, British membership of the EU.

Contrasting perspectives on integration

British governments have over time tended to prefer intergovernmental co-operation rather than supranational integration. There has also been a preference for negative integration in areas of low politics with a concentration on the effective operation of the single market and a distinct lack of enthusiasm for grander projects and discussion of the EU's *finalité*. Whether this preference for intergovernmental co-operation is sustainable in an era when issues of 'high politics', such as foreign and security policy and immigration and asylum policy, are moving 'closer' to the supranational method remains an open question, which will be investigated more closely when British responses to EU policy integration are analysed in Chapter 7.

Supranationalism implies a central authority with power over member states: the so-called 'Brussels Empire' that alarms Eurosceptics. A federal system would seek to preserve some measure of national and sub-national autonomy, but the exact balance is far from clear because of the ambiguities of federalism, the different territorial bases of political organization in the member states, and because of the controversial nature of this debate. The EU does show some signs of federation, albeit limited and perhaps best understood as a form of 'co-operative federalism' whereby member states and the EU share responsibilities because neither has the authority to tackle the challenges they face on their own.

What is clear is that there has been a remarkable process of political and economic integration in Europe since the Second World War and that the EU constitutes a truly unique form of international political organization. The chapters that follow look at this process and at Britain's role in it. The next chapter looks at the historical context of Britain's EU membership in which it is seen that Britain was distrustful of supranationalism and stayed out of the EC, thus failing to shape policy priorities that were to prove disadvantageous when it did decide to seek membership.

4

Joining the Club

Introduction

Britain's relations with the European Union since the 1950s need to be related to the character of that organization (supranational and with some lurking federal ideas) and to key developments in British domestic and foreign policy. The two went hand in hand as Britain stood aside from the first steps taken towards European integration in the 1950s, then re-evaluated its role and sought membership of the EC in the 1960s and 1970s. The chapter develops the 'Britain in Europe' theme by providing an overview of Britain's relationships with the EC from the post-war leader of a landslide Labour government, Clement Attlee, until accession in 1973. The chapter is particularly concerned with the factors that shaped British government attitudes towards supranational integration, the capacity to attain UK European policy objectives, and the ways in which these preferences and objectives changed over time between the late 1940s and the early 1970s. In the 1950s, the development of European integration is assessed alongside Britain's long-standing preferences for free trade and the maintenance of economic relations with the Commonwealth and USA, an aversion to supranationalism, and a desire to recover great power status. In the face of competing influences, British governments in the 1950s chose not to participate in the early moves towards European integration. This stance was re-evaluated in the early 1960s and led to membership applications in 1961–3 and 1967, both of which were rebuffed by President de Gaulle. A key underlying point is to demonstrate the ways in which national history and national self-understanding played (and still play) a key role in British relations with the EU.

From the contemporary vantage point it is easy to condemn the choices that were made by Britain's political elite when the first steps towards European economic and political integration were taken and the lack of 'European vision' implicit within them. Yet, whilst 20-20 hindsight is a great asset for the contemporary historian, in the 1950s it could not have been known that the ECSC would develop into what we now know as the EU. It would also have constituted a remarkable about-turn for the British government in the early 1950s to abandon its foreign and trade policy priorities and throw in its lot with the supranational European Coal and Steel Community and its progeny, the European Economic Community. It is more fruitful to explore the decisions that were made, the historical and institutional context within which they were taken, and then analyse their implications without necessarily having to embark on a hunt for the 'guilty men'.

East versus West

After the Second World War Europe was divided and faced severe economic and political challenges. To the east the Soviet Union consolidated its strength. To the west states looked to their principal ally, the USA, for help. As Story (1993: 11) puts it, 'Europe had become an object of world politics with the shots being called by the great powers.' American assistance to Europe came in the form of Marshall Aid, named after Secretary of State George C. Marshall, who developed the plan to rebuild west European economies. Around $13 billion worth of aid was distributed among west European countries between 1948 and 1952. West Germany was the main beneficiary of Marshall Aid, receiving $4.5 billion. This served to draw it firmly into the Western bloc. By establishing the Organisation for European Economic Co-operation (OEEC) in May 1948, the Americans sought to involve recipient countries in the Marshall Aid distribution process. Significantly, the British, then the strongest power in Europe, resolutely advocated intergovernmental co-operation in the OEEC rather than the institution of supranational structures with powers over member states.

The USA was keen to see the establishment in Western Europe of open capitalist economies with liberal-democratic political systems. It made sound commercial sense for the USA to seek to restore the economies of the west because it could then trade with them. Hence the USA was a sponsor of European integration and sought the inclusion of its closest European ally, the UK, into this organization. It was not only the external threat from the east that perturbed the Americans; there were also strong Communist parties in France and Italy. The restoration and consolidation of economic prosperity within a liberal, capitalist order was seen as a defence against Communism in these countries.

On Soviet insistence, Marshall Aid was not accepted in Eastern Europe. Both Czechoslovakia and Poland rejected it. This, and the Czech Communists' seizure of sole power in February 1948, led Britain, the Benelux countries (Belgium, the Netherlands, and Luxembourg) and France to form the Brussels Treaty organization in March 1948 whereby they pledged mutual military aid and economic co-operation. Also in March 1948 the three Western occupying powers in Germany – France, Britain and the USA – unified their occupation zones and convened a constitutional assembly, which introduced currency reforms that created the Deutschmark. This caused similar steps to be taken in the east of Germany by the fourth occupying power, the Soviet Union. A Soviet attempt to blockade Berlin in the winter of 1948 (which, although occupied by the four powers, was surrounded by the Soviet zone of occupation) was breached by Allied airlifts.

In April 1949 the Treaty of Washington established NATO. This firmly committed the USA to defend Western Europe. In September 1949 the Federal Republic of Germany (FRG) was created. In October 1949 the GDR was established in the east. The division of Germany provided firm evidence of the Iron Curtain that had fallen across the continent of Europe.

Intergovernmentalism versus supranationalism

It has been argued that British political elites made three fundamental miscalculations about the first steps taken in the 1950s towards European economic and political integration (Beloff, 1970):

1 British governments held the view that supranational integration was idealistic rather than practical and that it would inevitably fail. The EC's federalizing tendencies would soon founder on the rocks of member states' national concerns. The evidence for this is that the British refused to join the ECSC and the European Defence Community (EDC) and only sent a senior civil servant to the negotiations, which led to the Rome Treaties of 1957.
2 Britain believed that the problems of the post-war era could be met by establishing a free trade area (EFTA), and that supranational integration was unnecessary.
3 The British under-estimated the obstacles to accession once a distinct course of action had been decided upon. de Gaulle blocked the applications made by Macmillan (1961–3) and Wilson (1967).

The restoration of nation states after the Second World War had dashed the hopes of constitutional federalists who had sought a United States of Europe. In their opinion, only such a dramatic step could transcend the bitterness and divisions that had plagued the continent and generated two world wars in the space of 30 years. For them, ways forward in a Europe of nation states were unclear. In the meantime, nation states were re-established and became closely linked to the performance of welfare state functions that further served to consolidate the national state as the recipient of citizens' loyalty.

What was clear was that a basic divide was emerging between Britain, on the one hand, and the six countries that were to found the ECSC in 1951 on the other. The Attlee government was prepared to sponsor co-operation with other European countries, but primarily as a way of ensuring that Britain remained top dog. The Foreign Office view was that 'Great Britain must be viewed as a world power of the second rank and not merely as a unit in a federated Europe' (cited in Ellison, 2000: 16). The British had no intention of participating in a supranational organization, but supranational plans that fundamentally changed relations between European states were being hatched. The Benelux countries had in 1948 taken steps towards 'pooling' their sovereignty when they set up a customs union.

It has been argued that the European policies of the Labour government (1945–51) and Conservative governments of the 1950s directly contributed to the outcome that was supposed to be avoided: the fear that Britain would become, as Labour's post-war Foreign Secretary Ernest Bevin put it, 'just another European country'.

Early tensions between supranationalists and intergovernmentalists became apparent at the May 1948 Congress of Europe in The Hague, where over 700 prominent Europeans met to discuss the future of the continent. The outcome of the meeting was creation of the Council of Europe in May 1949. It was located in Strasbourg, on the Franco–German border, in order to symbolize reconciliation between these two countries. Britain's preference for intergovernmentalism prevailed in the Council of Europe: decisions in its Council of Ministers are taken on the basis of unanimity. It has come to be identified with the European Convention on Human Rights (ECHR), signed in November 1950. This, after the atrocities of the Second World War, signified a commitment to human rights as binding on sovereign states. By 2003 the Council of Europe had 41 members and was the largest pan-European grouping.

Schuman's plan

A core group of west European countries felt frustrated by Britain's opposition to supranationalism and, as the Benelux countries had already done in their customs union, sought economic integration. France and West Germany formed the key axis within this supranational project. Plans developed by the French foreign minister, Robert Schuman, were for a common market in coal and steel. The ECSC was an attempt to resolve the question of how to both restore West German economic prosperity, from which the French would benefit, whilst binding West Germany to a peaceful west European order. The Netherlands, Belgium and Luxembourg had already taken steps to pool their sovereignty, while for the Italians supranational integration could offer an external guarantee of economic and political stability.

Schuman's plan, proposed on 9 May 1950, led to the creation of the ECSC by the Treaty of Paris in April 1951. It created a common market for coal and steel and supranational structures of government to run the community. Schuman's ambitions were not limited simply to coal and steel. As he put it, 'Europe will not be made all at once or according to a single general plan. It will be built through concrete achievements which first create a de facto solidarity' (cited in Weigall and Stirk, 1992).

The ECSC broke new ground in two ways: it laid the foundations for a common market in the basic raw materials needed by an industrial society; and it was the first European inter-state organization to show supranational tendencies.

Schuman advocated step-by-step integration. A united Europe was the goal, but it would be achieved through 'spillover' effects (see Chapter 3). A leading ally of Schuman was the Frenchman, Jean Monnet, who became the first President of the High Authority of the ECSC (the forerunner of the Commission).

Britain was not opposed to the creation of the ECSC, but was opposed to British membership of it. As Hugo Young (1999: ch. 2) shows, there was strong opposition from Labour politicians and senior Whitehall mandarins to British participation in the 'institutional adventures' of Monnet and Schuman. Coal and steel had only recently been brought under state control, so ceding competencies in this area was an unattractive proposition. But more than this, integration also risked offending key trade unions; or, as Herbert Morrison put it: 'It's no damn good – the Durham miners won't wear it' (cited in Forster, 2002a: 299). That said, if supranational integration were to pacify Franco–German relations then it would be advantageous (it could hardly be argued otherwise). Also, the fact that the US government supported the ECSC affected the British government's stance.

A divide in interpretations of British responses to European integration in the early and mid-1950s has been identified between diplomatic historians and economic historians (Ellison, 2000: 5). Diplomatic historians focus on foreign policy and see UK policy as motivated by opposition to supranationalism, a strong preference for an Atlantic basis for European security, and a need to balance relations with Europe with those with the Commonwealth and USA (J. Young, 1993). Economic historians focus on financial policy and see that while the EC6 sought to develop a common market, Britain sought to maintain sterling's convertibility with the US dollar as a route to the re-establishment of former glories (Milward, 1992). Whatever the focus, a point that unites the two camps is the general view that Britain was not particularly successful in achieving either its diplomatic or commercial policy objectives.

The European Coal and Steel Community's institutions

The ECSC was a major innovation in international politics because participating states agreed to relinquish aspects of their sovereign authority to common institutions. This was an ambitious plan and there were those in Britain that saw it as doomed to fail because high-minded ambitions would founder on the rocks of hard-headed *realpolitik*. What these harbingers of failure did not grasp was that the ECSC was not solely motivated by high minded idealism but by calculations of national interest, particularly French ideas about how to develop peaceful relations with West Germany. Four main institutions were created to operate the ECSC:

1   The High Authority had two main tasks: to make policy proposals and to ensure that member states complied with their obligations. Member states were not allowed to give subsidies and aid to their national coal and steel industries and restrictive practices were outlawed. The High Authority was more than just a bureaucracy; it also had an important political role. Its nine members were not national representatives, but they were intended to advance the purposes of European integration.

2   The Council of Ministers was the legislature of the ECSC. There were six members of the Council, with each member state having one

representative. As member states were unwilling to lose complete control over key industries, decisions were usually made on the basis of unanimity, which meant that decision-making structures were weak because it was often difficult to get all participants to agree. The Council of Ministers introduced an important element of intergovernmentalism into the ECSC.

3   The Common Assembly was meant to provide a democratic input into the working of the ECSC. However, members of the Assembly were not directly elected, but were chosen from the ranks of national parliamentarians. They had a purely advisory role and possessed no legislative authority.

4   A Court of Justice was established to settle disputes between member states and the ECSC. When members signed the Treaty of Paris they entered into a binding legal commitment. The role of the Court was to interpret ECSC law in the event of disputes, and thus to define the parameters of supranational integration.

Although the ECSC's institutions created a supranational authority, member states were keen to have the final say in decisions that were taken. They ensured that this happened by making the Council of Ministers the decision-making body of the ECSC. Even today, decision-making power in the EU still resides to a large extent with member states in the Council of Ministers. As we see in the next chapter, this institutional hybridity has been a key feature of the EU's institutional system.

Two steps forward, one step back

Stanley Hoffmann (1966) has argued that European integration has tended to falter when it has had to deal with matters of 'high politics', such as foreign affairs and defence, and to prosper when confronted with matters of 'low politics', chiefly trade. In the early 1950s the morale of federalists was raised by the success of the ECSC, and they looked to build on this success by creating a European Defence Community. This represented a move into the domain of 'high politics' of defence, security and foreign policy.

In 1950, the leader of the opposition, Winston Churchill, had called for a unified European army acting in co-operation with the USA and West Germany. In office, though, Churchill's Conservative government of 1951 to 1955 was as hostile to supranationalism as had been its Labour predecessor, and it refused to join the EDC. The French Left was also opposed to rearmament of Germany within the EDC. The plan was killed off in August 1954 when it was rejected by the French National Assembly. Instead, in the same month, the six ECSC members plus Britain, as the west European, intergovernmental, pillar of NATO, established the West European Union (WEU). The WEU incorporated the vanquished axis powers of Germany and Italy into the collective defence structures of Western Europe.

All roads lead to Rome

The creation of the WEU could be portrayed as a triumph for intergovernmentalists and a setback for integrationists, although Milward (1992: 386) argues that the setback provided momentum for the negotiations that led to the Treaty of Rome and creation of the Common Market. By the mid-1950s integrationists sought a common market, like that set up by the Benelux countries in 1948. In June 1955 a conference of foreign ministers was convened in the Sicilian coastal town of Messina and a committee led by the Belgian foreign minister, Paul-Henri Spaak, was asked to look at options for further integration.

The British representative on the Spaak committee was a Board of Trade official, Russell Bretherton – 'the sacrificial agent' as Hugo Young called him – rather than a senior minister. This indicated the British government's lack of serious intent. The discussions centred on creation of a common market and an atomic energy authority. When, in November 1955, Spaak drew up his final report Bretherton asked that no reference to Britain's position be made. This was seen as tantamount to British withdrawal from the process, an impression that the British government was not concerned to dispel (J. Young, 1993: 47).

The outcome of the Spaak committee was two treaties of Rome signed by the six founder members (Belgium, France, Italy, the Netherlands, Luxembourg and West Germany) in March 1957: one established the European Economic Community (EEC) and the other set up the European Atomic Energy Authority (EAEA or Euratom). Thus, there are three founding treaties of the European Communities: the Treaty of Paris (1951) that created the ECSC and the two Treaties of Rome (1957) that established the EEC and Euratom. Subsequent treaties, such as the Single European Act (1986), the Maastricht Treaty (1992), the Amsterdam Treaty (1997) and the Nice Treaty, amend these founding Treaties.

The EEC became the predominant organization. Its founding Treaty was premised on 'an ever closer union of the peoples of Europe'. It sought the abolition of trade barriers and customs duties and the creation of a common external tariff, thereby making the EEC a customs union. The EEC was also designed to promote the free movement of workers, goods, services and capital within a common market. The member states transferred to the EEC powers to conclude trading agreements with international organizations on their behalf.

Four main institutions, modelled on those set up to run the ECSC, were created to manage the EC, as shown below:

1 The Commission, a supranational institution responsible for both policy proposals and implementation.
2 The Council of Ministers, the legislative authority.
3 The Common Assembly (now known as the European Parliament), with a consultative role and no legislative authority.
4 The Court of Justice, to umpire matters of dispute relating to EC law.

The EEC Treaty also made provision for a Common Agricultural Policy (CAP). Agriculture was an obvious candidate for a common policy for three main reasons. First, it would have been illogical to leave this important area of economic activity with member states. Second, the EEC and the ECSC addressed a range of industrial issues, such that an agricultural policy was seen as a balance to these concerns. Third, France, with its large agricultural sector, sought protection for its farmers as well as access to markets in other member states. Through the CAP France has been highly effective in dressing the national interest as the European interest and thus protecting one of its key economic sectors. The CAP had three founding principles:

- common agricultural prices in the EEC
- common financing (meaning an agricultural budget)
- community preference over imports.

Much of the Treaty framework was vague and depended heavily on the impetus given to integration by member states. The speed and direction of European integration have always depended heavily on their collective endeavour.

Many have argued that the 1950s were a decade of lost opportunities for the British. John Young detects national arrogance in the views of those such as the former Conservative politician, Anthony Nutting, who argued that 'Britain could have had the leadership of Europe on any terms she cared to name' (cited in J. Young, 1993: 52). The historian,

Mirian Camps, also claimed that the 1950s was a decade of 'missed opportunities' in which the leadership of Europe was Britain's 'for the asking' (Camps, 1964: 506). John Young (p. 52, emphasis in original) goes on to make a contrasting point very clearly:

> Britain could not have had the leadership of Europe *on its own terms* because Britain saw no need to abandon its sovereignty to common institutions, whereas the Six saw this as vital. Britain could only have played a key role in European integration, paradoxically, *if* it had accepted the continentals' terms and embraced supranationalism, but very few people advocated this before 1957.

The British response

By November 1955, the British were developing a plan that they hoped would lure the EC 'six' away from the supranational integration and towards the British preference for a free trade association without supranational pretensions. The result of Britain's alternative plan was the creation of EFTA, set up by the Stockholm Convention of July 1959. EFTA was in accord with the British preference for intergovernmentalism. The seven signatories – Denmark, Norway, Sweden, Portugal, Austria, Switzerland and Britain – established a free trade area which brought down barriers to trade between members and sought to keep in touch with EC tariff reductions. Europe was now at sixes and sevens.

By the early 1960s it had become apparent to the British that EFTA was peripheral to the fast-growing economies of the EC. A powerful trading bloc was emerging on Britain's doorstep from which it was excluded. In the 1960s the EC appeared to be going from success to success as the Common External Tariff was put in place and the CAP established. Britain was forced into a re-evaluation of previous policy and sought membership of the EC. However, as will be seen, de Gaulle was distinctly underwhelmed by the prospect of British membership and vetoed the first two British accession bids.

The origins of the European Community

A rapid process of European integration was instigated in the 1950s by the institution of the ECSC, the EEC and Euratom. An anti-Europeanism evident in British politics during the 1950s hardened into an anti-Common

Market stance motivated by a dislike of supranational integration's implications for the British political elites view of their country's place in the world (Forster, 2002a).

During the 1950s, supranational integration remained largely confined to the area of low politics and failed to break into the domain of high politics following rejection of the EDC in 1954.

Britain remained aloof from supranational organizations. However, this was not just the product of its distrust of supranationalism; as the former US Secretary of State, Dean Acheson, put it in 1960, the British had lost an Empire and were trying to find a role. Despite decolonization, the Empire/Commonwealth retained a powerful influence over many Conservative MPs and remained 'the main religion of the Tory Party' in the 1950s as R.A. Butler put it (cited in Forster, 2002a: 299). These historical ties and economic entanglements created some real tensions within the British elite when trade policies and relations with the USA, the Commonwealth and the European Community were discussed.

By the end of the 1950s a basic divide had emerged in Europe between the 'EC6' and the 'EFTA7'. The EU proved to be the magnet to which EFTA countries have been attracted. By 2002 most of the EFTA member states had joined the EC (Austria, Britain, Denmark, Portugal and Sweden). Norway rejected membership in referendums in 1972 and 1994, but is associated with the EU through the European Economic Area.

1960s: Britain says yes, de Gaulle says no

Britain is commonly referred to as awkward or reluctant, but other member states have been 'awkward' too. In the 1960s France under the leadership of de Gaulle unilaterally vetoed British accession and strongly opposed the development of qualified majority voting in the Council of Ministers. Kaiser (1996) argues that the UK had come to terms with majority voting as early as 1961. British policy towards the EC was re-evaluated in the 1960s. Both Macmillan (between 1961 and 1963) and Wilson (in 1967) pursued membership of the Community, only to be rebuffed by de Gaulle's veto. The other member states supported UK accession, but the General's '*non*' was enough to block British membership. It was left to Heath to lead Britain into the EC in January 1973.

De Gaulle's vision was of Europe as a third force between the super-powers of both east and west, ideally with him as its leader. He thought Britain would seek to dominate the EC and place it firmly in the American bloc. Britain and America shared a 'globalist' perspective, of which central features were commitment to an open world trading order and rejection of protectionism.

Four broad characteristics of British policy towards the EC in the 1950s should be highlighted: first, aloofness towards Europe based on a perception, as Churchill put it, that Britain was 'with them' against the greater foe of Communism, but not 'of them' in participating in integration. Second, there was opposition to the sovereignty-eroding implications of supranational integration. British national identity had, if anything, been strengthened by the experience of the Second World War. The sovereignty that had been so keenly defended then was not about to be ceded to supranational institutions in Europe. Third, the other side of this perspective was that accession would be a sign of failure and of Britain's diminished status in the world. Fourth, the development of an alternative policy focused on the Empire and the 'special relationship' with the USA, but by the early 1960s the British government was questioning its aloofness towards the EC. The 'special relationship' with the USA had been dented by the Suez crisis of 1956, when the USA had declined to support Britain's military intervention in Egypt. The relationship was beginning to seem more special in British eyes than in American, and post-war hopes of partnership had been replaced by an economic and military dependence by means of which Britain was consigned to a role of 'increasingly impotent avuncularity' (Edwards, 1993: 209).

Britain was also worried that its close ties with America could be supplanted by links between the USA and the EC. The USA feared that de Gaulle's 'third force' aspirations for Europe would weaken the Western alliance, and hoped Britain would steer the EC in a direction sympathetic to American interests. In July 1962 President Kennedy called for an Atlantic partnership between the USA and the EC, including Britain. He wanted to see an outward-looking and open EC and wanted Britain to be part of it.

In the 1960s the Commonwealth ideal that nations of the former Empire could co-operate on an equal footing took several dents. Divisions emerged between the 'black' and 'white' Commonwealth over, for example, Britain's less than wholehearted denunciation of the racist South African regime after the Sharpeville massacre of 1961. Conflict also arose between India and Pakistan over the disputed territory of Kashmir, and over the unilateral declaration of independence made by Ian Smith's regime in Rhodesia in 1965.

By the time Harold Wilson became Prime Minister in 1964, economic concerns impelled the membership bid. EFTA was not proving a success when compared to the dynamic economies of the EC, and Commonwealth trading patterns were changing as Australia and New Zealand looked to markets in the USA and Japan. Wilson had come to office espousing 'the white heat of the scientific revolution' that would modernize the British economy. Larger markets were needed for high technology industries – such as aircraft and computers – but exclusion from the EC meant separation from the supranational institutions that united fast-growing neighbouring economies.

On all usual economic indicators Britain was lagging behind the EC. For example, between 1958 and 1968 real earnings in Britain rose by 38 per cent, compared to 75 per cent in the EC. Fear of isolation is apparent in a memorandum sent by Macmillan to his Foreign Secretary, Selwyn Lloyd, in 1959: 'For the first time since the Napoleonic era the major continental powers are united in a positive economic grouping, with considerable political aspects, which, although not specifically directed against the United Kingdom, may have the effect of excluding us both from European markets and from consultation in European policy.'

1973: membership

In 1969 the political complexion of the two countries at the heart of European integration – France and West Germany – changed in a way advantageous to Britain's membership hopes. In France President de Gaulle resigned and was replaced by Georges Pompidou, who (as will be seen) favoured British accession. In West Germany the new Social Democratic government, led by Willy Brandt, was also keen to see enlargement of the EC.

However, prior to the accession of new member states the founder members laid down a budgetary framework for the Community at a heads of government meeting in The Hague in 1969. This was formalized by Treaty in 1970 and provided a classic example of rules that were not to Britain's advantage being determined in the absence of input from the British government. Britain was obliged to accept the *acquis communautaire* (the entire body of European law), including the budgetary arrangements. When Britain joined it contributed 8.64 per cent of the budget, rising to 18.72 per cent in 1977. Construction of the EC's 'own resources' was not to Britain's advantage as it effectively penalized countries with extensive trading links outside the EC and those that had efficient agricultural sectors. Goods entering the EC from non-member states encounter the EC's Common External Tariff, which then becomes part of the Community's 'own resources'. Having substantial trading links with non-EC countries, notably those in the Commonwealth, Britain was disadvantaged from the start by this measure. Britain's relatively efficient agricultural sector meant that much benefit was not secured from the main financial activity of the EC, the Common Agricultural Policy and its support system for (particularly French) farmers.

Negotiations on British accession began in June 1970 under the Conservative Prime Minister, Edward Heath. In July 1971 a White Paper was published. It noted some of the disadvantages of membership as follows:

1   It was estimated that food prices would go up by 15 per cent over a six-year period because the CAP contained a system of Community preference which would mean that Britain could no longer shop around on cheaper world food markets.
2   Increased food prices would contribute to a 3 per cent increase in the cost of living over a six-year period.
3   British contributions to the EC budget would amount to £300 million a year, making Britain the second largest contributor behind West Germany. British contributions would be high because it had extensive external trading links.

Although Heath was pursuing a policy developed by his Conservative and Labour predecessors who had come to the conclusion that EC membership was necessary if Britain was not to risk economic and political isolation, he was more than merely a pragmatic European. Indeed, Heath was a wholehearted advocate of British membership and remained a convinced Euro-enthusiast throughout his political career. In this he stands apart from many of his Eurosceptic opponents who started out as supporters of British membership of the EC before becoming vociferous critics.

Edward Heath's political outlook was shaped by formative experiences in his youth when he travelled extensively in Europe and saw the rise of Nazism at first hand, even being present at the Nuremberg rally in 1938 (Heath, 1998). Heath's maiden speech as an MP in 1951 had extolled the merits of the ECSC and advocated British membership. Heath remained a stalwart defender of the EU and a vigorous opponent of the Eurosceptics even after the tide within the Conservative Party had turned strongly against him in the 1990s. On pragmatic grounds, too, Heath was convinced of the merits of British accession. Even though there were some points of contention and some areas where EC and British priorities did not fit, he thought that Britain had little option but to enter the EC and try to shape it from within.

Geoffrey Rippon led the British negotiating team. The application was co-ordinated through the Cabinet Office in an attempt to prevent Whitehall rivalries and tensions scuppering the application. Since the first accession application in 1961, the pace of European integration had quickened considerably. By the early 1970s there were 13,000 typewritten pages of Community legislation covering key areas of EC activity such as the Common Agricultural Policy and the common market (by 2003 there were some 80,000 pages). The leading official negotiator, Sir Con O'Neill, summed up some of the frustrations of the negotiating team when he wrote in 1972 Foreign Office report that: 'None of its policies were essential to us. Many of them were objectionable.' But they had to be accepted if accession was to occur or, as O'Neill also put it, 'swallow the lot, and swallow it now' (cited in H. Young, 1999: 227). That said, the UK did secure some adjustments to EC rules that favoured Commonwealth trading partners for a five-year transition period.

Aside from the negotiation details, there was another crucial element to British accession: the support of French President, Georges Pompidou. Heath (1998: 367–70) had already established a good relationship with Pompidou. The British–French summit meeting, 19–20 May 1971, was central to UK accession. Pompidou supported UK accession for a variety of reasons. It would allow him to distinguish himself from de Gaulle (Pompidou did not share de Gaulle's distrust of the 'Anglo-Saxons'). Another French rejection of British membership could have irreparably damaged UK–French relations. Finally, when compared to the Labour leader, Harold Wilson, there was little doubt that Heath 'meant it' when he sought full membership and that he would not be distracted by the Commonwealth or USA. In the Salon des Fêtes of the Elysée Palace where de Gaulle had vetoed UK accession in 1963, Pompidou (standing alongside Heath) declared that:

> Many people believed that Great Britain was not and did not wish to become European, and that Britain wanted to enter the Community only so as to destroy it or divert it from its objectives … Well ladies and gentlemen, you see before you tonight two men who are convinced of the contrary. (cited in Heath, 1998: 372)

This gave firm impetus to the negotiations, which then required Parliamentary approval. This was secured on 28 October 1971 when

MPs voted by 356 to 244 in favour of accession to the Community, but the Conservative government relied on support from 69 Labour MPs who defied a three line whip to support accession. The House of Lords endorsed membership even more overwhelmingly by 451 votes to 58. The Treaty of Accession was signed in Brussels on 22 January 1972.

British accession occurred just as the economies of Western Europe were ending their long post-war period of economic growth. Britain could hardly have chosen a less propitious moment to dip a tentative toe into the waters of supranational economic and political integration. Oil price increases soon helped to plunge the British and European economies into recession.

Conclusion

This chapter has explored the attitudes of British governments towards European economic and political integration in the period from the end of the Second World War, the commencement of the Cold War and the onset of supranational economic and political integration, initially through the ECSC and then in the form of the EEC. Across the political spectrum and at the highest official level, there was scepticism about the European project initiated by the French and Germans. The chapter also sought to identify the policy preferences that underlay these attitudes, the capacity to attain these objectives and the ways in which preferences and objectives changed over time. It was shown that during the 1950s in neither commercial nor diplomatic terms was there a deeply held view at the highest political level that European economic and political integration was in the UK's interests. The UK was prepared to sponsor integration, but was not itself prepared to participate in the common structures of a supranational community. This was founded on a view that Britain's commercial interests did not lie exclusively with this European grouping and that a route to recovery of great power status could be found through the Commonwealth and the special relationship with the USA. By the 1960s it had become clear that the context within which these preferences were exercised was changing: the Commonwealth ideal and the special relationship had both been dented, the UK economy was growing at a slower rate than the EC countries, and European integration was proving to be a success. Taken together, these indicators of relative decline instigated some form of national identity crisis. Britain had won the war, but seemed to be losing the peace. But rather than being seen as a route to reclaimed influence,

European integration was seen by many as amounting to recognition of Britain's diminished place in the world. Any conversion to Europe was unlikely to be heartfelt.

These indicators of relative British decline cannot be ignored. The re-evaluation of British relations with the EU prompted a decision in the early 1960s to abandon the experiment in intergovernmental free trade centred on EFTA and for Britain to throw in its lot with the EC. The capacity to attain this objective was seriously undermined by the opposition of de Gaulle, because in his view Britain did not 'mean it' and would steer the EC in the direction of US interests. The change of government in France opened the door to UK membership, as too did Edward Heath's genuine and wholehearted desire for British membership.

These developments also have a broader long-term significance. First, as historical institutionalists point out, initial policy choices can have long-term effects because they establish a path for policy developments from which it can become more difficult to deviate over time. UK governments faced problems with European integration during the 1950s and 1960s because when push came to shove they did not *believe* in the European project to the extent that the member states did. When it did arrive, UK engagement was based on a pragmatic and instrumental view of European integration that remained strongly influenced by preferences for Atlanticism, intergovernmentalism and global free trade. The British political elite were also economical with the truth when it came to divulging to the British people the nature of the organization that Britain was joining. The EC was often portrayed as a common market devoted to trade objectives. The political implications had been clear since the 1950s, but were played down in the UK. This was unlikely to provide fertile ground for acceptance of more ambitious integration plans in the future.

A second point that builds on the historical legacy of these choices made during the 1950s and 1960s is that strong elements of continuity can be detected in Britain's relations with the EU. The maintenance of close ties with the USA, support for a vision of Europe that focuses on the central role of member states, and a preference for free trade and open markets all provide a link between British attitudes in the 1950s and aspects of New Labour's approach in the first decade of the twenty-first century. The next chapter develops these themes by analysing events since Britain joined the club in 1973 and the patterns of continuity and change that have been evident.

5

Full-Hearted Consent? Britain in Europe from Heath to Blair

Introduction

How can British relations with the EU since Britain joined the club in 1973 be explained? The previous chapter suggested the powerful legacy of post-war events. This chapter takes these analytical strands forward by exploring British relations with the EC/EU from the premiership of Edward Heath until that of Tony Blair. The chapter continues the Britain in Europe theme by exploring the preferences of British governments, the motivations for these preferences, the capacity to attain UK objectives and the ways in which preferences, motivation and capacity have changed over time. It will be shown how Britain engaged with important developments in European integration such as the Single European Act and the Maastricht Treaty. The chapter will link with the Europe in Britain themes by indicating the ways in which political changes in the UK (such as the development of Conservative Euroscepticism in the 1990s) had effects on Britain's relations with the EU and led to serious questions being asked about Britain's continued membership of the organization. The chapter will conclude with an overview of New Labour's EU policies and will ask whether they also indicate continued differential and conditional engagement with the EU and, as such, despite some of Blair's rhetorical commitment to Europe, are actually indicative of substantial continuities in Britain's EU policies.

1974–5: renegotiation and referendum

EC membership in 1973 was for Edward Heath his defining political accomplishment and the one of which he remained most proud. This counted for little when continued British economic decline and major industrial disputes led to the fall of his government in February 1974 and his replacement as Prime Minister by Harold Wilson. As leader of the opposition Britain's membership of the EC posed something of a dilemma for Wilson. As Prime Minister he had sought EC membership in 1967, but in Britain's adversarial political system he could use EC membership as a device to criticize the Heath government. Moreover, there was deep opposition to the EC within the Labour Party and labour movement. Wilson's strategy was to oppose the terms of accession as negotiated by Heath and pledge a future Labour government to renegotiation and a referendum. This caused tensions within the Labour Party at the highest level (most notably, for the Deputy Leader and convinced pro-European, Roy Jenkins). Wilson's reasoning was that a shift to a broader public debate could avoid deep Labour Party divisions being exposed to the public with the result being, as James Callaghan put it, that the referendum was 'a life raft into which one day the whole Party [might] have to climb' (cited in Forster, 2002a: 303). Labour were involved in some opportunistic u-turns when one considers their 1967 attempt to secure membership, but the depth of opposition within the Party made a referendum an attractive proposition. Harold Wilson gave responsibility for co-ordinating Labour's opposition to the accession treaty in the House of Commons to the confirmed anti-EC duo of Michael Foot and Peter Shore. The contrast here with Conservative Party management is interesting. Heath had marginalized opponents of the EC and excluded them from the membership negotiations. Labour at this time had anti-marketeers in senior positions within the government and involved in discussions at the highest level about Britain's future in Europe.

After Labour returned to power in February 1974 renegotiation talks were led by the Foreign Secretary, James Callaghan. Callaghan has been described by his biographer as emphasizing from the start 'his coolness about the European project and his intention of dissecting it in its fundamentals'. When officials suggested that there might be some leeway on the budget and the CAP, Callaghan rebuked them, asking if they had read the Labour Party manifesto, and stated that if they had then they would discover that the Labour government's aim was a fundamental renegotiation of the Treaty of Accession (cited in Morgan, 1997: 412–13). This was hardly likely to go down well with the other member states. That the Eurosceptic Peter Shore and the pro-European Roy Hattersley then carried out the detailed discussions may have appeased Labour's pro- and anti-Common Market brigades, but it baffled other member states.

Why should other member states accede to British demands? There were many good reasons why they might find them irritating. After all, unravelling the complex EU *acquis* to favour the British might prompt other member states to seek some compensation too. For instance, if the British were to get some help with their budget contributions, then why not the West Germans who were also big contributors?

Britain gained little through the renegotiation that it could not have gained through normal Community channels. The degree of acrimony engendered by the bargaining soured Britain's relations with other members for many years. For what they were worth, the House of Commons endorsed the renegotiated terms by 396 votes to 170 in April 1975. Ominously for the Labour government, and despite pro-Community speeches from both Wilson and Callaghan, a special Labour conference on 26 April 1975 voted by 3.7 million to 1.9 million to leave the EC.

The pledge to hold a referendum helped Wilson overcome divisions within the Labour Party. Indeed, it seems likely that this was the referendum's major purpose. During the referendum campaign of 1975 Wilson suspended the convention of collective Cabinet responsibility so Cabinet ministers could speak according to their consciences. The 'Yes' campaign commanded powerful political assets despite opinion polls at the outset pointing to a 'No' vote. It had strong support from Fleet Street and from influential business interests, which provided a large part of the £1.5 million spent in the quest for an affirmative vote. It also gathered a powerful coalition of centrist politicians, including Heath, Labour's Roy Jenkins and the Liberal leader, Jeremy Thorpe. By comparison, the 'No' campaign raised just £133,000. It found itself outgunned and was weakened by its disparate character: Tony Benn from the left of the Labour Party formed a decidedly uneasy temporary alliance with right-wingers such as Enoch Powell. The outcome, on 5 June 1975, was a two to one vote in favour of continued membership on a 64 per cent turnout (Butler and Kitzinger, 1976; King, 1977). The anti-EC National Referendum Campaign soon fizzled out with the rapid disappearance of its 12 regional offices and 250 local branches (Forster, 2002a: 304).

1976–9: Callaghan's difficulties

In April 1976 James Callaghan succeeded Harold Wilson as Prime Minister and inherited a Labour Party divided over EC membership. Labour's rank and file distrusted the EC even though some prominent Labour politicians, such as Roy Jenkins and Shirley Williams, were keen advocates of membership. There were two main areas of concern: first, it was felt that integration into a supranational community would restrict national sovereignty and the freedom of action of a Labour government; and second, the EC was seen as a 'capitalist club' with market-based purposes that offered little to working people. Arguments over EC membership were symptomatic of a creeping malaise within the Labour Party that saw the leadership frequently at odds with the membership and which culminated in a grassroots move to the left, with right-wingers splitting to form the Social Democratic Party (SDP) in January 1981.

In February 1975 the Conservatives replaced Edward Heath as leader with Margaret Thatcher. Thatcher had opposed the 1975 referendum, describing it, in a phrase that would come back to haunt her in her Eurosceptical dotage (when she called for a referendum on the Maastricht Treaty), as a device for demagogues. She argued for a 'Yes' vote on the grounds that Britain needed to foster economic links with the European markets on its doorstep.

Callaghan's pragmatism and Atlanticism meant he held no truck with the lofty rhetoric of European union. He had a poor reputation in EC circles as a result of his dogged pursuit of national interests during the British renegotiation, and failed as premier to ease tensions caused by Britain's entry to the Community.

From March 1977 Callaghan relied on support from the Liberals to sustain his administration. This support was conditional upon the insertion of a clause introducing proportional representation as the method of voting in direct elections to the European Parliament. Such a clause was duly inserted into the European Assembly Elections Bill of 1977. However, it provoked a Cabinet revolt and, on a free vote in the House of Commons, was defeated. It also delayed direct elections, which, to the irritation of other member states, were put back from 1978 to 1979.

The British Presidency of the EC in the first six months of 1977 did little to enhance Britain's reputation. Callaghan was hamstrung by a Eurosceptical party and by domestic economic problems. In a letter to the General Secretary of the Labour Party at the start of the British Presidency, he outlined three basic principles that informed the Labour government's stance on the EC:

- maintenance of the authority of EC nation states and national parliaments, with no increase in the powers of the European Parliament
- emphasis on the necessity for national governments to achieve their own economic, regional and industrial objectives
- reform of the budget procedure.

Contained within these policy principles is a clear restatement of Britain's suspicion of supranationalism and continued concern over the high level of budget contributions. Margaret Thatcher shared these concerns when she became Prime Minister in May 1979. Thus while she became well known for battling for a budget rebate and opposing extensions of supranational authority, Britain's reputation as an awkward partner both preceded and survived her.

British membership of the EC was advocated on pragmatic economic grounds. Many British people seemed to think that they were joining a Common Market – an economic organization that was little more than a glorified free trade area – although the political intent of the European Community had been clear since its foundation in the 1950s. The idea that the EC was essentially designed as a glorified free trade area was not true. Suffice to recall that Britain's alternative to the EC in the form of EFTA was just such an organization, but this largely failed. Yet the pragmatic acceptance of membership by Britain and the understanding propagated by some of the original purposes of the 'Common Market' mean that Britain has tended to judge the EC by utilitarian standards: what does it have to pay and what does it get out of it? Britain was paying a lot in the late 1970s and early 1980s and seemed to be getting little in return. Not surprisingly, enthusiasm for the EC did not run deep.

1979–84: the budget rebate

When Margaret Thatcher took office in 1979, the Conservatives were seen as a pro-European party. In her 1981 speech to the Conservative Party conference Thatcher reflected on British membership of the EC and noted that:

> it is vital that we get it right. Forty-three out of every hundred pounds that we earn abroad comes from the Common Market. Over two million jobs depend on our trade with Europe, two million jobs which will be put at risk by Britain's withdrawal [Labour's policy at the time]. And even if we kept two thirds of our trade with the Common Market after we had flounced out – and that is pretty optimistic – there would be a million more to join the dole queues. (Harris, 1997: 147)

But Thatcher's pro-Europeanism was distinct from that of her predecessor, Heath. While Heath 'lived and breathed the air of Europe', Thatcher tended to depict European unity as desirable in terms of anti-Soviet policy

(H. Young, 1989: 184). From the mid-1980s onwards, Thatcher began to take a more populist line on Europe and viewed the EC, its institutions and other European leaders with much suspicion (see Chapter 9 for more discussion of Euroscepticism).

Europe was, however, not a central political theme of the first two Thatcher governments (1979–83 and 1983–7), which focused on domestic economic policy and external events such as the miners' strike, the Falklands War (1982–3) and the US bombing of Libya (1986). Probably the most pressing issue was the British contribution to the EC budget. By the end of the 1970s Britain was the second largest contributor to the budget and was in danger of becoming the largest, paying over £1 billion a year, even though it had the third-lowest GDP per capita of the nine member states.

A series of often acrimonious negotiations – 'patient' and 'a little impatient diplomacy' as Thatcher put it in her speech to the 1984 Conservative Party conference – were held between 1979 and 1984. The then Commission President, Roy Jenkins, writes in his memoirs of long hours spent discussing the BBQ: the British Budget Question (or, as he preferred to put it, the Bloody British Question). He notes how Thatcher made a bad start at the Strasbourg Summit in 1979 when she had a strong case but succeeded in alienating other leaders whose support she needed if a deal were to be struck. Britain's partners in the Community were unwilling to receive lectures on the issue from Thatcher and were alienated by suggestions that the budget mechanisms were tantamount to theft of British money, particularly as Britain had known the budgetary implications when it had joined (Jenkins, 1991: 495). The issue was finally resolved at the Fontainebleau summit in June 1984 when a rebate was agreed amounting to 66 per cent of the difference between Britain's value added tax (VAT) contributions to the budget and its receipts. The next chapter shows that the UK remains the second largest contributor to the EU budget, behind Germany.

The Fontainebleau agreement was important as it meant that EC leaders could lift their sights from interminable squabbles over the budget and begin to think strategically about the future of the Community. 'More generally, the resolution of this dispute meant that the Community could now press ahead with the enlargement [to Portugal and Spain] and with the Single Market measures which I wanted to see', as Thatcher put it (Thatcher, 1993: 545). The British government's preferences had been clearly stated in a paper, entitled 'Europe: The Future', circulated at the Fontainebleau summit (HM Government, 1984). The paper called for the attainment by 1990 of a single market within which goods, services, people and capital could move freely. It very clearly reflected the deregulatory zeal that Thatcher brought to domestic politics. The legacy of these ideas about deregulation and liberalization have also been strongly felt in British government preferences towards European integration in the administrations that have come since Margaret Thatcher left office in 1990. Buller (2000) argues that the single market project was seen as a way of enshrining core Thatcherite principles at EC level. The fact that this Thatcherite vision of a liberalized, deregulated EC was not widely accepted by other member states can help explain the development of Conservative Euroscepticism in the late 1980s and through the 1990s.

There is another point here too. Thatcherism also changed the rules of the game of domestic economic and social policy and shifted ideas about the respective roles of the state and market. Even though they may not have been widely accepted at EU level they have had major effects on British domestic politics with implications that can be traced through to current dilemmas, such as New Labour's position on replacing the pound with the Euro.

1984–7: towards the single market

In Britain Thatcher had sought to 'roll back the frontiers of the state' and allow free enterprise and market forces to flourish. Thatcherism embodied what has been characterized as the amalgam of the free economy and the strong state (Gamble, 1988). For Thatcherites the EC was a stultifying bureaucracy that could do with a dose of Thatcherite free market vigour, whether it liked it or not.

In order to secure the single market promoted in the Fontainebleau paper Britain needed allies amongst its EC partners. There were potential allies at both the national and supranational level, as shown below:

1   The two key member states, France and West Germany, were amenable to single market reforms. The French Socialist government elected in 1981 had abandoned its reflationary economic policies in 1983 (under the then Finance Minister, Jacques Delors), and the Christian Democrat-led coalition of Chancellor Kohl in West Germany supported the creation of a single market
2   The new Commission President, Jacques Delors, took office in 1985 and seized upon the single market as his 'big idea' to restart integration and shake off the 'Eurosclerosis' of the 1970s and early 1980s.

The Commissioner responsible for the internal market, the former Conservative Cabinet minister, Lord Cockfield, assisted Delors in his ambitions.

A White Paper prepared by the Commission put forward 300 legislative proposals for the single market. These were later whittled down to 282. Heads of government at the Milan summit in June 1985 accepted the proposals. In the face of objections from the Danes, Greeks and British, an intergovernmental conference was convened to consider reform of the EC's decision-making process to accompany the single market plan.

Whilst Britain was hostile to strengthening Community institutions, France and West Germany asserted that attainment of the single market in fact necessitated increased powers for supranational institutions such as the European Parliament in order to ensure that decision-making efficiency and a measure of democratic accountability followed the transfer of authority to the supranational level. The British did not see it that way and thought the single market could be achieved without reform of the EC's institutions. In her memoirs, Thatcher recalled that, 'it would have been better if, as I had wanted originally, there had been no IGC [intergovernmental conference], no new treaty and just some limited practical arrangements'. The British government compromised on some issues such as increased use of qualified majority voting in order to secure more prized single market objectives. The resultant Single European Act (SEA) had three main features (the first of which was actively supported by the British government, while the latter two were not):

1 Establishment of a target date, the end of 1992, for completion of the internal market and attainment of the 'four freedoms': freedom of movement of people, goods, services and capital.
2 Strengthening of EC institutional structures, with qualified majority voting (QMV) introduced in the Council of Ministers to cover new policy areas relating to harmonization measures necessary to achieve the single market. Increased use of QMV ensured swifter decision-making. Unanimity was still required for fiscal policy, the free movement of persons and employees' rights legislation. The European Parliament's role was strengthened by introduction of the 'co-operation procedure', which gave power to suggest amendments to Community legislation. The Council retained the right to reject Parliament's amendments.
3 A new chapter of the Treaty was added covering 'Social and Economic Cohesion'.

The Thatcherite vision was of a limited 'regulatory' European state (as discussed in Chapter 3) within which the role of European institutions would be to police the single market without becoming involved in the core allocative and distributive questions that would remain largely the concern of national governments and market forces. The Commission's White Paper put forward by the Commission identified three kinds of barriers to trade that needed to come down if the single market was to be attained:

- physical barriers (mainly customs and border controls)
- fiscal barriers (indirect taxes vary in the Community and constitute a barrier to trade)
- technical barriers; these were very significant because member states had developed their own product standards which differed widely and formed a substantial barrier to free trade.

The single market programme and ideas about what it should involve provided a backdrop for Conservative Euroscepticism. For Thatcherites, the single market was an end in itself that could raise to a European stage the liberalizing and deregulatory elements of the Thatcherite project. For many other member states, the SEA was a means to an end, that end being deeper economic and political integration with the EC taking a bigger role in flanking areas such as social and regional policy, while also moving towards far more ambitious projects such as economic and monetary union. This gap between many other member states and the Thatcher governments centred on the respective roles of the state and market. This gap grew in the 1990s because of the acceptance among Eurosceptics that European integration would bring with it Brussels-imposed re-regulation of the UK economy.

1987–90: Thatcher's last hurrah

The final years of Margaret Thatcher's premiership were characterized by an almost incessant battle against spillover effects generated by the SEA. For the French and Germans, who had been key single market allies, adoption of a plan to complete the single market was a new beginning for integration. They sought to consolidate the success of the SEA by promoting integration in other areas. Plans were hatched for EMU and for Community social policies to ensure minimum rights for workers in the wake of the freedoms given to capital by the SEA.

Thatcher firmly set herself against the integrative consequences of the SEA. This was particularly evident in her response to questioning in the House of Commons following the Berlin summit meeting of EU heads of government in October 1990. During her responses, she departed from the pre-arranged and carefully worded text to launch into an attack on the integrative ambitions of other EC member states and the docility in front of this threat (as she saw it) of the opposition Labour Party. A section of Thatcher's response is cited below:

> Yes, the Commission wants to increase its powers. Yes, it is a non-elected body and I do not want the Commission to increase its powers at the expense of the House, so of course we differ. The President of the Commission, Mr. Delors, said at a press conference the other day that he wanted the European Parliament to be the democratic body of the Community, he wanted the Commission to be the Executive and he wanted the Council of Ministers to be the Senate. No. No. No.
>
> Perhaps the Labour party would give all those things up easily. Perhaps it would agree to a single currency and abolition of the pound sterling. Perhaps, being totally incompetent in monetary matters, it would be only too delighted to hand over full responsibility to a central bank, as it did to the IMF. The fact is that the Labour party has no competence on money and no competence on the economy – so, yes, the right hon. Gentleman [referring to opposition leader Neil Kinnock] would be glad to hand it all over. What is the point of trying to get elected to Parliament only to hand over sterling and the powers of this House to Europe? (*Hansard*, Vol. 178, Col. 869, 30 October 1990)

This statement exposed divisions within the Conservative Party and was the breaking point for the Leader of the House of Commons (as well as the ex-Chancellor of the Exchequer and Foreign Secretary), Sir Geoffrey Howe. Moreover, as the Conservatives languished in the opinion polls in 1990 and the disastrous 'poll tax' prompted massive civil disobedience across the country, many Conservative MPs began to see Margaret Thatcher as an electoral liability (Watkins, 1991). The final straw for Howe was Thatcher's response to questioning after the Berlin summit. He resigned from the cabinet and used his resignation statement to bitterly criticize her leadership style. Howe's speech was the beginning of the end for Thatcher's premiership. Howe (1995: 667) stated that 'the Prime Minister's perceived attitude towards Europe is running increasingly serious risks for the future of our nation. It risks minimizing our influence and maximizing once again our chances of being once again shut out.' Howe's statement prompted the long-standing opponent of Thatcherism, Michael Heseltine, to launch a leadership challenge, although he was deeply unpopular amongst many Conservative MPs who remained attached to Thatcherite ideas, even if the lady herself had left office. This allowed John Major to come through the middle as the candidate who would maintain the Thatcher legacy while bringing a more emollient style to government and international relations, or at least that was the thinking of many Conservative MPs. Major was perceived as the inheritor of the Thatcherite mantle, not least by Thatcher herself. Major had enjoyed a rapid ascent of the government hierarchy, including a remarkably brief stint as Foreign Secretary (July – October 1989), but his views on Europe were unclear. They remained so for much of his premiership.

1990–3: Major, the Exchange Rate Mechanism and Maastricht

Within the EC John Major adopted a more conciliatory tone than his predecessor and expressed the intention of placing Britain 'at the heart of Europe'. In particular there was an attempt to improve relations with Germany that had become frosty, not least because of a seminar organized by the Prime Minister at her country residence, Chequers, to 'analyse' the German character. In a summary of the meeting that was strongly disputed by many of the participants (see, for example, Urban, 1996), the following were identified in the minutes of the meeting as aspects of the German character: 'angst, aggressiveness, assertiveness, bullying, egotism, inferiority complex, sentimentality', accompanied by 'a capacity for excess' and 'a tendency to over-estimate their own strengths and capabilities' (Urban, 1996: 151). These conclusions, drafted by Thatcher's foreign policy adviser, Charles Powell, outraged many of those present who had actually focused during the meeting on the remarkable transformation and stability of the Federal Republic.

Much of the fear among Conservative Eurosceptics was based on the power of the German economy and reunified Germany's key role as the largest EU member state. This was the sub-text for development of the plan for EMU in the late 1980s. France, in particular, was a keen advocate of EMU because it was seen as securing Germany within the EU and thus, as Chancellor Kohl once put it, giving Germany a European roof rather than Europe a German one. The British Conservative government was deeply divided about the plan for EMU and its forerunners, the European Monetary System (EMS) and the ERM. Thatcher was growing more sceptical about European integration and opposed EMU as a threat to national sovereignty, while her Foreign Secretary Howe and Chancellor Lawson supported ERM membership. At the June 1989 Madrid summit Thatcher was pressured by her Chancellor, Nigel Lawson, and her Foreign Secretary, Sir Geoffrey Howe, to set a date for ERM membership. She resisted, but was forced to set a series of conditions that were to be met if Britain was to sign up to ERM (although these were not met when the UK did join a year later).

Chancellor Lawson saw ERM as strongly related to domestic anti-inflationary policy. As he put it in his resignation statement to the House of Commons on 31 October 1989:

> Full UK membership of the EMS ... would signally enhance the credibility of our anti-inflationary resolve in general and the role of exchange rate discipline in particular ... there is also a vital political dimension ... I have little doubt that we [Britain] will not be able to exert ... influence effectively and successfully provide ... leadership, as long as we remain outside. (cited in Balls, 2002)

Lawson and Howe both left their high offices for reasons linked to these divisions over Britain and Europe, but their successors (Major in the Treasury and Douglas Hurd in the Foreign Office) were equally strong advocates of British participation in the ERM. By June 1990 Thatcher was forced to concede because, as she put it in her memoirs, 'I had too few allies left to resist and win the day' (Thatcher, 1993: 772). ERM membership tied sterling to the Deutschmark at a rate of £1 to DM2.95 and required market interventions to maintain exchange rate parities at levels 6 per cent below or above this central rate. A crucial reason for membership was the attainment of domestic economic objectives and to add external credibility to anti-inflationary policies. The downside was that it was far from clear that these external commitments would tally with the domestic economic situation. There was little direct evidence to suggest that the ERM would necessarily bring stability. Moreover, the enormous economic consequences of German reunification and subsequent high German interest rates could well place unsustainable pressure on sterling's ERM parities. While German interest rates remained high then so too would British interest rates, even though the UK economy was struggling to emerge from recession and required lower interest rates. Stephens (1996: 259) argues that the main mistake was 'the elevation of exchange rate parity into a badge of pride ... ensuring that when defeat came it was devastating'. As will be discussed in Chapters 7 and 9, the ERM fiasco was to shatter the reputation of the Conservative Party for economic competence and impel Tory Eurosceptic rebellion (see Chapter 9).

Major also faced the issue of the IGCs convened to discuss deeper economic and political integration. Despite Major's softer style there were within the British government's negotiating position at Maastricht in December 1991 a number of continuities linking Thatcher and Major:

1   An opt-out from the Social Chapter. The Secretary of State for Employment, Michael Howard, had said that he would resign if the Social Chapter were accepted (Lamont, 1997: 133).
2   The right for the British Parliament to decide whether Britain would enter the third stage of the plan for EMU when a single currency would be introduced.
3   Promotion of the notion of subsidiarity which, in the eyes of the Conservative government, was a way of reinforcing national perspectives on Community decision-making.
4   Advocacy of intergovernmental co-operation rather than supranational integration as the basis of cohesion in foreign, defence and interior policy. Intergovernmental 'pillars' were incorporated into the Maastricht Treaty.

Unconstrained by high office, Thatcher remarked that she would never have signed the Maastricht Treaty. However, the treaty Major negotiated and signed could be seen as reflecting inherited policy preferences. In addition, Major also reaped the integrative whirlwind which Thatcher had helped initiate when she signed the SEA in 1986.

Major's deal at Maastricht temporarily assuaged Tory divisions over Europe and helped lay the foundations for his April 1992 general election victory. A conspicuous feature of the election campaign was lack of debate about Britain's place in the EU. Both Conservative and Labour Party managers knew their parties to be divided on the issue, and tacitly conspired to keep silent about it. Eurosceptics were thus not entirely unjustified in later complaining that the British people had not in fact endorsed Maastricht at the 1992 general election, and that they should therefore be allowed a referendum on the issue.

Safely returned to government, Conservative divisions over Europe could no longer be hidden and were to be exposed by a series of calamities in the summer and autumn of 1992 (analysed more fully in Chapter 9). An important point in relation to the Europe in Britain theme is that the

Major government was hamstrung by domestic divisions and unable to formulate either a clear or effective policy towards European integration. Major had to straddle the pro- and anti-EU wings of his Party and was unable to provide strong leadership. Thus while there were clear continuities in British preferences (intergovernmentalism and free trade with a Thatcherite twist) the capacity to achieve these preferences was chronically undermined by domestic political turmoil within the Conservative Party. Other member states became rather like rubberneckers observing a car accident: they would slow down and swerve to avoid the wreckage, but would continue with their own journey towards ambitious forms of economic and political integration. The Britain in Europe and Europe in Britain themes were connected by a rudderless government pre-occupied with domestic divisions, a series of setpiece confrontations (such as the Ioannina compromise) at which Major would draw a 'line in the sand' only to see it swiftly washed away, and Britain weakened in Europe because not only did it fail to articulate a clear line, but also because fundamental questions about British membership were being asked.

Chapter 9 discusses more fully the ways in which a determined band of Eurosceptics frequently defied the government by calling for a referendum on Maastricht and trying to block the passage of the Maastricht Bill through the House of Commons. Major was forced into a complex balancing act because he also had pro-European cabinet ministers such as Kenneth Clarke and Michael Heseltine in prominent government roles. The Eurosceptics' rebellion culminated in July 1993 when they contributed to a government defeat on a Labour amendment incorporating the Social Chapter into the Maastricht Treaty. This was a mischievous move by the Tory Euro-rebels who hated the Social Chapter, but loathed the Maastricht Treaty even more. Major's response was to 'go nuclear' and turn the issue of Maastricht into one of confidence in the government. In the face of near-certain defeat in a general election and the return of a pro-European Labour government, most of the Tory rebels returned to the party fold. This did little to ease divisions within the Conservative Party, which reached into the cabinet. For a participant's insight into the in-fighting, loathing, bitterness and acrimony that descended on the Conservative Party, see Gardiner (1999).

During the 1997 general election campaign, the deep divisions within the Conservative Party became all too evident. Even government ministers distanced themselves from the Party's policy to 'negotiate and decide' (more commonly known as 'wait and see') on EMU. Major felt powerless to dismiss the dissenting ministers because of the effects he feared such action would have on an already damaged Party (Geddes, 1997). In 1992, after Major had left the Maastricht negotiating chamber, one of his advisers unwisely claimed 'game, set and match' for Britain. With hindsight, this appears a rather rash judgement. Instead, the Maastricht deal lit the blue touch paper beneath the Conservative Party, which ignited to cause civil war within the Party and played an important part in Labour's landslide victories of 1997 and 2001.

'Modernization' under New Labour

Philip Stephens (2001: 67) has argued that while Tony Blair – 'the most instinctively pro-European Prime Minister since Edward Heath' – has been able to make Britain's case in Europe he has been unable to make the case for Europe in Britain. This remains a core dilemma for New Labour which is best represented by equivocation on the Euro.

In a speech delivered (in French) to the French National Assembly in October 1998, Blair noted that his first ever vote had been cast in favour of Britain's EC membership in the June 1975 referendum (although in 1983 he stood as a candidate for a Party committed to withdrawal). In government after 1997 Blair could expect far fewer EU-related problems than his predecessor because of his crushing parliamentary majority. To this advantage can be added the conversion to the merits of European integration experienced by many within the Labour Party and labour movement since 1983. Yet controversial and potentially divisive issues still linger, particularly on the question of the Euro. Moreover, a key victory for Eurosceptic campaigning was to ensure that the debate on the Euro would not just be for MPs, but that any decision to join would depend on a referendum. This takes a key EU issue beyond the realm of the House of Commons and the grasp of the party managers and places it in the public arena with all the associated uncertainties that this can bring.

The key point with regards to Labour's position on the EU is the transition from outright advocacy of withdrawal in 1983 to its current, more pro-EU position. Labour fought the 1983 election on the basis of a manifesto that developed an Alternative Economic Strategy for the UK that would involve large scale state intervention and controls over the economy. These were incompatible with continued EC membership. By the end of the 1980s, it was possible to argue that Labour was the more pro-European of the two main parties. Two factors explain the shift, one ideological and the other strategic. In ideological terms Labour underwent a dramatic shift in its EU policy after the catastrophic 1983 defeat.

The new party leader, Neil Kinnock, had been a staunch and eloquent left-wing opponent of the EC throughout the 1970s. He was now to begin a personal and political odyssey that would see him advocate the 'modernization' of the Labour Party, endorse positive engagement with the EC, and conclude with him moving to Brussels to become a European Commissioner. Almost as soon as Kinnock became party leader the commitment to outright withdrawal was watered down to a commitment to withdraw if satisfactory renegotiated terms could not be secured.

By the 1989 European Parliament elections, Labour was advocating active engagement with the EC at a time when the Conservative Euroscepticism was beginning to emerge in the late 1980s. The intellectual ballast for this pro-European ideology was provided by examples taken from other EU member states (particularly West Germany), whose economies and social welfare systems had performed better than the UK and who offered the prospect of a more consensual form of capitalism with a stronger emphasis on welfare and social protection. Labour's modernization in its early stages was thus linked to mainstream aspects of European social democracy. This domestic ideological shift was reinforced by supranational developments that saw the EC develop its 'social dimension'. No longer could the EC be passed off as a capitalist club that offered little to working people. Indeed, Thatcher's strong opposition to the social dimension sustained the left-wing view that perhaps Europe really could offer new opportunities for progressive politics (at least on the basis that my enemy's enemy is my friend). This was particularly so for the beleaguered trade unions that Thatcher labelled as the enemy within and that experienced a legislative onslaught through new employment legislation. European integration's opportunities for trade unions was a point made by the Commission President, Jacques Delors, in a 1988 speech to the TUC annual conference, much to Thatcher's annoyance as she was not happy to see the Commission President being so supportive of her opponents (Rosamond, 1998).

The second reason for Labour's shift to a more pro-European stance is linked to the strategic concerns of an opposition party facing a government that was becoming, as the 1980s progressed, more vocal in its opposition to European integration. The case for European integration had been a powerful feature of the political centre ground in British politics with a broad measure of agreement between centrist elements in all three main parties that Britain's place was within the EC. As the Conservatives appeared to abandon this centre ground then Labour could occupy it (facilitated by the ideological shifts outlined above) and portray themselves as a reinvented, moderate and mainstream party that had ditched the extremist policies which had been damaging in 1983. To be European was to be modern and to be modern was to be European.

This reorientation would suggest that the New Labour government elected in 1997 and re-elected in 2001 with overwhelming majorities would be more positive in its European policies. There were early signs that it might be. Tony Blair announced a new era of constructive engagement, while *The Observer* newspaper felt moved to herald the New Labour approach to foreign policy with the headline 'Goodbye Xenophobia'. The Labour government announced that it would sign up to the Social Chapter while the negotiation of the Amsterdam Treaty in June 1997 indicated both a new and more open British government approach (certainly when compared to the disastrous final years of the Major administration). This was marked by acceptance of both legislative and institutional changes such as the addition of a new employment chapter to the Treaty, the inclusion of a new Article 13 within the Treaty that greatly extended the anti-discrimination measures, as well as agreement to increase the use of QMV and bolster the role of the European Parliament. On a personal level, Blair seemed much more comfortable with other European leaders than his two Conservative predecessors.

It is, however, also possible to detect some continuity in New Labour's EU policy. For instance, the Amsterdam negotiations saw the UK government maintain a consistent line with that pursued by its predecessors on border controls, CAP reform and the role of NATO (Hughes and Smith, 1998; Fella, 2002). New Labour also hedged its bets on the Euro. Furthermore, as New Labour's enthusiasm for the German model of social capitalism faded then that of Blair and Gordon Brown at the Treasury seemed to grow for US-style market liberalization. Divisions became apparent between Blair's 'third way' and European social democracy (Clift, 2000; Gamble and Kelly, 2000).

Elements of continuity are also apparent. The first is the preference for intergovernmentalism and the maintenance of links with the USA. New Labour expounds a vision of Europe that enshrines the central role of the nation state as the key building block of international politics. The fact that New Labour sees the EU as a union of sovereign states is consistent with the attitudes of previous British governments. This combines with a continued emphasis on transatlantic ties and the UK's self-positioning as the USA's closest ally in Europe. These Atlantic ties came under close scrutiny during and after the war in Iraq when a serious division emerged between Britain and France. The status of the USA as the world's only superpower, combined with the neo-conservative foreign policies of the Bush administration and fears of US unilateralism, led to real tensions in the US–European alliance (Kagan, 2002). In a speech to the Foreign Office conference of British Ambassadors on 7 January 2003, Blair (2003) stated what the principles of British foreign policy should be:

> First, we should remain the closest ally of the US, and as allies influence them to continue broadening their agenda. We are the ally of the US not because they are powerful, but because we share their values. I am not surprised by anti-Americanism; but it is a foolish indulgence. For all their faults and all nations have them, the US are a force for good; they have liberal and democratic traditions of which any nation can be proud ... it is massively in our self-interest to remain close allies. Bluntly there are not many countries who wouldn't wish for the same relationship as we have with the US and that includes most of the ones most critical of it in public.

Blair then added that:

> Britain must be at the centre of Europe. By 2004, the EU will consist of 25 nations. In time others including Turkey will join. It will be the largest market in the world. It will be the most integrated political union between nations. It will only grow in power. To separate ourselves from it would be madness. If we are in, we should be in whole-heartedly. That must include, provided the economic conditions are right, membership of the single currency. For 50 years we have hesitated over Europe. It has never profited us. And there is no greater error in international politics than to believe that strong in Europe means weaker with the US. The roles reinforce each other. What is more there can be no international consensus unless Europe and the US stand together. Whenever they are divided, the forces of progress, the values of liberty and democracy, the requirements of security and peace, suffer. We can indeed help to be a bridge between the US and Europe and such understanding is always needed. Europe should partner the US not be its rival.

This intention to be a bridge illustrates the ways in which British politics remains between Europe and the USA (Gamble, 2003). The gap between Europe and the USA became more difficult to bridge in the run-up to, and aftermath of, the invasion of Iraq when major divisions emerged between the UK and the French and German governments. Tony Blair showed himself to be at least, if not more, pro-US than any of his post-war predecessors in Number 10 Downing Street, and this indicates strong transatlantic continuities in British foreign policy.

The second element of New Labour's approach to the EU is linked to the UK's socio-economic model and those in other EU member states (as well as the nascent EU approach). New Labour can be understood as 'open regionalists' (Baker, Gamble and Ludlam, 2002) in the sense that the majority of Labour MPs believe that economic and social objectives can best be attained within the framework of the EU and within a competitive and fair European economy. This reflects a re-evaluation of Party commitments undertaken when Kinnock and John Smith were the Party leaders. But there is another, 'third way' element of open regionalism as 'part of the means by which the party claims to be navigating between the polar opposites of old-style social democratic collectivism and neo-liberalism' with key importance attached to market liberalization as the basis for British full-hearted participation (Heffernan, 2002). Europe needs to become a little more British if Britain is to become fully engaged with it. Thatcher believed that the EC required a healthy dose of Thatcherism, whether it liked it or not. The fact that other member states baulked at this prescription then became a basis for Conservative hostility to European integration. New Labour now argue that participation in deeper integration depends on other member states 'modernizing' their economies and social welfare systems. Without these changes then the chances of New Labour endorsing membership of the Euro recede. New Labour are leading advocates of a European economic reform agenda that seeks more flexible and dynamic labour markets (HM Treasury 2001). Moreover, the adoption of economic reforms that mirror those that have been introduced in the UK has become a core component of the Treasury's evaluation of whether adoption of the Euro would be in Britain's interests. New Labour's commitment to Europe is conditional in the sense that it requires adaptation by other EU member states, although (as was the case with Thatcher) it is not necessarily clear why British strictures will be accepted by other member states.

British pragmatism in Europe

This chapter has examined the preferences and motivation of British governments, their capacity to attain these objectives and the reasons for the shifts in these preferences that have occurred over time. The chapter has sought to develop the 'Britain in Europe' theme through examination of Britain's relations with developing structures of EU governance while also broaching the issue of 'Europe in Britain' and the ways in which European integration has been absorbed as part of the organizational and ideological logic of British politics (a theme which will be developed more fully in later chapters). It has been shown that there are strong elements of continuity marked by continued preference for intergovernmental co-operation, the view that the nation state should remain the central unit within the EU and that the Atlantic partnership should remain a core element of the UK's international identity.

There have also been important shifts too. The Conservatives went from being a pro-European integration party, albeit based on a pragmatic acceptance of the EC as good for business to a hostility towards European integration that was strongly based on the Thatcherite legacy. Labour also fundamentally re-evaluated its stance on European integration and moved from advocacy of outright withdrawal in the early 1980s to a pro-integration stance by the early 1990s. Yet even this apparent shift from Conservative hostility to Labour pro-Europeanism contains some elements of continuity. Thatcherite Euroscepticism was informed at least in part by dismay that other EC member states were unprepared to accept Thatcherite strictures and that, for these other member states, the single market was a means to an end (that end being deeper economic and political integration) rather than an end in itself (i.e., Thatcherite deregulation and liberalization). New Labour too – following a brief flirtation with European social democracy – have defined their relationship to core EU economic objectives around the attainment by the EU of certain economic reform prerequisites. If these are satisfied then New Labour is prepared to engage with important developments such as EMU. New Labour, then, has maintained a long-standing British preference for conditional engagement with the EU.

6

Britain and European Union Institutions

Introduction

Although EU institutions can appear dull and their procedures arcane, this should not disguise the intensely political and sometimes controversial nature of their roles and responsibilities. This chapter explores the development of the EU's institutional system and pays particular attention to current debates about institutional reform in a wider Europe. It will also examine the ways in which British governments have sought to pursue their interests within these debates about institutional development. British governments have tended to prefer intergovernmental structures with an underlying understanding of the EU as an association of sovereign states while harbouring some reservations about grand designs and ambitious projects concerning the EU's *finalité,* such as a European constitution that might stress a 'federal vocation'.

The Spring 2002 EU-wide opinion polls conducted by Eurobarometer showed a comparatively low level of knowledge of EU institutions in the UK, as is illustrated by Tables 6.1 and 6.2 which show responses in the UK compared to the EU average when people were asked whether they had heard of the main EU institutions and what their levels of trust in these institutions were.

UK respondents declared relatively little knowledge about, or confidence in, EU institutions. This chapter's analysis of EU institutions tends to focus on government preferences regarding institutional design and development and thus contributes to the book's Britain in Europe theme.

The Brussels Empire?

EU institutions operate within a system within which powers are shared between the member states and EU institutions and exemplify the ways in which supranational integration challenges a vocabulary of political analysis based on nation state-centred forms of political organization.

Table 6.1 Knowledge of European Union institutions (%)

Institution	UK	EU15 average	Top of the form
European Parliament	86	89	Denmark, 98
Council of Ministers	36	63	Sweden, 90
Court of Justice	56	67	Denmark, 95
European Central Bank	56	73	France, 91
Convention on the Future of Europe	14	28	Luxembourg, 48

Source: Data from *Eurobarometer Standard Report* (Spring 2002).

There are five main EU institutions:

1   The Commission is comprised of 20 Commissioners (including two from Britain, Neil Kinnock and Chris Patten) and around 20,000 full-time staff. Neo-functionalist theorists saw the Commission as a potential driving force of integration. Under the Presidency of Jacques Delors between 1985 and 1995 the Commission entered the political demonology of British Eurosceptics. Since then the Commission's reputation has been dented by allegations of fraud

Table 6.2 Trust in European Union institutions (%)

	Trust		Don't knows	
	UK	EU15	UK	EU15
European Parliament	32	54	33	22
European Commission	45	65	37	28
Council of Ministers	35	61	48	33
Court of Justice	32	49	40	30
European Central Bank	25	47	46	31
Convention on the Future of Europe	12	25	62	54

Source: Data from *Eurobarometer Standard Report* (Spring 2002).

and mismanagement. The Commission remains central to the EU's
political and economic development.

2   The Council (or, as it is more commonly known, the Council of
Ministers), within which national governments are represented and
which combines both legislative and executive functions. British
governments have tended to see the Council as the most legitimate
basis for collective decision-making, rather than increased powers
for either the Commission or European Parliament.

3   The European Parliament is the only Community institution which is
directly elected and which is acquiring increased legislative authority alongside the Council. In Britain, low levels of turnout in its elections and of public awareness of its activities plague the Parliament.

4   The European Court of Justice, which interprets the growing body of
Community law, rules on the acts of institutions and thus plays an
important role in shaping the parameters of an integrated Europe.

5   The European Council, set up in 1974 to provide high-level political
leadership, which comprises heads of government who meet for two-
day summits at least once every six months.

The Commission

British Eurosceptics have often portrayed the Commission as an agent of
integration by stealth. For pro-Europeans it is necessary that the
Commission has a central role within the Union, not least to ensure
effective attainment of EU objectives. There is some continuity in
the preferences of British governments towards the Commission that
include those of the New Labour government. In October 1998 the
then Minister for Europe made it clear that, from the point of view of
the British government, the Commission was not a 'big political leader',
but was necessary to ensure the EU's smooth running and efficient
administration. If we probe beneath the surface of this observation we
also encounter a British perspective on the role of public officials and
administrators, albeit not one that is shared by all member states or necessarily evident within the Commission itself, a point to which we return
below. First, however, it is important to grasp the key elements of the
Commission's role.

When established as the High Authority of the ECSC in the early
1950s the Commission was seen to embody a technocratic, expertise-
based style that was at the time seen as the appropriate response to the

problems that faced west European countries. But, as Claudio Radaelli (1999: 1) has put it: 'At stake is the allegation of being a political system ruled by technocrats who ignore the basic thrust of democracy. Whilst democracy is based on legitimate consensus, free elections and participation, technocracy recognizes expertise as the sole basis of authority and power.' Yet, as Radaelli (1999) demonstrates, the actual picture is more subtle and nuanced with expertise playing an important role in EU decision-making because many EU issues are technical concerns and of low political salience, and this makes them particularly disposed to this decision-making style. Research into the views of senior Commission officials suggests that these officials are themselves aware of the changed environment in which they operate and that the era of 'benevolent technocracy in the tradition of Jean Monnet has come to a close' (Hooghe, 2001: 358).

Who's who?

Edward Page (1997: 119) has argued that one rather fundamental difficulty is that 'Commissioners are not commissioned by anyone to do anything in particular.' The 20 Commissioners appointed between 1999 and 2004 were nominated by the member states to pursue the rather vague and general objective of 'organizing Europe', but beyond that there was no guarantee of a shared conception of what this organization of Europe should involve or how it should evolve.

The President of the Commission, currently the former Italian Prime Minister, Romano Prodi, is appointed for 5 years and is responsible for the allocation of portfolios, although larger and more powerful member states expect to see their Commissioners in prestigious posts. Each Commissioner is supported by a personal cabinet, which supports his or her tasks and liaises with other Commissioners' cabinets. Upon appointment Commissioners are meant to forswear their national loyalties, but this is unrealistic: Commissioners cannot wipe their national political memory banks clean upon moving to Brussels and, anyway, it is seen as no bad thing if Commissioners are in touch with political developments in their country of origin.

There are currently 20 Commissioners: two each from the five largest countries (Britain, France, Germany, Italy and Spain) and one from each of the rest. The UK nominates two Commissioners: one from each of the two leading political parties. The current British Commissioners are the former Labour leader, Neil Kinnock, and the ex-Conservative Party chair and former Governor of Hong Kong, Chris Patten. The Nice Treaty proposed a reorganization of the Commission at the time of the next enlargement with bigger member states agreeing to nominate only one Commissioner in return for more voting power in the Council of Ministers.

Article 158 of the Treaty of Rome stated that: 'The members of the Commission shall be appointed by common accord of the Governments of the member states.' The Commission President and the Commissioners are nominated by the member states and their appointment then requires the European Parliament's approval. Following ratification of the Maastricht Treaty in November 1993 the third Delors Commission held office for two years until 1995. Since 1995 the appointment of a new Commission has been supposed to coincide with elections to the European Parliament (these are held every five years). The Maastricht Treaty stated that each new Commission must receive the assent of the European Parliament before it can take office. Approval is sought for the Commission en bloc, not for individual commissioners. The Santer Commission that took office in 1995 was the first to be subject to these new endorsement procedures.

Santer's appointment was riddled with problems. This appointment also illustrated the difficulties encountered by the Major government when dealing with other EU member states during a period in the 1990s when Euroscepticism was biting deep into the Conservative Party. The

Table 6.3   Presidents of the European Commission since 1958

Name of President and nationality	*Dates in office*
Walter Hallstein, West Germany	1958–67
Jean Rey, Belgium	1967–70
Franco Maria Malfatti, Italy*	1970–2
Sicco Mansholt, Netherlands	1972–3
Francois Xavier Ortoli, France	1973–7
Roy Jenkins, Britain	1977–81
Gaston Thorn, Luxembourg	1981–5
Jacques Delors, France	1985–95
Jacques Santer, Luxembourg	1995–9
Manuel Marin, Spain†	1999
Romano Prodi, Italy	1999–

*   Malfatti resigned to return to Italian politics and was replaced as interim President by Mansholt.

†   Marin was interim President following Santer's resignation.

British government initially vetoed the candidate preferred by other member states, the Belgian Prime Minister, Jean Luc Dehaene. Dehaene was deemed unacceptable by the British government because of his federalist views. That Santer's views were in fact very similar to those of Dehaene tells us that the British veto of Dehaene was closely linked to the Conservative government's need to be 'tough' on Europe to appease the Party's voluble Eurosceptic wing.

These intergovernmental wranglings alienated the European Parliament, which was keen to exert its new powers regarding Commission appointment. Santer was seen as second choice, while the European Parliament was annoyed by the intergovernmental shenanigans. Consequently, the European Parliament only endorsed Santer's appointment by 260 votes to 238.

Table 6.3 shows the Commission Presidents since 1958, while Table 6.4 shows the composition and portfolios of the 2000–2004 Commission.

Table 6.4   Members of the Commission, 2000–2004

Romano Prodi	President
	Vice-president
Neil Kinnock	Administrative Reform
	Vice-president
Loyola de Palacio	Relations with the European Parliament, Transport & Energy, Vice-president
Mario Monti	Competition
Franz Fischler	Agriculture, Rural Development & Fisheries
Erkki Liikanen	Enterprise & Information Society Internal Market
Frits Bolkestein	Taxation and Customs Union
Philippe Busquin	Research
Pedro Solbes Mira	Economic & Monetary Affairs
Poul Neilsen	Development & Humanitarian Aid
Günter Verheugen	Enlargement
Chris Patten	External Relations
Pascal Lamy	Trade
David Byrne	Health & Consumer Protection
Michel Barnier	Regional Policy
Viviane Reding	Education & Culture
Michaele Schreyer	Budget
Margot Wallström	Environment
Antonio Vitorino	Justice & Home Affairs
Anna Diamantopoulou	Employment & Social Affairs

Source: www.europa.eu.int/comm

Roles and responsibilities

The Commission has the following functions:

1   It holds the sole power of initiative in the Community pillar. Since the 1990s, however, its policy initiation role in the intergovernmental 'pillars' (JHA and CFSP) has been shared with the member states.
2   It implements policies and exercises executive responsibilities in pursuit of agreed objectives.
3   It manages the EU's finances.
4   It exercises external responsibilities in policy areas, most notably international trade negotiations where the member states have ceded authority to the Union to act as their representative.
5   It guards the legal framework and report breaches to the European Court of Justice.
6   It represents and negotiates on behalf of the member states in agreed areas, such as international trade.

In addition to these tasks, Neil Nugent (1999: 140) identified two other important but more informal roles for the Commission as a mediator and conciliator between member states and EU institutions in cases of dispute, and as the conscience of the Union committed to the goal of deeper European integration.

The Commission held 44 meetings in 2001. It presented 456 proposals, recommendations or draft instruments for adoption by the Council and Parliament. This comprised 43 directives, 182 regulations and 231 decisions.

1   Regulations are binding in their entirety and directly applicable to all member states.
2   A directive can also be issued which is binding as to the results to be achieved, but the form and method of implementation are left up to the member states.
3   Recommendations, decisions and opinions are also issued but they are not binding on the member states.

The Commission also presented 297 'Communications' and reports on EU activities, as well as four White Papers (including a highly significant one on European governance) and six Green Papers.

A distinct feature of the EU as a supranational system is the process by which Treaties between states are turned into laws that bind those states. Over time this has become an intensive process of law and politics connecting the 15 member states and reaching deep into their societies. Box 6.1 gives an example of one piece of legislation that caused particular problems for the British Conservative government, but this also shows the ways in which EU institutions act, the ways in which they interact with other member states, and the ways in which EU legal outputs feed into domestic politics.

Organization

There is no single model of European public administration. The British approach is centred on a Whitehall ethos of civil service neutrality, collective responsibility and information sharing across government.

The 20,000 Commission staff work in a unique multinational and multilingual environment. Officials come from countries with different administrative traditions, which can mean rather different understandings of roles and responsibilities. One illustration of the potential for clashes between different administrative traditions was provided by a report prepared by a British official within the Commission's personnel department. The report argued that 'The first shock of many staff recruited into the European institutions is to find that many of their underlying assumptions about behaviour, often barely made explicit in their own country since they seem so obvious, are not necessarily shared by colleagues' (cited in Stevens, 2002: 10). There can also be tensions and rivalries within the Commission. Stevens and Stevens (2000: 196) identify three sources of conflict: turf wars for influence and control over particular policy areas; ideological conflict over policy and solutions; and conflict over the distribution of resources. In such terms it is better to think of the Commission as a 'multi-organization' rather than a monolith (Cram, 1994). This is illustrated by Hooghe's (1997: 95) interviews with senior Commission officials about their perceived roles: 'Actors were often motivated by a number of issues: more or less supranational control, more or less Europe of the Regions, the prevalence of one DG [Directorate General] over another, the need for a mobilizing idea for the Commission versus running things efficiently, public intervention versus free market, and career concerns.'

The internal structures and organization of the Commission itself have come under scrutiny because of questions about efficiency and managerial competence. A Committee of Independent Experts (CIE) found that 'It is becoming difficult to find anyone who has even the slightest sense of responsibility ... The temptation to deprive the concept of

---

**Box 6.1   The Commission's policy role and impacts on British politics:
the case of social policy**

The legal background: The Treaty of Rome contained social policy provisions in Articles 118–123. The Commission's power of initiative gave it the right to bring forward policy proposals in these areas. The social policy provisions were mainly designed to ensure the transferability of social entitlements for workers moving within the EC. The Single European Act extended these competencies and thus strengthened the Commission's role within the EC's 'social dimension' through measures such as Article 118a, which stated the following.

1 Member States shall pay particular attention to encouraging improvements, especially in the working environment, as regards the health and safety of workers, and shall set as their objective the harmonization of conditions in this area, while maintaining the improvements made.
2 In order to help achieve the objective laid down in the first paragraph, the Council, acting in accordance with the procedure referred to in Article 189c and after consulting the Economic and Social Committee, shall adopt by means of directives, minimum requirements for gradual implementation, having regard to the conditions and technical rules obtaining in each of the Member States.

This article gave the Council the power acting by a qualified majority (i.e., via Article 189c) and on the basis of a Commission proposal the responsibility to adopt measures aimed at ensuring the health and safety of workers.
→

---

responsibility of all substance is a dangerous one. The concept is the ultimate manifestation of democracy' (CIE, 1999a, point 9.4.25; see also CIE, 1999b).

Reform attempts have been hindered because there is no European model for public administration and the Commission has a weak reform capacity (Page and Wouters, 1995; Cini, 1996; Stevens, 2002). While Commissioner Kinnock's reform efforts may not attract the same public attention as the 'bigger' political questions, they do have important effects on staff morale and on their ability to perform their tasks.

Reform attempts can also be related to more general trends in public administration and the rise of 'new public management' that places more emphasis on output and results. These trends had little impact at EU level in the 1980s and early 1990s because this was already a hectic period due to the resurgence of integration. Attacks on the Commission and EU administration could also be portrayed as a Eurosceptic assault

$\rightarrow$

The UK political background: EC social policy was a controversial issue for the Conservative government in the 1980s and 1990s. The UK government had agreed upon accession in 1973 to the social policy provisions of the Treaty of Rome and to the small extension of social policy competencies contained in the SEA. However, Margaret Thatcher refused to sign the 1989 Social Charter, a non-binding declaration of social policy principles. John Major then opted out of Maastricht's Social Chapter which extended the social policy provisions within the EU. The UK government was sensitive to what it saw as the Commission's 'creeping competence' and a quasi-socialist agenda that would re-impose social regulations 'rolled back' at domestic level.

The controversy: Social competencies were clearly established by Treaty (the Treaty of Rome and the SEA). These charged the Commission with responsibility for policy development. This created the scope for a clash between the Commission and the UK government. Commission President Jacques Delors was also keen to see development of the EC's role in these areas. The Commission proposed a Directive using Article 118a covering the organization of working time that regulated minimum periods of daily rest, weekly rest and annual leave. The UK government contested the legal basis for the Directive by arguing that the proper legal basis was the Social Chapter (from which the UK had opted out) and not Article 118a (which applied to the UK).

The outcome: The Court of Justice in Case c-84/94 of 12 November 1996 rejected the UK government's argument and argued that the Commission had acted properly and that the Directive did indeed apply to the UK. This outcome was portrayed by Conservative Eurosceptics as indicative of the EU's creeping competence, erosion of UK sovereign authority, and as contradicting the deregulatory thrust of Thatcherism.

on the idea of Europe. These arguments were less convincing when allegations of fraud and mismanagement were levelled at the Santer Commission. These particularly centred on the French Commissioner, Edith Cresson, and allegations of nepotism and financial impropriety.

The Santer presidency initiated reform efforts under three headings. The Sound and Efficient Management programme began in 1995 and was followed by a scheme for the Modernization of Administration and Personnel. In 1998 these were then all brought under the common heading of Designing Tomorrow's Commission, which produced a report that scrutinized Commission activities under the headings of 'structures', 'activities and resources' and 'working methods'. Efforts then centred on improving co-ordination within the Commission, better anti-fraud measures, the development of control systems for the evaluation of procedures and more decentralization. But the progress of reforms has been very slow. One reason for this is the opposition of the unions to the reforms. Another was the lack of clear leadership, which was not helped by the fact that the Commission was in some turmoil at the time.

A deeper underlying reason is the existence of different models of public administration within the Commission. There is no agreed model of European public administration. To illustrate the effects that this can have Stevens (2002) contrasts a 'public authority' model that is rule-based and stresses the independence of senior officials in pursuit of their responsibilities with a 'service provision' model that pays close attention to delivery and could involve performance related pay. The latter model would be recognizable in the UK context (as well as Denmark and the Netherlands), but not in those member states where a public authority model continues to hold sway (Austria, Belgium, Greece and Italy and, to a lesser extent, France, Spain and Sweden, according to Page and Wright, 1999: 273). The progress of reforms is likely to be slow because of the effect of the absence of a European conception of public administration on the very institution, the European Commission, which is supposed to embody this idea.

Policy implementation

The UK authorities have a good track record when implementing EU policy. In this regard, the UK is not particularly 'awkward'. The Commission does, however, face important constraints when seeking to implement, not least because it is not the Commission *qua* Commission that implements; rather, the Commission relies on implementing authorities in the member states. The Commission thus shares its responsibility for the management of policy implementation with the Council and with implementing agencies in member states. Another key constraint on policy implementation is the relatively small size of the Commission compared to national bureaucracies. The Commission has around 20,000 permanent staff. EU member states average 322 civil servants per 10,000 population, while the EU has around 0.8 civil servants for every 10,000 inhabitants (Nugent, 1999: 108). This makes the notion of a 'Brussels Empire' administered by a vast Commission rather absurd. Co-operation with national bureaucracies creates a 'dual executive' with responsibility for implementation and oversight shared by the Commission and the member states. This is a practical response to the scale of the tasks but can lead to problems of fragmentation that makes management and supervision of policy implementation difficult. The result is that whether or not EU law is properly implemented depends to a large extent on how efficient national bureaucracies are in taking account of the various directives and regulations that emanate from Brussels. The British track record has been good because a Whitehall ethos of collective responsibility and information sharing has enabled a relatively smooth adaptation by the British core executive to the requirements of membership (Bulmer and Burch, 1998).

The Commission is also responsible for guarding the EU's legal framework and ensuring that the Treaties and Community law are respected. If an infringement is spotted then the first thing that the Commission does is issue a letter of formal notice. This usually suffices, but if compliance still does not occur then the Commission can deliver a 'reasoned opinion'. The final recourse is to refer the case to the ECJ. In 2001, the Commission:

- initiated 1,050 infringement proceedings (1,317 in 2000)
- issued 529 reasoned opinions (460 in 2000)
- referred 162 cases to the Court of Justice (172 in 2000), of which 14 were against the British government.

Challenges since the 1990s

Since the 1990s, the Commission's internal structures and political role have been placed under the spotlight. The Commission must seek to balance its responsibilities to promote European integration with the need to maintain good relations with the member states. It must also display political astuteness because new EU issue areas such as foreign, defence and immigration policies cannot be passed off as the largely technical issues that many core Commission concerns (such as single market integration) have been in the past. In his speech to the European Parliament in 2000 that outlined the Commission's strategic objectives, Prodi highlighted the pressures confronting the EU as it sought to further develop its role:

> Until now, European integration has been a largely economic process establishing the single market, introducing the single currency. From now on it will be an increasingly *political* process. This is not a matter of choice it is a necessity: Europe's political integration must advance hand in hand with its geographical enlargement. The new frontiers of this integration are Justice and Home Affairs, the Common Foreign and Security Policy, defence co-operation and the crucial question of

fundamental political values. These issues go to the heart of national sovereignty and require an even greater level of political consensus than those which dominated the 1980s and 1990s. (Prodi, 2000)

Since the 1990s there has also been a shift in emphasis from creating institutional structures and establishing policy priorities to attempting to ensure that policy objectives are actually attained. Policy implementation has become a key EU challenge with a more general emphasis on developing patterns of European governance that mesh with more general state, social and market changes in Europe and the rest of the world. There has been discussion of new forms of European governance that seek to move beyond what were seen as the inflexible and hierarchical structures put in place during the 1960s to more network-based patterns of interaction that reflect the complex multi-level interactions between and within member states that now characterize the EU (Metcalfe, 2000; Commission of the European Communities, 2001).

Yet, as Cram (2000: 60) tellingly points out, it might be wrong to assume that the member states are firm supporters of a reformed, effective Commission able to operate effectively and perhaps challenge the member states' authority: 'Do member states really want a leaner more efficient Commission or does the current ambiguity and relative inefficiency rather suit them?'

The Council

For British governments the Council representing the national governments has tended to be seen as the most legitimate basis of EU decision-making. New Labour in power have maintained this long-standing preference reflective of the conceptualization of the EU as an association of sovereign states that have agreed to pool sovereignty. According to this thinking, these states remain the building blocks of the international political order.

The term 'The Council' is a plural noun for around 20 sectoral Councils covering the EU's areas of responsibilities. They comprise national ministers with specific responsibilities in those areas. The most important is the General Affairs Council composed of foreign ministers, although the agriculture Council, the budget Council and ECOFIN (economics and finance ministers) rank close behind.

In formal terms, most EU business is done within the Council, but in reality the support administration, COREPER (Council of Permanent Representatives), and vast numbers of Working Groups do most of the background and preparatory work. The Council could actually be characterized as the dignified element of a more complex process that predominantly occurs at the level of officials rather than ministers. National ministers are unlikely to have the time to involve themselves in the minutiae of policy proposals. For the UK government, the point of engagement with the Council, other EU institutions, and other member states is the UK's Permanent Representation (UKRep) in Brussels. Box 6.2 outlines the organization and roles of the UK's Permanent Representatives.

Most Council business is conducted within the Justus Lipsius building on the Rue de la Loi/Wetstraat in Brussels, although all member states have their national delegations housed not too far away. Westlake (1999: xxiv) reports that around 80 per cent of business is conducted in the Council's working parties, 10 per cent in COREPER, 5 per cent in the Council and 5 per cent in corridors. By this reckoning, the corridor is as important as the formal Council setting (with up to 24 km of corridor within the Justus Lipsius building: Westlake, 1999: 14). To this can be added the

---

Box 6.2   The UK in Brussels: the role of UKRep

The UK's Permanent Representative has overall responsibility for the work of UKRep and represents the UK on the Committee of Permanent Representatives (COREPER). Until January 2003 this post was held by Sir Nigel Sheinwald, who left to serve as the Prime Minister's special adviser during the Iraqi war and then became Ambassador to the USA. This indicates the high profile nature of the Permanent Representative's role.

The UK Permanent representative sits on what is called COREPER II, which deals with high political issues such as foreign and defence policy, economic and financial policy, the budget, Justice and Home Affairs, and Development.

The Deputy Permanent Representative sits on COREPER I, which deals with specialist Councils such as the Internal Market, Consumers, Industry, Environment, Social Affairs, Telecommunications, Energy, Transport, Fisheries. (Because of its complexity and centrality there is a special committee that deals only with agriculture.)

UKRep is then broken down into specialist units that deal with Political Affairs, Institutions, Agriculture and Fisheries, Industry and the Internal Market, Social Environmental and Regional Affairs, Economic Affairs, Finance and Tax, External Relations, Development and Trade, Justice and Home Affairs.

The Scottish, Welsh and Northern Ireland executives are also represented in Brussels with staffing related to the competencies of these executive authorities.

rather more difficult to gauge – but nevertheless essential – impact of the telephone, fax and email.

Roles and responsibilities

Some UK ministries are more Europeanized than others. This differential engagement between the British state and the EU means that areas such as agriculture and fisheries have become intensively Europeanized while the EU has much less effect on areas such as education (see Chapter 8 for a fuller discussion). Some ministers encounter their European colleagues on a regular basis, others less so. Some ministries – the Foreign Office, for instance – tend to be more enthusiastic about European integration while others, such as the Treasury, harbour more scepticism. The point here is that the UK's conditional and differential engagement is indicated by the ways in which Europe has not become fully embedded within the preferences, interests and identities of key departments of state, such as the Treasury. Nevertheless, routine trips to Brussels are a key part of the job description for national ministers. When they get to Brussels they encounter a rather different form of politics from that experienced in Whitehall and Westminster.

There is no public gallery from which the Council of Ministers can be observed. If there were, then viewers would see a room of around 100 people: the Presidency and supporting officials, the ministers from the 14 other member states and their officials, the Commission's representatives, members of the Council's secretariat and legal service, plus the translators needed to ensure that the ministers understand events. The whole event can seem rather chaotic as officials scuttle in and out of the meeting. The Council works in all 11 of the EU's official languages with simultaneous translation plus rapid translation of important documents into the official languages.

The agenda for Council meetings is drawn up by the member state holding the Presidency (the EU Presidency currently rotates between the member states on a 6-month cycle). In formal terms, the Commission holds the sole power of initiation within the Community pillar. In practical terms, there are other influences on the EU's agenda. A member state can take the opportunity of holding the Presidency to push for its own particular priorities. The European Council composed of the heads of government can charge the Council with specific tasks. The Council and Parliament can pressure the Commission to make proposals. COREPER also has a strong influence on the Council agenda.

The Council faces time constraints. The usual one-day meeting format does not make it easy for all issues to be resolved. A consequence is that lunch has become an important part of the meeting. The occasion can be used to progress Council business in a more informal setting where, as a former British Commissioner put it, 'the conversation is free and intimate – often astonishingly so' (Tugendhat, 1986: 159). If progress is really slow then the meeting may go to a late sitting. The ex-Labour minister, Gerald Kaufman (1980: 166), wrote that if the attendants were bringing trays of coffee then all was probably well. If, however, they were bringing trays of whisky then a late sitting was likely. If the worst comes to the worst then ministers can 'stop the clock' at midnight on the day that a decision is to be reached and then keep going until agreement is secured. The agriculture council became notorious for such marathons, although they are now more rare.

The Council within the European Union system

Martin Westlake (1999: xxiii) contends that a caricatured view of the Council has developed as 'a monolithic institution, negative in instinct, labouring in confidentiality, forging secretive deals, restrained by unanimity and blinkered by notions of national sovereignty'. Westlake argues that this is a misrepresentation and that the Council is both more complex and less negative: more complex because it combines legislative and executive roles, lacks a standard decision-making procedure, and has developed its own idiosyncratic processes in particular issue areas; less negative because it has 'organically developed a series of – sometimes very delicate – mechanisms which together embody one of the most revolutionary developments in Europe's long and frequently bloody history; the peaceful sharing of national sovereignty between increasingly complex nation states for the achievement of common goals'.

There is no clear separation of powers within the EU system: legislative and executive responsibilities are shared. For instance, the Council of Ministers exercises legislative authority, but shares this role with the European Parliament. The Council has executive responsibilities, but shares this role with the Commission. These legislative and executive responsibilities place the Council at the core of the EU's institutional system and make it central to the development and elaboration of EU policies. At the same time, power is shared, inter-institutional relations are a central concern, and so too is the requirement to strike a balance between national and collective interests: 'The Council ... embodies a sense of collective purpose, collective commitment and collective ideas. It is the forum for reconciling the distinctive purposes and powers of the member states with the needs for recurrent and disciplined joint action' (Hayes-Renshaw and Wallace, 1997: 2).

The Council could be seen as a rather insulated environment linked to a Brussels political scene within which officials can spend as much time interacting with colleagues from other member states as they do with co-nationals back in national capitals. National officials based in Brussels will develop particular sectoral expertise and interact quite intensively with colleagues from other member states. Moreover, within each Council, particular modes of operation can develop that are distinct to that Council and its members (Westlake, 1999: 60).

Decision-making

The key decision-making issue within the EU has been the extent to which issues should remain reliant on a unanimous vote or should be subject to qualified majority voting or QMV (which requires around a 72 per cent majority in a weighted voting system). The UK has not been an enthusiastic advocate of QMV, but has realized that if EU objectives are to be attained in areas such as single market integration then it is necessary to move towards QMV and not risk one country having the power to block.

Disputes about Council decision-making induced one of the EC's first crises when de Gaulle blocked plans for the use of qualified majority voting. The use of the national veto to protect vital national interests was enshrined by the Luxembourg compromise of January 1966, but the problem was that reliance upon unanimity was a block on decision-making. The difficulty of securing unanimous agreement among member states could make it near impossible to achieve substantive action. The shift towards QMV that has occurred since the SEA of 1986 has been central to the resurgence of integration and has been seen as a way of

Table 6.5   Distribution of weighted votes in the Council of Ministers in EU of 15

Germany, France, Italy, United Kingdom	10 votes each
Spain	8 votes
Belgium, Greece, Netherlands, Portugal	5 votes each
Austria, Sweden	4 votes each
Denmark, Finland, Ireland	3 votes each
Luxembourg	2 votes

unblocking decision-making procedures and ensuring attainment of EU goals, particularly single market integration.

Both the Amsterdam and Nice treaties increased the number of issues covered by qualified majority voting. Nice, for instance, made an additional 30 issues subject to QMV, although sensitive issues such as social security and taxation remained subject to unanimity. Qualified majorities are based on a system of weighted votes. Table 6.5 shows the

Table 6.6   Qualified majority voting in the enlarged EU after 2004 (projected)

Country	Votes	Population per vote (million)
Germany	29	2.03
UK	29	2.04
France	29	2.03
Italy	29	1.99
Spain	27	1.46
Poland	27	1.43
Netherlands	13	1.21
Greece	12	0.88
Czech Republic	12	0.86
Belgium	12	0.85
Hungary	12	0.84
Portugal	12	0.83
Sweden	10	0.89
Austria	10	0.81
Slovakia	7	0.77
Denmark	7	0.76
Finland	7	0.74
Ireland	7	0.53
Lithuania	7	0.53
Latvia	4	0.61
Slovenia	4	0.49
Estonia	4	0.36
Cyprus	4	0.19
Luxembourg	4	0.11
Malta	3	0.12
Opened negotiations in 2000		
Romania	14	1.61
Bulgaria	10	0.82

distribution of votes for the EU of 15 while Table 6.6 shows the planned distribution of votes in an enlarged EU. The Treaty of Nice introduced a 'triple lock' system. The basis for this deal was agreement by larger member states to agree to appoint only one Commissioner while voting was re-weighted in their favour in the Council. The 'triple lock' works as follows: any Council requires a specified number of votes (71.3 per cent of those cast rising to 74 per cent when membership hits 27 states); QMV will have to be supported by at least half the member states; and any member states will be able to request verification that the QMV represents at least 62 per cent of the EU population. If this 'demographic cushion' test is failed then the proposed measure will fall.

The ways in which QMV has influenced decision-making are interesting because they are often more informal than these precise rules suggest. Few votes are actually taken within the Council because many of the points for consideration are so-called 'A points' upon which agreement has already been reached in COREPER. When 'B points' are considered then the member state holding the Presidency will strive to be familiar with the positions of the member states and have an appreciation of what is required to reach agreement. More often than not, the Presidency will observe that the necessary majority has been achieved and, if no member states dissent, then the matter will be agreed. Under existing rules, a blocking minority would usually require a coalition of two big states and two smaller ones. QMV has thus altered the environment within which decisions are taken and affected the calculations of national ministers and their officials. If a member state knows that it is in a minority of one then it may try to wring concessions, but will often realize that it can be better to live to fight another day.

The readjustment of QMV was a source of conflict between the British government and other EU member states at the time of the 1995 enlargement. Most member states favoured an automatic reassignment of the qualified majority to reflect the impact of the three new member states with the effect that a qualified majority would remain at around 70 per cent of the votes cast and a blocking minority would be 30 per cent. The UK, backed by Spain, argued that the blocking minority should not be readjusted and that it should remain at its former level of 23 votes (25 per cent of the total after enlargement). At the Greek town of Ioannina in March 1994 it was agreed that when there were between 25 and 30 per cent of the votes against a particular proposal then the Council Presidency would seek a compromise. Some saw the Ioannina compromise as a new Luxembourg compromise. Its effects have been much more limited. It did, though, contribute to the debate about the balance of votes between larger and smaller member states.

Changes in the Council's role

There have been important changes in the Council's role since the 1990s as the EU has developed responsibilities for foreign and security policy and for internal security matters such as policing, judicial co-operation, immigration and asylum. These are areas in which decision-making has been strongly focused on the Council with very limited roles for the European Parliament, Commission and European Court of Justice.

To this developing Council role can be added concerns about legitimacy and democracy. The national ministers who represent the member states in the Council are members of elected national governments. As such, they are accountable to national parliaments. A problem is that the participation of these ministers in European level decision-making can be difficult to scrutinize and only indirectly legitimated by national elections. However, it has been argued that if the Council were made more open then the deal-making might be driven to new, unaccountable venues because national ministers could have good reason to ensure that their negotiating positions are not exposed to the full glare of public scrutiny.

The issues of scrutiny, accountability and transparency of Council decision-making are key issues that relate to the EU's so-called 'democratic deficit'. The idea here is that as powers and responsibilities have been transferred to Brussels then similar transfers of the scope for scrutiny and accountability have not followed these. Much discussion of the democratic deficit is overblown. Regular EU decision-making processes and safeguards are at least as, if not more, open as those at national level. However, discussion of the democratic deficit related to the Council highlights a fundamental ambiguity in the Council's role in that it is both a decision-making body and a forum for negotiation between member states. In its legislative role the Council can be likened to a national parliament, whereas in its executive role it can be likened to a Cabinet. National parliaments are televised and records of discussion and voting are publicly available. Cabinets, on the other hand, tend to be secret and information about their activities can be as much to do with leaks as about formal disclosure.

When the Council is in negotiating mode then secrecy has some advantages: 'Ministers and their officials build coalitions, exercise leverage and do deals benefiting from the veil of secrecy that mostly cloaks their actions, as do ministers within national governments' (Hayes-Renshaw and Wallace, 1997: 7). When the Council is legislating then this confidentiality can appear anomalous and, at worst, can breed suspicion or hostility. Hayes-Renshaw (1999: 40) argues that quite significant steps have been taken towards greater openness with the post-Maastricht provisions for disclosure of information and public access to Council meetings. But core EU legislative and executive processes do remain shrouded in secrecy.

In sensitive areas such as the CFSP and JHA pillars there has been a particular reluctance to disclose information, although it must be said that national governments are not prone to openness in these areas either so it is unfair to pillory the EU for failing to attain standards of which national governments also fall short. Text box 6.3 identifies some of the issues at stake as calls for openness and transparency meet the EU's expanded internal security role.

The Council Presidency

The country holding the Presidency of the Union chairs the Council of Ministers. The draft European Constitution proposes to change this with a President elected by the member states serving for up to 5 years. The Presidency rotates among the member states every six months. As Westlake (1999: 45) puts it, 'the modern Presidency is at one and the same time manager, promoter of political initiatives, package broker, representative to and from the other Community institutions, spokesman for the Council and for the Union, and an international actor'. Every member state regardless of its size, economic power or political weight holds the Presidency. This involves preparing the agenda for meetings, chairing hundreds of meetings, seeking consensus between member states, liaising with other EU institutions, and organizing at least one meeting of the European Council (with the mounting security costs that this now entails). This is a task to test the diplomatic mettle of even the largest member states. It can also be the opportunity for member states to bask in the lime-light of international prominence and for some national leaders to try on the mantle of international statesman or woman, for six months at least.

The British Presidency of January–June 1998 saw one meeting of EU heads of government in Cardiff in June, as well as 43 meetings of the Council of Ministers. In addition, the first 'European Conference' was held in London on 12 March 1998. This comprised heads of government

Box 6.3   **Case study of European Union transparency and openness**

Background: The EU has developed foreign and internal security competencies in the 1990s that signify a move into high politics. The EU has also
developed (since the Maastricht Treaty) rules on transparency and openness.
The UK government has been an advocate of intergovernmental co-operation
in these areas, has tended to oppose supranational integration, and has been
cautious about too much transparency, which it feels might reveal sensitive
negotiating stances. In such terms it could be argued that intergovernmental
co-operation without empowerment of supranational institutions such as the
Commission and the European Court of Justice strengthens the executive
authorities of the member states. UK governments have not tended to have
too many problems with this.

The issue: Internal and external security concerns and bi-lateral relations
with the US were important during the 1990s and acquired a much higher
profile in the aftermath of the September 11 terrorist attacks on New York
and the Pentagon.

The actors: Co-operation on these security issues is dominated by the member states. Supranational institutions are weak. Moreover, opinion polls indicate that 'personal security' concerns are high on the agenda for many EU
citizens. There are, however, campaigning organizations in favour of developing an EU civil liberties agenda that seeks a balance between EU commitments to freedom and security and that does not concede too much ground
to security practices which undermine civil liberties. One such campaigning
organization is the UK-based Statewatch.

The events: In December 2001 the Council refused Statewatch access to the
agendas of EU–US Senior Level Group and the EU–US task force because
the USA vetoed access. Statewatch appealed and in March 2002 some 35
agendas were released, but with 458 sections of information blacked out.
This was not Statewatch's first experience of difficulty accessing documents
about these sensitive issues of high politics. In July 2002, after a four-year
fight, Statewatch complained to the European Ombudsman to obtain the
agendas of 10 EU–US high-level planning meetings between September
1996 and February 1998. The significance of these discussions became
apparent when it was revealed that the agenda for EU–US discussions
included the World Trade Organisation (WTO), the transatlantic business
dialogue, the transatlantic labour dialogue, China, Russia, Ukraine, Turkey,
data protection, EU reform, Kyoto, Plan Colombia, climate change, justice
and home affairs, drugs and organized crime.

The significance: The disclosure of the agendas for discussion demonstrated
the key issues dealt with in rather secretive intergovernmental forums.
Statewatch argued that there should be public disclosure of the subject matter discussed. The member states preferred to maintain a greater cloak of
secrecy. This provided a test for EU transparency and openness, although it
should also be noted that these internal and external security concerns are not
particularly transparent at national level either. Opaque EU processes could
further blur the picture.

from present and potential future members of the EU, except for Turkey, which boycotted the meeting because it was unhappy that it was being pushed further down the queue of prospective members. As is usual, the British government outlined a series of priorities for their Presidency. In the space of just six months the Presidency cannot determine the Community's agenda and must be sensitive to the importance of certain key issues as well as the opinions of other member states, particularly that which last held the Presidency and that which will hold it next. In effect, there is a troika of the past, current and future Presidencies to ensure continuity and co-ordination.

The most important issue facing the British presidency was preparation for EMU and introduction of the single currency. This caused some difficulties because the British government had not committed itself to participation in the single currency. Labour market flexibility and economic reform were also priorities for the British government, informed by the view that the kinds of 'modernization' advocated by new Labour could also benefit the European economy (HM Treasury, 2001). The British also resolved to push forward on other long-standing concerns, such as reform of the CAP. Finally, enlargement was prioritized.

The European Parliament

The 1999 elections to the European Parliament in Britain were notable in three respects (see Table 6.7). First, they were the first UK-wide elections to use proportional representation (PR). Second, the elections seemed to provide light at the end of the tunnel for William Hague's beleaguered Conservative Party. The Conservatives received 35.8 per cent of the votes cast, compared to Labour's 28 per cent. But neither the use of PR nor Hague's victory was the story: the most notable feature of the 1999 European elections was that a meagre 24 per cent of the electorate bothered to vote (see Table 6.8 and Figure 6.1). More than this, the governing Labour Party barely fought a campaign. Never could there have been a starker representation of conditional and differential engagement and the failure of European integration to become embedded as a core concern for the general public.

The European Parliament's role

The European Parliament (EP) is the only directly elected institution at EU level. Since the accession of Austria, Finland and Sweden in January

Table 6.7   Results in the United Kingdom of the 1999 elections to the European Parliament

Party	Votes	% of votes	MEPs
Conservative	3,578,218	35.8	36
Labour	2,803,821	28	29
Liberal Democrat	1,266,549	12.7	10
UK Independence	696,057	7	3
Green	625,378	6.2	2
Scottish National	268,528	–	2
Plaid Cymru	185,235	–	2
Democratic Unionist	192,762	–	1
SDLP	190,731	–	1
Ulster Unionist	119,507	–	1
Pro Euro Conservative	138,097	1.4	–
British National	102,644	1.0	–
Liberal	93,051	0.9	–
Socialist Labour	86,749	0.86	–
Others	333,753	–	–
Total Electorate	44,495,741		
Votes	10,681,080		
Turnout (UK)	24.0%		

Source: Reproduced from European Parliament UK Office (www.europarl.org.uk).

Table 6.8   European Parliament elections: voter turnout across the European Union (1979–99) (%)

	1979	1984	1989	1994	1999
EU	63	61	58.5	56.8	49.4
Austria	–	–	–	67.7 (1996)	49.0
Belgium	91.6	92.2	90.7	90.7	90.0
Denmark	47.1	52.3	46.1	52.9	50.4
Finland	–	–	–	60.3 (1996)	30.1
France	60.7	56.7	48.7	52.7	47.0
Germany	65.7	56.8	62.4	60	45.2
Greece	78.6 (1981)	77.2	79.9	71.2	70.2
Ireland	63.6	47.6	68.3	44	50.5
Italy	85.5	83.9	81.5	74.8	70.8
Luxembourg	88.9	87	87.4	88.5	85.8
Netherlands	57.8	50.5	47.2	36	29.9
Portugal	–	72.2 (1987)	51.1	35.5	40.4
Sweden	–	–	–	41.6 (1996)	38.3
Spain	–	68.9 (1987)	54.8	59.1	64.4
UK	31.6	32.6	36.2	36.4	24.0

Source: Reproduced from European Parliament UK Office (www.europarl.org.uk).

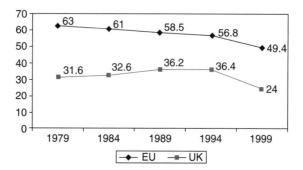

Figure 6.1   Turnout in elections to the European Parliament (United Kingdom and European Union average, 1979–99) (%)

Source: Author's Calculations from data held by the European Parliament UK Office (www.europarl.org.uk).

1995 there have been 626 members. The EP's role should not be under-estimated. It possesses shared budgetary authority with the Council and has seen increased legislative authority since the 1980s, both of which raise the EP's profile and move it alongside the Council at the heart of the EU decision-making process.

The EP has six main roles, as set out below:

1   As the Treaty provides, to scrutinize and amend legislation and to act as a co-decision-maker. At the very least, the Parliament must be consulted on Commission proposals, as the *Isoglucose* decision of the European Court of Justice in 1979 made clear. In the 1990s, the EP has become a co-decision-maker with the Council in most Community pillar areas.
2   Since the Maastricht Treaty, to endorse the appointment of the Commission president and the other Commissioners (en bloc, not individually).
3   To decide along with the Council the EU's budget.
4   To scrutinize the Commission.
5   To question the Council and Parliament.
6   To convene committees of inquiry.

Prior to ratification of the SEA the Parliament had the right to be consulted on legislation. By a two-thirds majority it could vote to sack the Commission and reject the budget. In addition, by the Treaty of 1970 that established the EC's budgetary framework, the Parliament was made joint budgetary authority, alongside the Council of Ministers.

The SEA introduced the co-operation procedure which allowed Parliament a second reading of proposed legislation in specified areas, and the right to suggest amendments (which were not binding on the Council of Ministers). The SEA also gave the European Parliament power of assent over new members of the Union.

Since the 1990s, the EP's powers have been further augmented by the introduction in the Maastricht Treaty of the co-decision procedure. Maastricht also gave the Parliament power of assent over appointment of the Commission and allowed it to request the Commission to submit any proposal when it decides, by an absolute majority, that new legislation is required.

The co-decision procedure has placed the Council and EP at the centre of the legislative process. The EP can no longer be dismissed as a talking shop. Since the 1990s the EP has acquired increased powers to the extent that that the member states acting collectively can no longer control the legislative agenda (Pollack, 1999). The EU legislative system seems to be evolving into a bicameral legislature centred on the EP/Council axis.

The European Parliament and popular legitimacy

Since 1979 the EP's powers have increased, but turnout in elections has declined. This places the EP in a legitimacy bind: it claims to represent the people of Europe, but the people of Europe demonstrate little interest in its activities. Moreover, when EU citizens participate in EP elections they tend to do so in national political contexts and on national political issues. It has been argued that turnout for European elections is lower than that at national elections because European elections are 'second order' – they do not change governments – compared to 'first order' national elections that can (Reif and Schmitt, 1980).

The extension of powers to the EP by co-decision could be a double-edged sword. Co-decision does give the EP a much more significant legislative role; but to exercise this role the EP must often retreat into processes of conciliation and negotiation with the Council that reduce rather than increase the EP's ability to reach out to groups and organizations within the EU that could be affected by the legislation (Lambert and Hoskyns, 2000; Warleigh, 2003).

Despite the continued strong national component in European Parliament elections, political parties within the EU are coalescing in transnational groupings. Article 138a of the Maastricht Treaty noted the important role that transnational political parties can play in the integrative process: 'Political parties at European level are important as a factor for integration within the Union. They contribute to forming a European awareness and to expressing the political will of the citizens of the Union.'

After the 1999 elections the European People's Party, of which the Conservative Members of the European Parliament (MEPs) are members, was the largest party grouping in the European Parliament (see Table 6.9).

The 37 Conservative MEPs constitute a Eurosceptic group within the avowedly federalist European People's Party. Labour MEPs and Northern Ireland Social Democratic and Labour Party MEPs are in the party of European Socialists. The shift to PR in the 1999 Euro elections contributed to increased Liberal Democratic representation and to representation at the fringes. Neither the Greens nor the UK Independence Party (UKIP) have enjoyed much success in national parliamentary elections, but they were able to secure nine seats between them at the 1999 elections. The UK Independence Party members joined the Europe of Democracies and Diversities groups, but tensions within the UKIP saw one MEP switch to non-affiliated along with Ian Paisley from the Northern Ireland Democratic Unionist Party.

The Court of Justice

The ECJ has been viewed by Eurosceptics in a similar light to the Commission, as an agent of integration by stealth pursuing a federalizing

Table 6.9 Political groups in the European Parliament, 1999–2004

Party	Seats
European People's Party	234
Party of European Socialists	175
European Liberal, Democrat and Reform Party	52
Confederal Group of the United European Left	50
Greens/European Free Alliance	43
Europe of the Nations	22
Europe of Democracies and Diversities	16
Non-affiliated	32

Source: Reproduced from European Parliament UK Office (www.europarl.org.uk).

agenda. Pro-Europeans argue that the ECJ has been a vital institution for securing adherence to key EU goals, particularly single market integration.

Supranational European integration involves the creation of a body of law at European level that over-rides national law. This section explores the ECJ's role and looks at core Community legal principles. It still makes sense to refer to 'Community' rather than 'Union' law because of the EU's pillared structure and the fact that the ECJ is largely excluded from the intergovernmental pillars for Common Foreign and Security Policy and Justice and Home Affairs.

The EU legal system and the role of the ECJ have been central to a process of economic and political integration that has turned treaties between states into laws that bind these states and that has thus *constitutionalized* the relations between EU member states (Stone Sweet and Sandholtz, 1999). One result of this is that relations between European states (which scholars of international relations have characterized as anarchical) have become more hierarchical and rule-based. This intensive multilateralism is a key feature of the European legal and political order (Caporaso, 1996).

The EU 'constitution' currently resides in the Treaties and the legislation produced since the 1950s. Rather than being the kind of document that could be placed in a person's pocket, it is more likely to require a medium-sized truck to carry it around. A task for the EU's constitutional convention was to try to come up with a clearer statement of core principles. There is, however, already a well-established legal framework at EU level. This framework stems from the core EC purposes, which have been primarily economic and concerned with development of the common market, creation of the single market and, more recently, with EMU. The ECJ in Luxembourg has, therefore, been primarily involved with economic and commercial issues. This contrasts with the European Court of Human Rights (ECHR) in Strasbourg, which is an entirely separate institution attached to the intergovernmental Council of Europe. It is not uncommon for the ECJ and ECHR to be confused, but they have very different remits and exist within different kinds of legal order.

The shift towards greater competencies for the EC/EU since the 1980s has placed increased strain on the Court of Justice. The Court consists of 15 judges, one from each member state, and nine advocates-general. Judges are appointed by agreement of member states for a period of six years, with partial replacement every three years. The advocates-general assist the judges by analysing the arguments of parties in dispute. The increased ECJ workload led to the creation by the SEA of a Court of

First Instance, which has power to hear and determine on points of law only, with a right of appeal to the Court of Justice. The Court of First Instance is not competent to hear cases brought by member states or Community institutions.

The ECJ has the following responsibilities:

- the interpretation of the Treaties
- to determine if any act or omission by the European Commission, the Council or any member states constitutes a breach of EU law
- to decide on the validity and meaning of Community legislation.

There are a number of core principles of Community law that illustrate the ECJ's core economic concerns, and these will be explored in turn.

Direct effect and supremacy

The most significant cases in this respect were *van Gend en Loos* (1963), *Costa* v. *ENEL* (1964) and *Simmenthal* (1978). These provided that it was possible for national law to be over-ridden if it conflicted with Community law. In English law it was confirmed in 1974 by *Aero Zipp Fasteners* v. *YKK Fasteners (UK) Ltd.* In making the judgment, Mr Justice Graham noted that, 'This [European Communities] Act to put it very shortly enacted that relevant Common Market Law should be applied in this country and should, where there is a conflict, override English law.'

Member state liability

Francovich (1991) established that where member states breached Community law resulting in damage to individuals then the member state was obliged to compensate individuals for damages incurred. In *Hedley Lomas* (1996) the ECJ ruled that this was the case when member states' restrictions in breach of Community law harmed an exporter of live animals.

Rights of individuals

The ECJ has, for instance, made rulings on equal pay provided for by Article 119 of the Treaty of Rome. In *Defrenne* (1971) the ECJ ruled that all courts of member states should apply a direct effect of this principle so that all citizens could benefit from it. In the case of *Barber* v. *Guardian Royal Exchange* (1990) the ECJ extended the application of Article 119 to occupational pension schemes and ruled that differences between men and women in access to occupational pensions were a breach of Article 119 (this decision did not apply to state pensions).

EC freedoms

The key decision was *Cassis de Dijon* (1979), which established the principle of mutual recognition and as such was central to the creation of the European single market. Cassis de Dijon is a French liqueur. Cassis was, though, denied access to the German market because its alcohol content was too low at 20 per cent to make it a liqueur by German standards (25 per cent was required). The ECJ ruled that if Cassis was legally manufactured and sold in France as a liqueur then it could be legally sold in other member states too. The importance of this was that it removed the need for a mountain of regulations to specify product standards for all goods traded within the EC. The ECJ has also acted to ensure that the EU's four freedoms (free movement for people, capital, goods and services) apply to all EU citizens. This has led to action against member states and companies that have tried to circumvent Community law. *Binsbergen and Reyners* (1974) provided for the freedom to provide services and freedom of establishment. *Nouvelles Frontières* (1986) provided that EU deregulation should also apply to the air industry.

The European Council

The European Council was established in 1974 to provide political leadership at the highest level. It is composed of the heads of government who meet at least twice a year to plot the EU's political course. The European Council is thus central to the 'history-making decisions', to the grand declarations, to the photo opportunities and, more recently, to the protests and high security that accompany any high level political gathering.

The European Council was institutionalized in Paris in 1974 and formalized by the SEA in 1986. It meets twice a year, though extra meetings can be held in the event of exceptional circumstances, and it generally convenes in the country holding the Presidency of the Community. When Britain held the Presidency in the first six months of 1998 the European Council met in Cardiff in June. In addition, a European Conference was convened in March 1998 comprising present and future EU member states.

Article D of the Maastricht Treaty outlined the European Council's role to: 'provide the Union with the necessary impetus for its development and shall define the general political guidelines thereof'. The European Council served as an important vehicle for the 'preference convergence' that under-pinned the resurgence of integration in the 1980s.

There were four meetings of the European Council in 2001. A glance at the agenda for these meetings shows: how some items recur (such as enlargement); the issuance of declarations that set the political course; the affirmation and reaffirmation of political and economic priorities; the addressing of a range of foreign policy issues; and response to political crisis.

The Gothenburg European Council of 15 and 16 June was a fairly routine meeting focused on enlargement and sustainable development. A range of foreign policy issues was discussed: relations with Russia, the western Balkans, the Middle East, Algeria, East Timor and the Korean peninsula. The presence of the US President, George W. Bush, in Gothenburg on 14 June for a US–European summit led to a declaration that restated the core values and shared objectives of the transatlantic community.

An extraordinary session was held in Brussels on 21 September following the terrorist attacks on the USA. Solidarity with the USA was declared and the European Council analysed the international situation resulting from these events and decided on the measures needed to stimulate EU action. It adopted an action plan spelling out the tasks to be undertaken by the Council in its various compositions and asked the Commission to analyse the impact of the attacks on economic prospects.

An informal meeting in Gent on 19 October was originally intended to be devoted to enlargement issues and preparations for the introduction of Euro notes in January 2002, but instead it refocused attention on the response to the September 11 terrorist attacks. Three declarations were adopted: on the preparation for the introduction of the Euro, on the economic situation and on the follow-up to the attacks and the fight against terrorism.

The meeting in Laeken on 14 and 15 December adopted a declaration on the EU's future, known as the Laeken declaration. This identified the principal challenges facing the Union: a better division and definition of competence, simplification of instruments, more democracy, transparency and efficiency and moves towards a Constitution for European citizens. It also convened a constitutional convention to report to an intergovernmental conference headed by Valéry Giscard d'Estaing. The meeting also confirmed the objective of concluding accession negotiations by the end of 2002 so that new member states could take part in the 2004 European Parliament elections, and adopted a declaration on the operational capability of the common European security and defence policy.

Looking to the future

The EU's institutional structures are 'hybrid' in the sense that they contain both intergovernmental and supranational elements. British governments have long preferred to highlight the centrality of intergovernmental institutions such as the Council and European Council, and to be wary of increased powers for the Commission and the European Parliament. That said, institutional changes since the 1980s have contributed to the consolidation of supranational decision-making processes that could be seen to run counter to this British preference for intergovernmentalism. The Council now increasingly decides more issues on the basis of QMV, which means less possibility for national vetoes. The European Parliament has through co-decision-making become more closely involved in law-making, while the ECJ has also continued to leave its mark on the legal parameters of a politically and economically integrated EU.

These political and legal entanglements have developed progressively over time and are difficult to roll back. The EU institutional system has evolved into a more advanced form of supranational governance that has become part of an EU system while also reaching into domestic politics in EU member states. Analysis of the EU's institutional system reveals the conditional nature of British engagement tied to a particular, self-consciously pragmatic understanding of the limits of European integration and a preference for intergovernmental co-operation. At the same time, analysis of these institutions also demonstrates the ways in which a unique supranational decision-making system has evolved above the nation state with law-making powers that bind participating states. Chapter 8 returns to these points when the impacts of the EU on the organization of the British state are explored.

The future evolution of the institutional system is obviously a key concern. In this respect it is also possible to detect elements of New Labour's approach to European integration that are not particularly 'new', but in fact reflect rather longer-standing British preferences. Until 2002 the British government seemed more determined to block rather than actively participate in the Constitutional Convention. This attitude changed as it became clear that the Convention on the Future of Europe chaired by Giscard d'Estaing had significant momentum and that it would be better for the UK government to seek to influence the outcome from inside rather than snipe from the sidelines. The British government's representative on the Convention was the then Secretary of State for Wales (and the ex-Foreign Office Minister for Europe), Peter Hain. Hain's evidence to the House of Commons EU scrutiny committee in November 2002 showed the intergovernmental manoeuvrings within the Convention and the relative consistency of British attitudes towards EU institutions marked by a reluctance to empower EU institutions and a suspicion of grand projects focused on European integration's *finalité*. Hain identified British opposition to the idea of a Commission President elected either by MEPs or by the people of Europe. Hain made it clear that the British government saw the Commission President not as a 'big political leader of Europe', but as an administrator responsible for the Commission's smooth running. The British government was arguing for a separate proposal by which EU heads of state would elect a president for a five-year term.

This proposal was contained in the draft constitution for the EU prepared by the Cambridge law professor, Alan Dashwood. The Dashwood draft constitution drops references to 'ever closer union' and instead characterizes the EU as a 'constitutional order of sovereign states' founded on the principles of subsidiarity, proportionality, conferred powers and loyal co-operation. The idea is that powers would be reserved to the member states unless specifically provided for by treaty, although terms such as subsidiarity have been notoriously difficult to define (as was discussed in Chapter 3). Although officially independent, the Dashwood document was understood as a UK government sanctioned attempt to steer the discussions in a direction favoured by the British government. As one British government official put it, 'you need to hold the strings if you're going to fly a kite' (*The Guardian*, 16 October 2002). British participation in the Convention was shaped by Hain's confident assertion that Britain could make and win arguments about the EU's future (with the implicit reference to a failure to make and win arguments in the past). Many of the dilemmas that face the UK when considering institutional reform recur when the focus turns to key EU policies, which are the subject of the next chapter.

7

Britain and European Union Policies

Introduction

This chapter surveys the development and impact of key EU and explores the UK's role in their development and their effects on UK public policy. The chapter thus combines the Britain in Europe and Europe in Britain themes as we begin to explore the ways in which Europe hits home. There is no typical EU policy sector. Each is shaped according to particular circumstances, notably the amount of autonomy member states have been willing to cede by Treaty to the Union and the configurations of institutions and interests that develop in particular policy areas. Some policy areas, such as agriculture, are more supranationalized than others, such as foreign policy co-operation which retains a strong intergovernmental focus. The chapter begins by mapping well-established areas of EU competence (the budget, the CAP, and single market integration). It then moves onto assess newer issues (the environment and social policy) and then examines issues of 'high politics' (EMU, foreign and defence policy, and justice and home affairs).

The budget

The EU budget has been a long-standing bugbear for British governments because the UK is second behind Germany in the league table of net contributors. Figure 7.1 shows the net contributors and net beneficiaries to the EU budget. Since 1984, the UK has received a rebate on its budget contributions. Figure 7.2 breaks down the net and gross contributions.

The EU is not a club to which member states pay a subscription; rather, it has a system of independent financing (Laffan, 1997). A 1970 Treaty laid the foundations of the current system. The budget framework

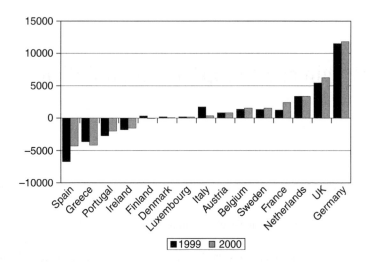

Figure 7.1   Net receipts/contributions of EU member states 1999 and 2000
(€ million)
Source: Reproduced from HM Treasury (2002: 11).

was not in the UK's interests because it favoured countries that traded more extensively with other member states (the UK had more extensive global trading links) and that had relatively inefficient agricultural sectors (the UK's was relatively efficient).

The sources of 'own resources'

The 1970 budget treaty was negotiated before UK accession and was widely acknowledged as not in Britain's interests. Edward Heath, for example, maintained that it would be better for Britain to join the EC and then try to shape it from within. Britain's budget contributions were to be a key test of this ambition.

The 1970 budget treaty had established three sources of the EU's 'own resources':

1   Customs duty levies on imports to member states. In 2002, these levies amounted to around 15 per cent of the total budget.
2   Levies on agricultural trade with non-member countries. These are not levied at a fixed rate. Instead they fluctuate, and are designed to raise the price of imported agricultural goods relative to those prevailing in the EU. In 2002, these accounted for around 2.5 per cent of the total budget.

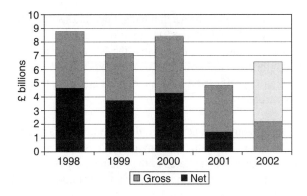

Figure 7.2   Profile of UK gross and net contributions from the EU budget 1996–2002

Source: Reproduced from HM Treasury (2002: 10).

3   A proportion of member states' sales tax (VAT – value added tax – in the UK). The rate was set at 1 per cent of the sales tax base, which rose to 1.4 per cent after 1986 to help pay for the accession of Spain and Portugal, and then decreased to 1 per cent between 1995 and 1999. At the 1999 Berlin summit, it was agreed that the maximum call-in rate of VAT would fall to 0.5 per cent by 2004. In 2002, the VAT contribution amounted to around 35 of the total budget.

A fourth source was added in 1988.

4   An amount proportional to each member state's share in total Union gross national product (GNP). This allows the EU to balance the difference between planned expenditure and the amount yielded by the three traditional sources of own resources. In 2002 the GNP contribution accounted for around 45 per cent of the budget.

The budget procedure is governed by five rules:

1   The rule of unity means that all revenue and expenditure must be incorporated in a single budget document (there are special financial arrangements for CFSP and JHA).
2   The rule of universality means that budget revenue is a common pool used without distinction to finance all expenditure.

3   The rule of annuality means that budget operations relate to a specific financial year for which the EU executive can be held to account.
4   The rule of equilibrium means that the EU cannot run a deficit and is not authorized to borrow to cover its expenditure.
5   The rule of specification means that each appropriation must have a given purpose.

The Council and Parliament share decision-making authority over the budget. The Council has the final say on what is known as 'compulsory expenditure', which is that related to the original purposes of the Union as set out in the Rome Treaty. In the main, this is agricultural expenditure. The European Parliament has the final say on 'non-compulsory expenditure', which is that spent on areas into which the EU has moved since the founding Treaties. In the main, this is money targeted to what is known as 'social and economic cohesion' (such as regional development aid).

Agriculture still consumes almost 50 per cent of the budget, but there has been growth in spending on 'structural operations' that target regional and social inequalities. The Commission's 'Agenda 2000', published in 1997, envisaged that the budget would remain at 1.27 per cent of the Union's GNP until 2006 and argued that the challenges facing the EU could be met from within current spending ceilings, but that this would necessitate reform of key policy areas, particularly the CAP. The financial perspective put in place by the heads of government at the 1999 Berlin summit to cover the years 2000–6 set the budget ceiling at 1.27 per cent.

UK governments have been determined (i) to protect the budget rebate, although this has drawn the ire of other member states that are big contributors and resent the UK's special status and (ii) to ensure tight control of EU finances with the ceiling maintained at current levels and without big increases in contributions from the richer member states. The Treasury tends to view EU spending in the UK as reimbursement of contributions made rather than new money (see Chapter 8 for further analysis).

The member states agreed at the 1999 Berlin summit that the ceiling for the EU budget would remain at 1.27 per cent of the combined GNP of the member states. In 2002, appropriations to the EU budget amounted to €100 billion (£63 billion). This equals around 2.5 per cent of the combined public spending of the member states. By contrast, the UK government consumes around 38 per cent of GNP because of heavy commitments to the welfare state and other major items of expenditure such as defence that the EU does not have responsibility for. The allusions to Westphalian forms of state flounder when the EU's limited budgetary resources are borne in mind.

Agriculture

Agriculture is one of the most Europeanized activities within the British government. The Ministry of Agriculture, Food and Fisheries used to conduct its own mini-foreign policy as it liased closely with other member states on this key EU competence. Without the CAP it is debatable whether the Ministry of Agriculture, Fisheries and Food (MAFF) would have survived as long as it did (Marsh, Richards and Smith, 2001). Bovine Spongiform Encephalopathy (BSE) and foot and mouth disease dealt MAFF fatal blows and its activities were merged into the new Department for Environment, Food and Rural Affairs (DEFRA).

In the UK the CAP has become a by-word for wastefulness and inefficiency. The UK agricultural sector has also experienced a series of crises and also prompted high levels of political mobilization around 'countryside' issues that range from hunting to the power of the large supermarket chains. These are often not EU issues, but because agricultural policy is a core EU matter then the question needs to be asked whether the CAP is part of the solution or part of the problem for British agriculture.

Common Agricultural Policy objectives

The CAP's establishment in 1962 and phased introduction by 1968 marked the establishment of a supranational decision-making process in an important area of economic activity. It was based on a *unified market* with free movement of agricultural products within the Common Market; *Community preference*, which means that EU agricultural products are given preference and a price advantage over imported products; and *financial solidarity*, which means that all expenses and spending which result from the application of the CAP are borne by the Community budget. Article 39 of the Treaty of Rome outlined five objectives for the CAP:

- to increase agricultural productivity
- to ensure a fair standard of living for the agricultural community
- to stabilize markets
- to ensure the availability of supplies
- to ensure reasonable prices to consumers.

These objectives were to be attained by institution of common prices for agricultural produce within the Union. Prices are decided annually by the Council of Ministers in the first half of the year, on the basis of proposals made by the Commission's agriculture Directorate General. The weakness of the system was that prices tended to be set too high which presented farmers with a relatively inelastic demand curve and stimulated over-production with the effect that agricultural surpluses built up (the infamous wine lakes, butter mountains and so on; for details see Grant, 1997).

The CAP functioned as a welfare state for farmers with reallocations from consumers to producers backed by powerful agricultural interest groups with close links to national governments. Wastefulness, market distorting effects and the impending EU enlargement to countries with relatively large and inefficient agricultural sectors have led to pressure for change. External pressures have been exerted by the liberalization of world trade, which draws attention to the protectionist CAP.

Two other factors play a growing and important role. First, there is heightened consumer awareness of food safety and environmental issues (the BSE crisis, foot and mouth and genetically modified foods are all examples of this). Second, the CAP has been indicted as a protectionist and market-rigging arrangement that harms farmers in Third World countries. For instance, subsidies on sugar exports by EU farmers have distorted the international terms of trade and had devastating effects on other sugar producing countries such as Brazil, Malawi and Zambia.

There are, however, major difficulties with CAP reform because it is essentially an intergovernmental process within which national governments and agriculture ministries (often closely aligned with farming interests) are key players.

The thwarted reform agenda

In the 1980s the British, Dutch and Danish governments pushed for change as they had small and relatively efficient agricultural sectors, which gained little from the CAP. The accession of Greece, Portugal and Spain in the 1980s, all of which have relatively large agricultural sectors, placed additional strain on the CAP, although the accession of states that would benefit from the policy was hardly likely to be an impetus for reform.

Opposition from member states and agricultural interests have made it difficult to secure changes. Rather, a series of measures can be identified over the last 20 years or so that have sought to rein in agricultural expenditure and deal with some of the more serious problems. The perception of these problems has also changed. In the 1980s, over-production was top of the agenda. Now, environmental concerns, food safety and fair trade with Third World countries are important too.

The Commission's Agenda 2000 document called for a new decentralized model of agriculture which would in theory give member states the ability to settle issues for themselves by taking better account of a particular sector or local conditions, although the Commission warned that this should not go so far as to renationalize agricultural policies (Commission of the European Communities, 1997). Commission proposals of March 1998 sought further price cuts; increased direct aid with an increased national level component to better reflect local circumstances; simplification of the rules; the reinforcement of action on the environment with current aid linked to less intensive farming methods; and rural development as a 'second pillar' of the CAP, backed by Community funding for rural development schemes. It was difficult for the member states to agree on substantive change to the CAP at the 1999 Berlin summit because of French sensibilities in light of the impending 2001 presidential elections. Discussion of substantive reforms was effectively postponed until 2005.

In its mid-term review of the reform agenda, the Commission proposed a further CAP makeover (Commission of the European Communities, 2002b). Key elements were 'decoupling', which means cutting the link between production and direct payments, and better monitoring of compliance which means that payments are made conditional on environmental, food safety, animal welfare and occupational safety standards. The key point with these proposals, as with all others, is that they are subject to the Council of Agriculture Ministers where it has been difficult to secure support for substantive reform. A quick look at the political context in the member states illustrates some of the broader problems with substantive change. President Chirac in France and the centre-right government elected in 2002 are unwilling to upset farming interest groups and have opposed radical changes. Changes were also delayed prior to 2002 because of looming German federal elections that could have seen the return to power of the Christian Democrats, which has traditionally been linked to farming interests. The 2001 elections in Italy also saw a change from a green to an extreme right agriculture minister in the new Berlusconi government who moved the Italian government into the anti-reform camp. There was also some reduction in pressure on the EU to get its own house in order when

US President Bush signed the Farm Bill, which will greatly increase subsidies to US farmers.

Britain and the Common Agricultural Policy

Sectoral woes in the UK have been compounded by major crises caused by the BSE crisis and the 1997 outbreak of foot and mouth disease. In March 1996 following the announcement of a possible link between a cattle disease, BSE, and its human equivalent, Creutzfeldt-Jakob disease, the Commission imposed a complete ban on the export from the UK of cattle and beef products such as gelatine. The British government took the Commission to the Court of Justice, but in May 1996 the Court upheld the Commission's ban. The Florence European Council of June 1996 put in place a timetable for lifting the ban, including the slaughter of an estimated 85,000 animals aged over 30 months and deemed at risk because of their association with infected cattle. The effects on the UK beef industry were substantial. In 1995 Britain exported beef worth £594 million and live calves (another very controversial issue because of the animal rights implications of transporting live animals) worth £73 million. It was reported that between 1996 and 1998 some 1,000 jobs were lost and that the ban had cost £1.5 billion, including government eradication measures. In June 1998 the Commission recommended that the export ban be lifted for de-boned beef from cattle aged 6–30 months and born after 1 August 1996. Exports from Northern Ireland had been allowed to recommence from 1 June 1998, although the French authorities continued to block UK beef exports until October 2002. The foot and mouth outbreak began in February 2001. The Commission imposed an immediate ban on the movement of animals susceptible to foot and mouth, which led to further devastation in the UK agricultural industry coupled with the effective closure of the countryside in large parts of the country, which hit tourism hard.

A report prepared for the government on the future of British agriculture by Sir Don Curry indicates important strands in official UK thinking on the CAP (Curry, 2002). The report is damning of the CAP, which it sees as dividing producers from their market, distorting price signals and masking inefficiencies (Curry, 2002: 20). The report proposes the removal of market price support and associated production controls. It also calls for a reduction in direct payments and 'decoupling', with direct payments untied from production. To promote the economic development of rural communities, the Curry report called for the transfer of resources from Pillar I of the CAP (subsidies to farmers) to Pillar II (support for rural development and environmental protection). The UK government has proposed that by 2006 there should be a 4.5 per cent transfer of resources from Pillar I to Pillar II, but the Curry Report argues that the government could go further. The introduction of the Euro has presented some additional problems for the British agricultural sector. As the report notes: 'Because of the way European payments are made, British farming is really a Euro-area industry operating in the wrong currency' because subsidies are denominated in Euros and thus depreciate in value as sterling appreciates. As things stand, the government offers compensation to farmers to cover losses incurred as a result of currency changes (£400 million between 1999 and 2001).

It seems that the CAP is part of the problem for British farmers and rural communities rather than part of the solution. That said, it would be unfair to blame the EU for all the problems of Britain's rural communities. The BSE and foot and mouth crises were linked to changes in regulatory structures governing British agriculture while the closure of village post offices, the removal of rural bus services or a ban on fox hunting are not the EU's responsibility. Even so, in the face of the serious obstacles to substantive reform it is difficult to see how major CAP changes can occur.

Britain and European Union environmental policy

British environmental policy cannot be understood without reference to the EU (Lowe and Ward, 1998; Jordan, 2000). Lowe and Ward's (1998) analysis of British environmental policy since the 1970s shows how an agenda largely driven by domestic concerns has been Europeanized in key respects. An initially sceptical and defensive reaction from British governments in the 1970s and 1980s (Golub, 1996) has been subsumed by the sheer weight of EU policies and initiatives. This has meant greater emphasis on the codification of legal standards and the clearer formulation of national policy in response to these EU standards. European Court of Justice decisions and Commission enforcement have intensified the pressure to adapt to EU-wide standards, particularly in areas such as water quality standards.

Environmental policy was an issue that ascended the EU agenda in the 1970s, reflective of the increased concern about 'post-material' quality of life issues. Environmental policy was formalized as an EU competence by the Maastricht Treaty, while Amsterdam enshrined the principle of sustainable development (Lenschow, 2001). The Nice Treaty was greeted with some dismay by environmental pressure groups because it was seen to switch power to larger member states, away from smaller 'greener' states and from the Commission.

A looming issue is that of how the EU will reconcile its commitment to sustainability with the accession of 10 new member states from central, eastern and southern Europe that have undergone economic and political transformations within which the environment has not always been a top priority. The attitudes that these new member states will adopt – will they be leaders or laggards? – is an important and open question (Jordan and Fairbrass, 2001).

The effects on British environmental policy are interesting because they illustrate the ways in which a particular policy sector can become Europeanized and the effects that this can induce in domestic policy structures (this point is developed more fully in the following chapter when the role of the Department of the Environment is assessed). Since 1972, the EU has adopted six environmental policy action programmes focused on areas such as waste management and limiting air and water pollution. The fifth action programme, running from 1992 to 2000, adopted a 'horizontal approach' that cut across sectors and sought to integrate the environment as a key concern in a range of policy areas, including agriculture, industry, tourism and energy. The sixth action programme (which will run until 2010) identifies climate change, nature and biodiversity, and the management of natural resources and waste as key concerns.

The effects on British environmental policy tend to differ by sector. Some areas, such as land use planning, housing and local government finance, remain largely untouched by the EU while others, such as water quality, are extensively Europeanized with highly prescriptive Europe-wide standards to be enforced at national level. The impact of the EU on environmental policy-making was to 'break open' the pre-existing policy community. Responsibility also shifted away from local government (which did have prime responsibility for implementation) towards other public bodies, including central government and agencies. Many of these groups then act almost as pressure groups at EU level pursuing a 'British' agenda. Lowe and Ward (1998) argue that the effects of this Europeanization have been largely beneficial because standards have risen as a result of EU obligations, although benefits in some areas are offset by costs in others, such as the detrimental effects of the CAP. The UK has moved since the 1970s from a defensive and sceptical posture and the stigma of being labelled the 'dirty man of Europe' to a more pro-active and policy-shaping role.

The single market

One area in which the UK has positively engaged with European integration is the single market. This meshes with UK preferences for deregulated, flexible and liberalized economies. The Conservative governments of the 1980s and New Labour governments since 1997 both argued that the European economy needed to become more British ('Thatcherized' in the 1980s and early 1990s, 'modernized' since 1997). If liberalization, deregulation and privatization were successfully entrenched at EU level this would impose strong constraints on future governments and rule out a return to state economic interventionism (Buller, 2000).

The organization of the single market

The Treaty of Rome provided for the creation of a 'common market' based on the free movement of goods, persons, services and capital. The creation of the single market after 1987 was a progressive extension of the idea of the common market in the sense that the SEA provided for the creation of a single market defined as an area without internal frontiers within which the free movement of people, services, goods and capital would be assured.

The UK Conservative government was favourable to the single market project, but did not agree that such measures would require major institutional changes or further policy integration. For the British government the single market was an end in itself, not a means to an end. Figure 7.3 shows that an initial point of intergovernmental preference convergence around the terms of the SEA soon turned into divergence as the expansive post-SEA agenda developed and the EC discussed ambitious plans such as EMU and a strengthened social dimension. The gap between UK preferences and the plans of other key EC member states was filled by the development of Conservative Euroscepticism.

Main features of the single market

The SEA contained both policy and institutional reforms. As well as putting in place a timetable for the realization of free movement, it also sought to establish more efficient decision-making processes. It did so by extending the use of qualified majority voting (QMV) in the Council

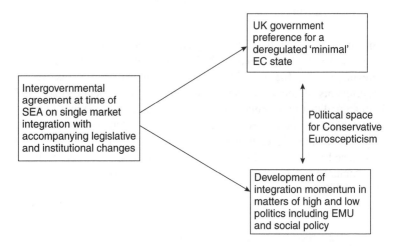

Figure 7.3   Preference divergence and the 'space' for Euroscepticism

with exceptions for sensitive areas such as taxation, free movement of people (affecting immigration policies) and the rights of employed people (affecting trade union rights). The White Paper also set a target date of 31 December 1992 for completion of the single market. Not all measures were attained by this date, but there was substantial movement towards the completion of the single market.

The single market centres on the 'four freedoms': free movement for goods, people, services and capital, and these will be considered in turn below.

Free movement for goods involves the abolition for trade within the single market of customs duties and charges. The ECJ has played an important part in ensuring that trade regulations in member states do not hinder either directly or indirectly intra-Community trade. The 1985 White Paper also proposed the removal of physical barriers (border and customs checks).

Free movement for persons is a sensitive issue because, while allowing nationals of member states to live and work in other member states, the measure also affects national immigration policies. Within the single market, the free movement of workers is of central importance. Article 39 of the EC Treaty provides that the 'freedom of movement for workers shall be secured within the Community'; this involves 'the abolition of any discrimination based on nationality between workers of the Member States as regards employment, remuneration and other conditions of work and employment'. The ECJ has been active in ensuring that Article 39 applied broadly and has extended the principle of freedom of movement to persons seeking employment.

Free movement for services is linked to the right of establishment: that is, Community nationals or Community businesses are given equal treatment when operating in other member states. The right of establishment also allows self-employed persons and Community businesses to set up and perform their activity in another member state. UK governments have been keen to see deregulation applied to the banking and insurance sectors too because of UK strength in the financial services industry.

Free movement for capital involves the prohibition of restrictions on capital movements (investments) and on payments (payment for goods or services).

The Commission publishes a biennial 'Scoreboard' to publicize compliance and non-compliance which allows identification of the single market laggards and the leaders. The UK along with Sweden, Denmark, Finland, the Netherlands, Belgium and Spain was praised for making good progress. France, Greece, Germany and Ireland were chastised for lagging.

Britain and the single market

British governments have continued to emphasize the benefits that business gains from the single market. In fact, this is one of the few areas in which British governments have been consistently positive about EU membership. More than 50 per cent of Britain's trade is with other EU member states. Table 7.1 shows that EU states comprise seven of both the top ten destinations for British exports and sources of imported goods. The USA does, however, remain Britain's largest trading partner.

Advocates of EU membership emphasize the benefits of the single market. They contend that more than 3 million British jobs and one-seventh of all UK income and production are linked to trade with other EU member states. Outside the single market, the UK would have little influence on the shape and future development of the European economy. The single market thus constitutes a highly significant economic development with important political implications within which British governments have sought to exert influence over the scope, shape and form of economic integration.

Opponents of Britain's EU membership argue that many of the advantages of the single market would accrue whether or not the UK was a EU

Table 7.1   The United Kingdom's top ten export and import countries, 2000 (£million)

Export destinations	Amount	Import sources	Amount
USA	29,505	USA	30,352
Germany	23,115	Germany	28,412
France	18,890	France	18,802
Netherlands	14,250	Netherlands	14,927
Ireland	14,140	Belgium	11,203
Belgium	9,369	Italy	10,064
Spain	8,243	Japan	9,376
Sweden	8,168	Ireland	9,375
Switzerland	3,917	Spain	6,796
Japan	3,767	Hong Kong	5,977

Source: Data from HM Customs & Excise (www.uktradeinfo.com).

member. The core issue is whether or not a credible alternative scenario can be identified. Some argue that Britain could remain in the European Economic Area, which is closely linked to the EU single market, and that as the world's fourth largest economy the UK has nothing to fear from a go-it-alone strategy. It has also been argued that the UK could position itself as a low regulation, privatized economy on the edge of the EU and become a magnet for inward investment (Gamble, 1998). It has even been argued that the UK could become a member of the North American Free Trade Area (NAFTA) instead of the EU, although despite the close relationship between UK and US governments this seems highly unlikely. Lurking beneath the 'Hong Kong' and NAFTA scenarios is a fear that the UK economy will be 'continentalized' rather than the European economy becoming 'Anglicized' in the sense that Brussels will be the source of regulations that undo the Thatcherite reforms which many opponents of EU membership hold dear.

Britain's New Labour government has its own distinct views on the kinds of economic reforms that the EU needs to undertake. The Blair governments have been enthusiastic advocates of the 'new economy' agenda agreed at the Lisbon summit of EU leaders in March 2001. This expresses the objective of making the EU the world's leading knowledge-based economy by 2010. This has also involved New Labour forming alliances with right-wing governments in Italy and Spain rather than with social democrat governments in pursuit of a liberalizing and deregulating agenda. This can be seen as indicative of the gulf between New Labour and the main strands of European social democracy (Gamble and Kelly, 2000).

Britain and European Union social policy

EU social policy came to symbolize Thatcherite resistance to European integration's post-single market spillover effects. Thatcher went so far as to characterize EU social policy as inspired by Marxist ideas about class warfare, while the Tory tabloids directed their ire at Commission president Jacques Delors as the harbinger of what they saw as an EU economy suffocated by Brussels red tape. Social policy was part of a commitment to 'social cohesion', including both social and regional policies. (Chapter 8 explores the regional dimension of this commitment to 'inclusion' more closely.)

The politicization of EU social policy in these terms has also led to over-exaggeration of EU social policy's effects. Two points are particularly pertinent. First, the EU is not a welfare state and does not have responsibility for core welfare state functions such as education, health and employment related benefits. It is highly unlikely that the EU will develop these kinds of welfare state responsibilities given diverse forms of welfare state organization within the EU. Second, EU social policy has been largely concerned with ensuring that the single market works smoothly. Thus the focus has been on ensuring that when people exercise their right of free movement within the EU, they take their social entitlements with them (Geyer, 2000).

When the UK joined the EC in 1973 there were social policy provisions contained in Articles 118–23 of the Treaty of Rome to which Britain became subject. This included a commitment to gender equality and the creation of a European Social Fund. Plans to further develop these social policy competencies occurred in the SEA's wake. The Social Charter was a non-binding declaration, but even so the British government refused to sign. The Charter crystallized divisions between the British Conservative government and other member states. The British Prime Minister, Margaret Thatcher, saw in the Social Charter not the moderation of mainstream European Christian Democracy but remnants of Britain's old system of industrial relations with 'beer and sandwiches' for trade union leaders at 10 Downing Street. She was not prepared to invite union leaders in through the front door of Number 10 and was determined that they would not gain entry through a 'back door' opened by Brussels. For this reason, British trade unions cast off their previous hostility to European integration (understood as a capitalist club that offered little to workers) and, instead, began to extol the virtues of integration. This process was accelerated by a speech made to the 1988 Trades Union Congress (TUC) conference by the Commission's President, Jacques Delors, who called on

British trade unions to be active in the construction of a more closely integrated Europe. Delors' presence at the TUC conference and his message to the assembled trade unionists enraged Margaret Thatcher and further damaged relations between her and the Commission President (Rosamond, 1998).

John Major followed the line of his predecessor by opposing any extension of Community social policy. Major secured an opt-out from Maastricht's Social Chapter. The result of British opposition to extended social policy competencies was that the Social Chapter, embodying many rights outlined in the non-binding Social Charter, became an agreement between the other 11 members.

The Amsterdam Treaty added a new Title VII covering employment to the Treaty of Rome, while the promotion of employment was added to the list of Community objectives as a 'matter of common concern' (Article 2 of the EC Treaty). The new objective consists in reaching a 'high level of employment' without undermining competitiveness. In order to attain this objective, the Community is given responsibility to complement the activities of the member states, involving the development of a 'co-ordinated strategy' for employment. The Amsterdam treaty extended QMV, although social security remained subject to unanimity and levels of pay remained excluded from EU competence.

Tony Blair's Labour government opted back into social policy following their election in June 1997. This need not necessarily indicate a 'third way' embrace of European social democracy. As discussed in Chapter 5, New Labour in power have sought an economic reform agenda for Europe that matches key components of UK 'modernization'. This has become particularly evident in the debate about the Euro because the UK has linked structural economic reform of the European economy to British participation (HM Treasury, 2001). This is a complex matter because it goes straight to the heart of relations between states and markets in EU member states. However, there may well not be enthusiasm in other EU member states for UK-style market liberalization, which could challenge national welfare states.

Economic and Monetary Union

The creation of an economic and monetary union has had, and continues to have, massive implications for British politics. Sterling's ejection in September 1992 from the Exchange Rate Mechanism shattered the reputation for economic competence of the Conservative government

and contributed to their electoral decimation in 1997 and 2001. Whether
or not Britain replaces sterling with the Euro remains a key unresolved
question in British politics with far-reaching significance for ideas and
practices of national sovereignty. John Maynard Keynes pointed out
that: 'Whoever controls the currency, controls the government.' Control
of key aspects of economic and monetary policy passes to the Council
of Ministers and the European Central Bank in Frankfurt. Advocates of
European integration contend that economic sovereignty is a chimera in
the modern era of economic interdependence and that member states can
only exercise effective economic sovereignty as part of an EMU.
Opponents argue that EMU is poorly conceived and not in the UK's
interests. The issue also focuses attention on the relationship between
the Prime Minister, Blair, and the Chancellor of the Exchequer, Brown,
at the heart of the Labour government.

EMU is important because it cannot be passed off as a largely technical
concern. Control over the currency and economic policy go to the heart of
national sovereignty. The entry into circulation of the single currency in
January 2002 is a visible representation of the drive to closer European
integration. There are those who argued that EMU was unrealistic and
doomed to fail (the early slide in the value of the Euro was grist to this
argument, although its more recent increases in value have not tended
to be seen by many UK financial commentators as vindication).
Furthermore, the same points were made about other ambitious steps in
the creation of an integrated Europe. The sceptics might be correct this
time. Perhaps the Euro is riddled with structural flaws and is doomed to
fail. But perhaps too it is worth bearing in mind that a mistake of British
governments over the last 50 years or so has been to doubt both the intent
of other European governments and the prospects for integration to succeed. British governments have then tended to watch from the sidelines
while policy and institutional priorities are established in their absence.

The origins of Economic and Monetary Union

The over-arching questions are (i) whether such a European currency
union can work, and (ii) the implications of such arrangements for
democratic government. Although there is no precedent for a monetary
union on such a scale, the historical omens are ambivalent because as
many currency unions have collapsed during the twentieth century as
have been created. In Europe, the Belgium–Luxembourg monetary
union survived until the creation of the Euro, but the Austro–Hungarian

empire, Czechoslovakia and Yugoslavia all saw political disintegration accompanied by monetary disunion.

Title II of the Treaty of Rome called for 'progressively approximating the economic policies of member states'. A Monetary Committee was established to seek monetary policy co-ordination, although there was no clear intention to set up a currency bloc in Europe. By the late 1960s the basic structures of the Common Market had been set in place and heads of government, meeting in The Hague in 1969, took steps to form an EMU to protect the CAP because common agricultural prices depended on currency stability, so that instability and exchange rate fluctuation would threaten its basis. Luxembourg's Prime Minister, Pierre Werner, was commissioned to bring forward a plan for EMU. He proposed three stages culminating in an irrevocable fixing of exchange rates and free circulation of people, goods, services, and capital. However, Werner's plan was undermined by events in the 1970s when dollar instability created by the burgeoning US budget deficit was compounded by the 1973 oil crisis and the failure of EU governments to agree a co-ordinated economic and political response.

The French and German governments remained convinced of the merits of further economic integration. In 1978 the Bremen summit established the European Monetary System (EMS) and its Exchange Rate Mechanism (ERM), with the Ecu as a parallel unit of exchange and forerunner of a single currency. The EMS aimed to formalize economic cooperation between the member states leading to eventual convergence. The Ecu was based on a 'basket' of member state currencies and related to their economic strength. Each national currency was valued in relation to the Ecu and, thus, to all other EU currencies with central rates of exchange.

The British joined the EMS in 1979, thus making sterling one of the component currencies of the Ecu, then joined the ERM in October 1990 and left rather unceremoniously on 16 September 1992 when sterling was placed under unsustainable pressure on 'Black Wednesday' (Stephens, 1996).

As discussed in Chapter 5, ERM entry caused tensions within the final Thatcher government between the Prime Minister, her Chancellor, Nigel Lawson, and her Foreign Secretary, Sir Geoffrey Howe, who were both pro-ERM. In her memoirs Thatcher (1993) recounts being bounced into the ERM at the Madrid summit against her will when Lawson and Howe ganged up on her, as she saw it. They were not key members of her government for much longer, although Thatcher's own political demise was not far removed and was closely connected to these arguments about EMU.

For its advocates, ERM membership was viewed as an external constraint that would inhibit any return to the 'boom and bust' policies of the 1980s when rapid economic growth had been followed by sharp recession. If the UK was tied to a credible external mechanism such as the ERM then this could impose anti-inflationary discipline on the UK economy. This reasoning also informed the selection of an exchange rate with the Deutschmark when Britain eventually entered the ERM which turned out to place unsustainable pressures on sterling. Sterling entered the ERM on 5 October 1991 at a rate of DM2.95 to the £. This was unsustainable because of the strength of the Deutschmark. 'Black Wednesday' saw the pound face frenzied selling on international currency markets with interest rates increased to 15 per cent (with devastating effects on mortgage holders). At 7.40 p.m. on 16 September the Chancellor of the Exchequer, Norman Lamont, announced that 'Today has been an extremely difficult and turbulent day' and that Britain's ERM membership was suspended (it has not been reactivated since). The ERM experience remains a strong card for those arguing against joining the EMU, yet it is also worth recalling that membership of the ERM was linked to domestic economic policy and the desire to impose anti-inflationary disciplines. The political choices made by the British government were key elements in their humiliation on Black Wednesday. The economic policy implications were important too. A latent Treasury Euroscepticism and the belief that economic policy 'credibility begins at home' were reinforced (Dyson, 2000). Moreover, this humiliation was to unleash a strong Euroscepticism within the Conservative Party, which was to have deeply damaging effects on the Party (for analysis of this policy disaster by the Treasury's Chief Economic Adviser see Balls, 2002).

Key features of Economic and Monetary Union

EMU implies a single currency, common economic policies and mechanisms for inter-regional exchange. Two political factors have been identified as central to whether or not a currency union can work (Cohen, 1998). First, can a hegemon guarantee stability of the system? One argument advanced for EMU is that it actually reduces the hegemonic power of Germany, although the criteria for EMU were heavily German-influenced. Second, does a sense of community exist among participating nations? The Maastricht ratification process suggested a gap between political elites and the peoples of Europe that could place pressure on EMU and the Euro if it fails to deliver prosperity. Moreover, the stability and growth pact designed to punish countries running 'excessively' inflationary policies was seen as a straitjacket on economic growth and condemned as 'stupid' by the Commission President, Prodi.

The drive towards EMU had a strong intergovernmental basis, although the UK (as so often at the key moments in the history of European integration) was absent from the table. Moreover, the motive for EMU can be seen to have a strong *raison d'état* centred on French concerns about Germany's post-Cold War development. Following German reunification in November 1989 the French were keen to hasten movement towards EMU in order to subsume potential German economic domination within structures of collective economic management. There were some doubts in Germany as many thought the foundations of German economic success – an independent Bundesbank committed to price stability – could be put at risk by participation in EMU. The driving forces behind the proposal were Paris and the Commission with support from Italy, Belgium and Spain. Germany's main reason for agreeing to participate was political: commitment to EMU was a way of showing continued faith in European integration (or, as Chancellor Kohl observed, putting a European roof over Germany rather than a German roof over Europe). Germany also attempted to ensure that the economic priorities of the EMU plan matched those that had under-pinned post-war German economic success. This included the 'growth and stability' pact, of which ironically it was then to become one of the first victims as the German economy suffered a serious slowdown and high levels of unemployment.

The EMU plan

In June 1988 the European Council set up a Committee for the Study of Economic and Monetary Union, chaired by the Commission President, Delors. Its report, submitted in April 1989, put forward a three-stage plan for EMU (Committee for the Study of Economic and Monetary Union, 1989). This formed the basis of the timetable agreed at Maastricht. The three stages on the path to EMU were as follows:

1   Stage One prescribed that all countries were to enter the ERM. Sterling finally joined on 8 October 1990 but market pressure forced it out on 16 September 1992.
2   Stage Two set out that by 1 January 1994 all currencies were to enter the ERM's narrow band (2.25 per cent).

3   Stage Three specified four convergence criteria (price stability, non-excessive government debt, stable currency and low interest rates) deemed necessary for countries wishing to participate in the third stage of EMU, when a single European currency would be established and an independent European Central Bank set up to run monetary policy.

At Maastricht the British and Danes secured opt-outs from this third stage of EMU. The Maastricht timetable was cast into doubt by the ERM crises of 1992 and 1993. The pressures of costly German reunification, which pushed up German interest rates and made the Deutschmark strong, caused these crises. In turn, this put other ERM currencies under pressure to maintain their ERM parities with the Deutschmark. This was particularly difficult for economies in recession or struggling to emerge from it – such as the British, Spanish and French – that were forced to maintain high interest rates in order to sustain their ERM membership, even though such policies neglected the needs of their real economies.

The events of 1992 and 1993 made it impossible to proceed to the third stage of EMU in 1997. After the delay in 1996 and 1997, the Commission was asked to bring forward further recommendations on progress towards convergence as early as possible. This it did in a report accepted by the Commission on 25 March 1998. This report was the culmination of a two-year debate about convergence. There was some creativity in interpretation of the criteria, which allowed countries making progress in the direction of attainment to be deemed to have converged. This should not disguise the quite substantial degree of economic convergence that did occur among participating member states.

At a meeting of heads of government in Brussels between 1 and 3 May it was agreed that eleven member states met the criteria. On 1 January 2002 Euro banknotes and coins entered circulation with a complete changeover to the Euro in public administration. By July 2002 national currencies had been cancelled as legal tender.

For and against Economic and Monetary Union

Recent British experience means that pro-single currency advocates face an uphill task. What are the arguments in favour? Participating member states and pro-Euro advocates identify four main merits of EMU.

1   The reduction of transaction costs generated by currency exchange.
2   The reduction of uncertainty caused by exchange rate fluctuations which undermine the ability of business to plan ahead.
3   The co-ordination of EU economies would create the world's most powerful trading bloc. At things are, the EU has more than 370 million people. This stands to rise to more than 400 million linked by a single market and single currency as enlargement occurs.
4   From a British point of view, scepticism about core EU objectives has in the past led to Britain being excluded when the 'rules of the game' are established. These rules are then not necessarily in the UK's interests and can make adaptation a more difficult process.

Opponents of the Euro also have four main arguments:

1   On political grounds, the creation of an EMU cedes economic authority to distant and unaccountable institutions at EU level. (Although this could be an argument for strengthening EU institutions to make them more democratic and accountable, opponents of EMU tend to see the nation state as the best level for effective economic decision-making.)
2   On economic grounds, the EMU creates one-size-fits-all economic policies that may not suit all participating states. The level of interest rates set by the European Central Bank in Frankfurt may not fit with economic priorities in an EU that encompasses 15 (and soon many more) European countries.
3   Far greater fiscal and political integration may well be necessary if an EMU is to work effectively.
4   The emphasis on stability and low inflation within the Euro-zone through the 'Stability and Growth' pact punishes member states which indulge in spending deemed 'excessive' by the Commission. This is a real dilemma, as Chancellor Brown found out when UK government spending plans were questioned by the Commission because of the prospect of running up levels of government deficit that were pushing Euro-zone limits.

A further economic argument from a British point of view is that Europe needs to embrace the kinds of economic reforms undertaken by Britain since the 1980s if the European economy is to be flexible enough to withstand economic shocks. There is a view within the Treasury that the Euro-zone needs to become more 'Anglicized' before UK membership can occur (Dyson, 2000).

Britain and Economic and Monetary Union

The UK opt-out only postponed a decision on entry. The ERM disaster holed the Conservative government beneath the waterline. New Labour shifted from 'wait and see' to 'prepare and decide' and launched a national changeover plan so that if the decision were made to join then the UK would be ready. The government has sought to make it clear that the decision will be an economic rather than a political one. The Chief Economic Adviser to the Chancellor, Ed Balls, drew lessons from history to argue that 'getting the politics right demands that we get the economics right' (Balls, 2002; see also Keegan, 2003). Many commentators believe that the politics cannot be easily detached from the economics, especially when the 'five economic tests' allow a significant margin for interpretation. The argument is that an implicit sixth test, 'Can a referendum be won?', is also central to the calculations.

The government position was made clear in a statement made to the House of Commons by Chancellor Gordon Brown (see Box 7.1). The statement professed to outline the government's policy, although Philip Stephens (2001: 73) has argued that 'the October 1997 statement was not so much a policy as a conscious decision not to have a policy unless and until the Chancellor said otherwise'. The immediate build-up to this statement saw the government's spin machine veer towards meltdown as apparently contradictory pronouncements emerged from the Treasury, 10 Downing Street, the Foreign Office and the 'minister without portfolio', Peter Mandelson. This reignited tensions within the Labour leadership dating back to Mandelson's support for Blair in the 1994 leadership contest. The concession to the advocates of the Euro was space for a change in the event of 'unforeseen circumstances'. The deeper and more far-reaching significance was that the Treasury, through its evaluation of the five tests, was placed at the heart of any future decision on whether Britain was ready to join the Euro.

This statement effectively postponed the Euro-issue for the lifetime of the first Blair government, but Blair stated that a decision would be made by June 2003. The timetable for possible membership is as follows. To begin with, five economic tests must be satisfied. The Treasury has the responsibility to determine whether these have been met (and because they are vague it also has the power to expedite or delay the referendum). The five economic tests seek to ascertain:

- sustainable convergence between Britain and the economies of a single currency
- sufficient flexibility to cope with economic change

- the effect on investment
- the impact on the UK financial services industry
- the impact on employment.

In June 2003 Chancellor Brown announced that just one of the tests (on financial services) had been met. Philip Stephens (2001) has argued that the claim that the decision is economic rather than political is

---

***Box 7.1* Statement by Gordon Brown, Chancellor of the Exchequer**

I shall deal in turn with the question of principle of economic monetary union, the constitutional implications and the economic tests that have to be met.

I start with the question of principle. The potential benefits for Britain of a successful single currency are obvious in terms of trade, transparency of costs and currency stability. Of course, I stress that it must be soundly based. It must succeed. But if it works economically, it is, in our view, worth doing. So in principle, a successful single currency within a single European market would be of benefit to Europe and Britain. Secondly, it must be clearly recognized that to share a common monetary policy with other states represents a major pooling of economic sovereignty.

There are those who argue that this should be a constitutional bar to British participation in a single currency, regardless of the economic benefits that it could bring to the people of this country. In other words, they would rule out a single currency in principle, even if it were in the best economic interests of the country.

This is an understandable objection, and one argued from principle, but in our view it is wrong. If a single currency would be good for British jobs, British business and future prosperity, it is right in principle to join. The constitutional issue is a factor in the decision, but it is not an overriding one. Rather, it signifies that, in order for monetary union to be right for Britain, the economic benefit should be clear and unambiguous.

I therefore conclude on the question of principle that if, in the end, the single currency is successful and the economic case is clear and unambiguous, the Government believe that Britain should be part of it.

There is a third issue of principle – the consent of the British people. Because of the magnitude of the decision, we believe, again as a matter of principle, that, whenever the decision to enter is taken by Government, it should be put to a referendum of the British people. Whenever this issue arises, under this Government there will be a referendum. Government, Parliament and the people must all agree.

We conclude that the determining factor as to whether Britain joins a single currency is the national economic interest, and whether the economic case for doing so is clear and unambiguous.

Source: *Hansard*, Vol. 299, Col. 583–4, 27 October 1997.

disingenuous because the tests are vague and open to interpretation (although see Balls, 2002, for a counter-argument). The House of Commons' Treasury select committee noted a lack of precision about what is required. As one expert remarked: 'The Chancellor's tests are so loosely defined that anyone will be able to say that they have either been passed or failed according to the dictates of political expediency' (House of Commons Treasury Select Committee, 1998). This may be exactly what the Chancellor had in mind because the political controversy surrounding EMU membership would make it a risky proposition to bind the government to one position or another. This is particularly the case during Labour's second term when the emphasis is on the delivery of improved public services. Stephens (2001: 73) notes that a more insidious effect of the five tests is that the government has cast itself as a passive bystander rather than a leader of the debate. If Britain is to join the Euro then the case must be made. The government has shown little inclination to engage with the British people on this issue, perhaps because of concern that a Euro referendum would be divisive and detract from the pursuit of other objectives that could secure a third term (the next chapter looks at the role of the Treasury more closely).

Maastricht's intergovernmental 'pillars'

The Maastricht Treaty saw the EU move into areas of high politics, a process which was continued by the Amsterdam Treaty. But member states trod cautiously when they decided to incorporate aspects of foreign and security policy and justice and home affairs into the Union. Supranational institutions were peripheral to decision processes in the intergovernmental 'pillars' added by the Maastricht Treaty. Did this mark the permanent establishment of a new form of intergovernmental co-operation or were the pillars temporary measures easing the transition to fuller integration for these contentious policy issues? The Amsterdam Treaty showed that most member states see the pillars as part of a transition to greater supranationalization and not as permanent features of the Treaty framework. Britain and Denmark are the member states that seem most reluctant to share this vision.

The Common Foreign and Security Policy

When push comes to shove does Britain look to Europe or the USA? The war in Iraq exposed huge divisions within the EU as the UK sided with the USA (along with the governments but not the people necessarily of Spain, Italy, Denmark, the Netherlands and most of the accession states). The war also exposed a huge division (at least in the run-up to the conflict) between the government's pro-war stance and much deeper public scepticism and hostility towards this pro-US position. The conflict also raised some rather fundamental issues about the nature of European power. The EU as an organization has been deeply committed to multilateralism – not least because that is a notion central to the EU's self-identity – and to respect for international law. The invasion of Iraq was a direct challenge to these precepts and deeply disturbing to many EU governments and their citizens for precisely these reasons.

The possibility of an EU CFSP also raises the issue of what kind of power the EU is. A prevailing view was that the EU was a civilian or 'soft' power centred on economic concerns, as opposed to a military power: an economic giant but a political dwarf, as one observer put it (Buchan, 1993). As Hedley Bull (1979: 151) stated: 'Europe is not an actor in international affairs ... and does not seem likely to become one.' Since then, there have been moves to consolidate a stronger EU presence in international affairs through formal co-operation on CFSP and the creation at the Cologne summit meeting of EU heads of government in June 1999 of a European Security and Defence Policy (ESDP) with a plan for the creation of a European Rapid Reaction Force by 2003. This debate must also involve some discussion of the kind of power that Europe *should* be because this goes to the heart of questions about the EU's international identity as a new kind of international actor (Manners, 2002).

The ways in which the EU and the member states deal with CFSP issues has also been affected by the post-Cold War context that challenges traditional notions of threat and appropriate response centred on a Europe riven by an ideological divide between east and west. During this Cold War period, west European security was guaranteed by the USA through NATO during the Cold War. Since the end of the Cold War, British governments have remained strong supporters of this Atlantic framework for European security and see any EU responses as nested within it.

Common Foreign and Security Policy development

In 1970 the six EC member states instigated foreign policy co-operation known as European Political Co-operation (EPC). EPC attempted to establish an external political profile to match the EC's burgeoning economic power and ensure, where possible, co-ordination. In 1987 the SEA strengthened EPC by establishing a secretariat to support its operations. The Maastricht Treaty boldly declared in Article J that: 'a common foreign and security policy is hereby established'. In reality the common foreign and security policy (CFSP) pillar was a formalization of existing EPC procedures rather than a radical new venture, but it does contain some innovations with potential for future development. Within the pillar arrangements foreign and security policy was to be decided by a system of 'joint action' with unanimity as the decisional modus operandi. However, once 'joint action' has been agreed in principle, majority voting could be used for measures of detail. Any decision (say) to send election monitors must be made unanimously, but subsequent decisions about numbers involved, and so on, can be decided by qualified majority. These provisions also allow for the discussion of defence issues previously confined to NATO, EUROGROUP (of European defence ministers) and, from 1984, the revived West European Union (WEU), the European constituent of NATO. In the 1980s the French and Germans were keen to establish a stronger European defence profile. They intensified their own co-operation by setting up the 4,000-strong Franco–German brigade, based in Bavaria. Other nations remained wary. The Maastricht CFSP 'pillar' sought to strengthen the WEU by moving the latter's headquarters, its secretariat, to Brussels, setting up a planning unit and inviting all non-WEU members of the European Community (Denmark, Greece and Ireland) to join. The European Council and Council of Ministers, acting unanimously, were to be central decision-making authorities for both foreign and defence policy. Although the differential memberships of the EU and WEU (five of the EU states were only observers in the WEU) makes this difficult, NATO is still supreme on the defence side, as the I-FOR (Implementation Force) operation in Bosnia showed.

War in the former Yugoslavia was a severe test for EU foreign policy. The carnage and chaos in Bosnia indicated that the EU failed the test. The USA at first urged Europeans to take the lead in mediating a peaceful solution to a European problem. Yet by 1993 the war's scope and intensity appeared to be beyond the ability of the Community to resolve. 'This is the hour of Europe', Luxembourg's foreign minister, Jacques Poos, had proclaimed in June 1991 after brokering another short-lived ceasefire. The Union's failure to resolve a bitter dispute on its doorstep proved a chastening experience. The economic strength of the Union served as a useful asset in peacetime but offered little in the face of bitter ethnic and religious dispute.

Amsterdam added some new provisions to the foreign and security policy pillar. A new post of High Representative was established. This was seen as a way of answering the criticism attributed to Henry Kissinger that Europe did not have a phone number. A Policy Planning and Early Warning Unit back the Council's High Representative, currently the former NATO Secretary General, Javier Solana. The Council is also given power to adopt by unanimity a 'common strategy' to be implemented by joint actions and common positions adopted by QMV, although decisions having military or defence implications will still rely on unanimity. Amsterdam also strengthened the 'soft security', peace-keeping and humanitarian intervention role of the EU by adding the WEU's 'Petersberg tasks' (humanitarian and rescue tasks, peacekeeping and combat-force in crisis management, including peacemaking) to the issues for which the CFSP would be responsible.

The Treaty of Nice contains new CFSP provisions relating to a European defence and security policy that covers all matters relating to EU security, including the gradual formulation of a common defence policy. The EDSP is thus part of the CFSP. Arrangements have also been made for regular EU–NATO consultation.

The CFSP is decidedly intergovernmental. The member states in the Council and European Council hold the upper hand while the Commission is weak. The Commission is 'fully associated' with the CFSP, but does not have the exclusive right to submit initiatives. Instead, these come mainly from the Presidency, a member state or the High Representative. The European Parliament is only consulted and briefed on developments. The basic instruments of CFSP differ from the 'directives' and 'regulations' of other more supranationalized policy areas. Instead, the CFSP instruments are common strategies, common positions, joint actions, decisions, and the conclusion of international agreements.

Britain and the Common Foreign and Security Policy

By 2003 it was absolutely clear that Tony Blair's prime allegiance was to the USA. His apparent enthusiasm for common EU measures in areas such as foreign and defence policy was framed by a belief that these needed to be linked to strong transatlantic ties. Very early in his first term in office, Blair took a step that was wrongly seen by some of his opponents as questioning Britain's commitment to NATO and the USA. In a March 1998 speech to the French National Assembly he identified defence and security policies as areas in which France and the UK were well equipped to co-operate. In December 1998 in St Malo this declaration was given more substance when Blair and President Chirac called for full and rapid implementation of Amsterdam's CFSP provisions. Where would these kinds of steps leave the British? On the one hand, the CFSP presents some difficulties. There is Britain's long-standing preference for intergovernmental co-operation, which could be accommodated within existing structures, but which is challenged by more ambitious ideas about closer European integration in these areas of 'high politics'. Second, there is the question of Britain's 'special relationship' with the USA which, even though it is more special in the eyes of Downing Street than the White House, is still much referred to and has been given added resonance by the post-September 11 'war on terror' and conflict with Iraq. In such terms, Britain's national interests seem not to be particularly Europeanized. Whether Britain's perceived 'national interest' can be accommodated within European defence and security structures thus remains an open question, but one that is clearly open to serious doubt (Howorth, 2000).

Justice and Home Affairs

The end of the Cold War not only changed thinking about foreign and defence policy, but also about internal security. A new series of challenges has been identified, such as large-scale migration or international organized crime, which have been seen to threaten the borders of EU member states and require some form of collective response because of their transnational nature. Two points need to be borne in mind. First, perceptions of security and insecurity are based on fears that may or may not have a basis in objective social reality. For instance, people imagine that the scale of immigration is far bigger than it actually is, but even though the general public over-exaggerate the extent of immigration, the fear of it (irrational or imagined as it may be) creates perceived threats that have very real social and political effects. This means that we need to explore the ways in which issues become seen as security concerns. Second, Europe's security/insecurity agenda has changed since the end of the Cold War with a new focus on what has been called 'societal security' which centres on the control of population rather than the control of borders. New forms and types of security control and new types of monitoring, surveillance and observation have developed.

There was informal co-operation on internal security dating back to the creation of the Trevi Group of interior ministers in the 1970s.

Maastricht's third pillar (covering JHA) formalized this co-operation and brought it within the EU. This recognized immigration, asylum, policing and judicial co-operation as matters of common concern and put in place structures for intergovernmental co-operation from which the Commission, ECJ and European Parliament were largely excluded. Co-operation was to occur in nine areas: asylum; external frontier controls; immigration; combating drug addiction; combating international fraud; judicial co-operation in civil matters; judicial co-operation in criminal matters; customs co-operation; police co-operation. The existing informal structures were included in a complex five-tier structure: specific working parties, steering committees, a Co-ordinating Committee set up under Article K.4 of the Union Treaty, the Committee of Permanent Representatives and the Council of Ministers for Justice and Home Affairs. An additional complication was the Schengen provisions. Schengen was initially set up in 1985 by France, Germany and the Benelux countries as a swifter route to full free movement. It then became a laboratory of the kinds of measures that the EU would need to introduce if the single market was to be accompanied by internal security measures. The problem was that not all EU member states were Schengen states (the UK has also refused to join).

The JHA pillar contained provisions for decision-taking mechanisms, but these were based on intergovernmentalism and required unanimity, which was difficult to achieve and very rarely forthcoming. This meant that provisions for 'joint positions', 'joint actions' and conventions in international law were difficult to realize. This also led to pressure for change because the measures were inefficient while also criticized for being undemocratic and unaccountable.

Amsterdam added a new Chapter to the Treaty creating 'an area of freedom, justice and security'. Immigration and asylum were moved from the intergovernmental pillar to this new chapter. Five-year deadlines were imposed for decisions to be reached on many key issues relating to entry, control and residence. The role of the Commission, Court and Parliament is increased, but unanimity in the Council will remain the basis of decision-making for at least five years. How unanimity will be reconciled with the five-year deadline for decisions only time will tell, although it is worth noting that when the SEA timetabled a plan for attainment of the single market it also made provision for QMV to facilitate decision-making. Police and judicial co-operation continue to fall under the reshaped third pillar, to which the Treaty of Amsterdam has added the prevention and combating of racism and xenophobia. The decision-making process was changed with 'joint actions' replaced by 'framework decisions', which are more like directives and the corresponding implementing measures. Amsterdam also brought the Schengen agreement into the EU with measures either placed in the new Title IV or the recast third pillar. The UK, Denmark and Ireland opted out of Amsterdam's Title IV.

Britain and Justice and Home Affairs

Co-operation on JHA is a tricky issue for the British government. There is recognition that this is an area in which there is public support for measures that tackle phenomena that are clearly transnational and require some kind of collaborative response. At the same time, there is a marked reluctance by the British authorities to cede control over the UK's external frontiers as would be required by full accession to Schengenland (i.e., an area of free movement within which border checks between participating countries are removed). The reason for this is that British immigration controls have exploited the island geography to exert strong controls at the external frontiers with less strong internal security mechanisms such as identity cards. Full adherence to Schengen would thus change this security mechanism and jeopardize the historically preferred response in UK to the regulation of international migration.

Britain chose to optout of the new chapter added by the Amsterdam Treaty covering free movement, immigration and asylum because of the implications of these provisions for external frontier controls. That said, since Amsterdam the UK has been keen to be associated with a whole raft of internal security measures agreed at intergovernmental level that do not go so far as to threaten the ability of the UK authorities to exert control at the country's external frontiers. Indeed, the introduction of national identity cards has been proposed by the Labour government and, if introduced, would bring the UK into line with the internal security paradigm that operates in other EU member states where internal checks rather than external controls are the norm. Asylum seeking migration has been a particularly salient concern with the UK government supporting European integration and QMV in this area as a way of resolving this domestic political concern. It could be suggested that the JHA area is one in which the level of integration belies the formal situation in the sense that the UK has adapted in quite significant ways to the developing EU internal security paradigm because these are seen to offer concrete benefits even though they confront tricky issues such as notions of sovereignty linked to control of external frontiers.

This adaptation suggests that, to a certain extent, subterfuge can be a path to compliance with EU norms and institutions and also demonstrates that the effects of European integration can be shielded from the general public. This is facilitated in an area such as JHA where there is already a tendency to secrecy.

Conclusions

This chapter has explored Britain's differential engagement with core EU policies and suggested that we need to pay some attention to the factors that have influenced British governmental preferences. Almost all aspects of domestic policy now possess a European dimension, although some are more institutionalized at EU level with associated consequences for domestic policy-making of common policies. Over time, a historical path has been established that links the UK polity to neighbouring European states via intensive ties that reach across the economies, political and social systems in these countries. The historical choice for Europe made in the 1970s has very real implications for the UK both in terms of attempts to shape the EU agenda and also in terms of national level adaptation to EU requirements.

First, we can explore the capacity of UK governments to shape the EU agenda. It has been argued that member states will seek to 'upload' their domestic policy approaches to EU level (i.e., to make their approach the EU approach because the costs of then 'downloading' this policy are low as it already fits with domestic political and administrative organization). Member states can then be 'pace-setters', 'foot-draggers' or 'fence-sitters' (Börzel, 2002: 196–208). Pace-setting involves attempts to actively shape the EU agenda and presupposes well-established national policy preferences and the capacity to push them through. In the area of single market integration the UK can be seen as a consistent pace-setter, although not all member states will be keen to follow the UK down the road to market liberalization. The UK has been either a foot-dragger where it has resisted integration, or a fence-sitter and neither taken the lead nor actively resisted. In some areas such as the CAP the UK has been a thwarted advocate of reform when other member states have been foot-draggers. In addition to this, the UK has also opted out of various EU policies (the Social Chapter, the final state of EMU, Title IV of the Amsterdam Treaty). This opt-out accommodates UK preferences, but also the preferences and capacity of other member states to push ahead.

Over time the 'path' of EU integration has more closely linked the UK to the EU, although points of tension centre on the British preference for market liberalization that unites both Conservative and New Labour governments and does not always rest easily with the views of other member states on the future shape of the EU economy. These tensions have other effects. They inhibit the capacity of European integration to become fully embedded as a constitutive component of the interests, preferences and identities of key political actors in the UK. This will become clearer in the next chapter when the effects of European integration on the organization of the British polity are examined. Some departments have become 'European', while others (such as the Treasury) continue to harbour doubts about 'the European project'.

8

The British State and European Integration

Introduction

This chapter examines the impact on the British state of European integration: the ways in which the British state has organized for Europe and the impacts of European competencies on the organization of the British state. A 'Whitehall ethos' and the impact of devolution since 1997 are to the fore because these processes filter and refract Europeanization. The story is not one of straightforward adaptation; particularly in central government there were well-established 'British ways of doing things' before accession occurred. Since 1973, the level of engagement with the EU has had important effects on both the functional (responsibilities exercised by the British state) and territorial (locations at which this power and authority is exercised) dimensions of British politics. At the same time, these effects are not uniform and it would be a mistake to adopt too sweeping an approach to the analysis of 'Europeanization' and assume that the EU alone has transformed British politics. As was suggested in this book's introduction, European integration will be filtered through domestic logics of politics and policy-making and there are grounds for expecting core elements of established national 'ways of doing things' to endure. In British central government, for instance, the persistence of a 'Whitehall ethos' can be detected while other changes may have domestic rather than supranational logics, such as the rapid development since 1997 of a constitutional reform agenda (devolved government in Scotland and Wales and new regional structures in England) that was driven more squarely by domestic political factors.

Contextual factors

Underlying this chapter's analysis are some contextual factors, which it is important at this initial stage to elaborate upon. Above all, there has been a marked change in the framework that under-pins analysis of the British state with a move away from concern with 'government' as formal structure towards the analysis of 'governance' as an activity that goes beyond the boundaries of the state to include a range of public, private and voluntary actors (Rhodes, 1997; Marsh, Richards and Smith, 2001). This points towards changed location of political processes away from the traditional focus of Parliament and Whitehall. This in turn is embedded within an EU debate about governance that includes ideas about effective delivery of EU objectives within new forms of state-like organization that have quite strong regulatory and/or post-modern dimensions.

This trend towards new patterns of governance is one to which Eurosceptic rhetoric has been slow to adapt because of its strong focus on the classic locations of power, authority and accountability: namely, Parliament and the notion of parliamentary sovereignty. It is not just European integration that challenges these traditional constitutional relationships. The deregulation and privatization of state activities, the profusion of agencies fulfilling state tasks, the growing influence of international organizations such as the International Monetary Fund and World Trade Organisation, and the power of neo-liberalism as an organizing principle for the international economy have also had powerful effects on the sovereign authority and capacity of the British state. As such, Europeanization constitutes one element of what has been called the 'hollowing out' of the British state (Jessop, 1994). This implies that 'external' shifts arising from European integration and 'internal' shifts associated with local government reform, devolution and the increased role of the private sector in the delivery of government services have seen powers move 'up', 'down' and 'out' from the central state with the effect that it has been eaten away and replaced by a differentiated polity 'characterized by functional and institutional specialization and the fragmentation of policies and politics' (Rhodes, 1997: 3; see also Rhodes, 1994). Holliday (2000) contests this 'hollowing out' thesis and argues that the core of British central government is now more substantial and integrated than ever before. This survey of the Europeanization of central government demonstrates the maintenance of a core EU policy grouping centred on the Foreign and

Commonwealth Office (FCO), Treasury and the Cabinet Office. On the issue of the Euro this network is even more intensively focused on the Treasury and Downing Street. In other areas, however, the increased demands of the EU, as well as the technical nature of many EU issues, has required specialist involvement by government departments and associated networks of expertise.

Europeanization, according to Bulmer and Burch (1998: 603), has both inter-state and intra-state dimensions. This chapter is particularly concerned with the intra-state dimensions understood as: 'the impact of EU policies, rules, practices, and values upon member state activities in respect of both the making and implementation of policy'. This implies that while power moves 'up' to Brussels, these EU competencies feed into national processes of policy-making and implementation as well as 'down' to sub-national levels of government.

The potential impacts on central government were noted just prior to accession in 1972 by the then British Ambassador, Nicholas Soames (1972, cited in Jordan, 2000: 2) when he observed that 'each department will be responsible for its own European thinking, for knowing the European rules and for having a feel for [the EC's] aspirations ... [W]hole departments must now be learning to "think European" and to take account at all times of the obligations imposed by membership.' This can prompt the allusion to multi-level or multi-location governance (as represented in Figure 1.3). Given the role of private and voluntary actors and the cross-cutting linkages that operate across these levels it would be wrong to sustain a morphological approach that focuses too strictly on levels (the supranational, national and sub-national are the three most commonly used) without also recognizing the intensive exchanges across, within and between these levels, which provides a complex picture within which decisions are made at various locations within this multi-level polity.

Taken at face value, this multi-level picture would appear to imply reduced powers for central government because competencies previously exercised are now exercised in other places. Thus Europeanization can be seen as one important part of a wider process of the internationalization and sub-nationalization of the British state that 'appears to be fundamentally altering structures and processes of British government' (Page, 1998: 803) as the UK becomes 'caught up in a multi-level framework of rules and negotiations' with national governments 'holding the gate between domestic and international politics for a shrinking number of policy areas' (H. Wallace, 1997: 452). The impact is generally regarded as significant but, as Bulmer and Burch (1998: 603) note, the precise effects are often rather fuzzy.

We now move on to consider more closely the impacts on the functional and territorial distribution of power and authority, but at the same time we must remember the point already made when introducing the concept of Europeanization that there is a need to be specific when discussing the effects of European integration on British politics. The concept loses meaning if it is used in too sweeping a fashion to refer to all changes that have affected the British polity without distinguishing between other possible causes that may have little or nothing to do with the EU. As will be seen, European integration has had important effects on the British state, but there has also been considerable resilience of established ways of doing things, while European integration did not drive other recent innovations such as the establishment since 1997 of devolved government.

Central government

When asked to judge the EU's impact on British institutions, Tony Blair's Europe adviser and Head of the European Secretariat in the Cabinet Office, Sir Stephen Wall (2002: 16), said that he thought European integration had had a 'fairly radical impact' and that this was particularly evident since the 1980s:

> When I was dealing with European issues in the early 1980s, you had two or three departments that really knew about Europe: the Foreign Office (because the Foreign Office was responsible for dealing with foreigners), the Ministry of Agriculture (because the CAP was an important part of life) and the DTI [Department of Trade and Industry] (because an important part of trade and industry had aspects of the single market). The Home Office, for example, had no experience of the EU. Basically, negotiations within Whitehall were infinitely more difficult than negotiations in Brussels because people tended to come with absolutely firm departmental positions: that was the British position that had to prevail in Brussels. But then, of course, over the years, more and more people have had experience of serving in the UK Representation. Now when you have discussions in Whitehall, clearly we have British positions, but we also (and majority voting has been a factor) have learnt that you can't just say 'well this is the British position'. You have to say 'who are our allies?' 'How do we make alliances?' 'What is the endgame going to look like?'

All Whitehall departments now find that some of their competencies have an EU dimension. Some departments have stronger European links than others: agriculture and fisheries, for instance, are areas where there is a common European policy rather than national policies. For many years the old Ministry of Agriculture, Fisheries and Food (now part of the Department of Environment, Food and Rural Affairs, or DEFRA) had close and intensive ties with EU institutions and other member states which meant that a small part of British foreign policy was exercised by MAFF ministers and officials. This gave MAFF a *raison d'être* that allowed a relatively small department to survive even when its core functions centred on subsidies and market intervention had become deeply outmoded ideas in Whitehall. The Foreign Office and DTI are also departments with close EU links. Other departments, such as what was the Department of the Environment, have developed EU ties more recently. The development of EU internal security responsibilities (crime, border controls, asylum) impinges on the work of the Home Office, which has led this quintessentially *domestic* department concerned with the core sovereign concerns of the British state to become to some extent Europeanized.

Over time, the intensity of British relations with the EU and the effects on the British polity have intensified. Following the creation of the EC in 1958 the key players were the Treasury, the Board of Trade, the Foreign Office, MAFF, the Commonwealth Relations Office and the Colonial Office. The Foreign Office played a key role, particularly when UK attentions turned to membership in the 1960s. Indeed, Marsh, Richards and Smith (2001: 215) argue that the EC gave the Foreign Office a new lease of life following the trauma of the end of empire. Accession negotiations were led by the Foreign Office while relations with the EEC within Whitehall were co-ordinated by the Treasury with three tiers of committees at various official levels. At the top level was the Economic Association Committee (EQ) chaired by the Prime Minister. It was within EQ that the agenda shifted from association to membership (Bulmer and Burch, 1998: 608). When membership was decided upon in 1961 then the Common Market Negotiations Committee replaced EQ. Following General de Gaulle's 'non' in 1963 a European Unit was established within the Cabinet Office, which was renamed during the 1970s as the European Secretariat, and which co-ordinated negotiations and discussions across Whitehall.

Upon accession in 1973 it was agreed that there would not be a separate Ministry for Europe because this would cut across the traditional functional and territorial distributions of responsibility within Whitehall with their emphasis on co-ordination and collective responsibility. Heath also wanted to encourage national ministers to see Europe as integrally connected to domestic politics and not as a foreign policy issue. In this response can be detected the way in which central government responded to European integration in a way that made sense in relation to established organizational practices and can thus be initially viewed as a 'thin' institutional constraint, although over time as EU competencies have grown this constraint has become much 'thicker' and become much more deeply embedded as a part of Whitehall's standard operating practices. Wallace and Wallace (1973: 261) predicted 'gradual adaptation rather than ... radical change'. EC accession in 1973 did not induce a collective attitude shift across Whitehall; rather, 'opinions were divided and "neutralism" towards the Community was sometimes the most positive of attitudes in some departments' (Willis, 1982: 25).

Britain organized for Europe in the following way: it was decided that the Foreign Secretary would represent the UK on the General Affairs Council and would chair a cabinet committee on EC matters – the Overseas and Defence Policy Committee, or ODP (E) – that would report to the cabinet. The European Unit in the Cabinet Office would seek to co-ordinate across Whitehall. The Foreign Office would play the leading role in negotiations with other member states and with the EC institutions through the UK Permanent Representation in Brussels (UKRep). UKRep is particularly important because it is the British government's voice in Brussels and deals with the Commission, other EU institutions and other member states' permanent representations.

This basic structure is still recognizably in place today. At the contemporary core of Britain's relations with the EU sits a powerful elite of government departments: the Foreign Office, 10 Downing Street, the Cabinet Office and UKRep (Burch and Holliday, 1996). ODP (E), chaired by the Foreign Secretary, discusses core policy concerns and reports to the Cabinet. The Treasury has sought to extract EMU from ODP (E) and make this a matter for bilateral discussions between the Chancellor and Prime Minister (Dyson, 2000). The European Secretariat in the Cabinet Office seeks co-ordination across Whitehall and the diffusion of information. Every Friday there will be a meeting between the FCO, the head of the European Secretariat in the Cabinet Office, the UK Permanent Representative and relevant government departments with issues on the EU agenda. Yet, as EU competencies grow, it becomes more difficult for this central co-ordinating machinery to keep a tight grip on all aspects of policy. Moreover, departments of state have become much more proficient and experienced in their dealings with the

EU because of the increasing number of policy issues that now possess a European dimension.

The UK has managed to develop a strong and effective co-ordinating mechanism for the development and pursuit of British interests that has been admired in other member states. The FCO continues to play a key role. In the early days of British membership the FCO's main responsibility was to co-ordinate Britain's relations with the EC. This changed as more sectoral, specialist and technical Councils developed competencies that required input from national ministries with appropriate expertise. At the same time, as the EU moved into areas of high politics such as CFSP post-Maastricht, the FCO became more involved in this area of EU activity. The Foreign Secretary continues to play a key role: 'In nine cases out of ten, it is he who concludes ministerial correspondence and ministerial discussions on any particular issue' (Wall, 2002: 17). (The 'one out of ten' issue is currently the Euro, which is managed bilaterally by the Prime Minister and the Chancellor of the Exchequer.) Finally, the FCO plays a strategic role that has seen it move away from attempts to muscle in on the Franco–German relationship and, instead, seek issue-by-issue alliances with other member states. This has led the UK to align itself with Italy and Spain over market liberalization, while there is also optimism that the new member states will be UK allies (particularly given the strong pro-US stance of the governments of many accession states although their stances on regional development and agriculture may not make them natural UK allies on these issues).

The main emphasis within Whitehall has been placed on securing cross-departmental agreement on major issues. This sets the UK apart from other member states where coalition governments lead to ministers from different political parties and more difficult co-ordination. Bulmer and Burch (1998: 607) argue that Whitehall has made a much smoother transition to EU membership than Parliament (as will become clearer when the Parliamentary arena is analysed in the next chapter). The important thing, however, is that both Whitehall and Parliament must work together because it is no good having a smoothly working and well-oiled central government machine if there is a lack of political leadership. Administrative and technical expertise cannot fill a political vacuum such as that which existed during much of the 1990s, or more recently on the single currency. Or, as one official more bluntly puts it: 'there's no point having a Rolls Royce machinery if the driver's a lunatic' (cited in Bulmer and Burch, 1998: 607). During John Major's premiership, for instance, the paralysis caused by deep divisions within the Conservative Party precluded the longer-term planning of EU policy. Blair's EU adviser, Sir Stephen Wall (2002: 16), made it clear that:

> What civil servants like is strong leadership. If you have a situation where people feel that that doesn't exist, and with regards to Europe in the last year or so before 1997 that was the perception, then you will find that they are unhappy and seek to follow what they believe to be the consensus line in the national interest.

Impacts of European integration

Bulmer and Burch (1998) identify four measures of institutional change: formal institutional structures, procedures and processes, codes and guidelines and cultural/normative change. In these areas they find that central government's adaptation to the EU has been in accordance with established patterns of domestic government. The main changes that they found regarded adaptation to the specific requirements of EC law and to the demands of negotiation and bargaining at EU level. In other respects, they argue that the main aspects of the Whitehall process have remained intact with continued emphasis on the search for a 'line' and emphasis once this line has been agreed on collective responsibility and the sharing of information across Whitehall. This has led to a growing institutionalization of the EU, but in accordance with the traditional Whitehall approach. This echoes the finding of Burch and Holliday (1996: 606) that points to the ways in which 'a pervasive Europeanisation of British central government has been consistent hitherto with the "Whitehall model" of government ... European integration has been absorbed into the "logic" of the Whitehall machinery'.

The Whitehall machinery favours 'unity, loyalty and consensus seeking' with an emphasis on prior cross-departmental agreement and information sharing (Dyson, 2000: 903). An additional norm has also been transplanted into the Whitehall machinery: effective transposition of EU legislation into national law. The UK has not been a particularly 'awkward state' when it comes to the implementation of EU decisions, which reinforces the point made by Wilks (1996) that it is useful to distinguish between the UK as a sometimes 'awkward partner' but often a less awkward state in terms of the capacity to adapt to EU requirements.

The case of the Department of the Environment (DoE) is interesting in this respect as the DoE shifted from an initially sceptical and defensive reaction to a more proactive role within the EU. Moreover, the structure of environmental policy-making was extensively Europeanized. Jordan (2000) studied the DoE's relations with the EU between 1970 and 1997 and the ways in which the Department's organization structured the scope and depth of Europeanization. This emphasizes the shaping effects of a Whitehall ethos and established standard operating procedures on adaptation by the British state to European integration's effects.

The leadership provided by secretaries of state can also be an important factor. For most of John Major's 1992–7 premiership the DoE was run by John Gummer, one of the stronger pro-Europeans in the cabinet. Gummer moved to the DoE from MAFF, which he saw as more tuned in to the EU than the DoE, which he thought tended to see the EU 'as something over there … The Department hadn't quite learnt that they had to take responsibility for what they had agreed. It was a question entirely of coming to terms with reality' (Gummer, cited in Jordan,

---

Box 8.1 **Case study of Council negotiations: Article 13 and European Union anti-discrimination law**

The issue: The Treaty of Rome made provision to counter discrimination based on nationality and on gender. There was growing pressure during the 1990s to extend these provisions to recognize other forms of discrimination evident in EU member states.

The British policy position: Between 1965 and 1976 Britain put in place race relations legislation that extended UK anti-discrimination law to combat both 'direct' and 'indirect' discrimination and allow scope for positive action. These provisions were in the civil code where the burden of proof is lower. Many other member states had anti-racist and anti-discrimination laws, but in the criminal code where the burden of proof is much higher. The Conservative government before 1997 had used subsidiarity arguments to block proposals for expanded EU competencies to cover racial discrimination. The New Labour government were prepared to sign signed up to Article 13 of the Amsterdam Treaty because it reflected both their more pro-EU stance and because the UK already had a fairly developed policy framework in this area and the costs of adaptation were not expected to be too high.

The Treaty article: Article 13 of the Amsterdam treaty stated that:

> Without prejudice to the other provisions of this Treaty, and within the limits of the powers conferred by it upon the Community, the Council, acting unanimously on a proposal from the Commission, and after consulting the European Parliament, may take appropriate action to combat discrimination based on sex, racial or ethnic origin, religion or belief, disability, age or sexual orientation. The Commission then brought forward two proposals: a 'race equality directive' and a directive combating all forms of discrimination in employment.

$\rightarrow$

$\rightarrow$

The negotiations: The seven-month period between policy proposals in December 1999 and agreement on Directives in June 2000 has been described as 'a record for the adoption of a piece of Community law requiring substantial legislative changes at national level' (Tyson, 2001: 111). The Directive also concerned an entirely new policy domain, required Council unanimity and had an inter-sectoral character that required inter-ministerial co-ordination in the member states which also contributed to make these directives 'least likely cases'. For the British, UKRep officials holding the social policy brief conducted this negotiation, but this was a cross-sector issue and so input also came from departments such as the Home Office and the Department of Education and Skills. The UK had no problem with the content of the proposed Directives because their measures to combat direct and indirect discrimination and allowance of scope for positive action fitted with UK priorities. The costs of adaptation were likely to be low. The UK also found itself in the unusual position when EU social policy was being discussed of being a policy leader rather than a laggard. There was, however, a UK bottom line: the proposed legislation was not to encroach on the activities of the UK immigration authorities who use forms of ethnic profiling to identify potential infringers of UK immigration laws.

The outcome: The two Directives agreed in June 2000 fitted well with UK domestic priorities and as such were a fairly costless way to indicate New Labour's commitment to the EU. The measures also put in place a framework for EU action that drew from British policy ideas and experiences and that far exceeds in its scope the level of provision in many other member states. In this area, the EU can be said to have 'levelled up' rather than 'levelled down' to a lowest common denominator policy (see Geddes and Guiraudon, 2004, for more details).

2000: 24). Jordan shows that the DoE has engaged more positively with the Commission's Directorate General dealing with environmental policy and with the European Parliament. The DoE also made more effort to get its officials to work in Brussels and gain experience there. Jordan (2000: 26) concludes that 'Europeanisation has significantly reduced the DoE's ability to make domestic policy independent of other actors, but it has provided new points of leverage over more powerful domestic departments, allowing the DoE to project its influence onto a broader European plane.'

A key aspect of adaptation across all policy issues has been the requirement to consider the views of other member states and to have an awareness of who Britain's allies on particular issues might be and how particular issues might work out with regards to existing policy frameworks. One example of how this can work out in practice is provided in Box 8.1, which looks at the British stance in the negotiations on

Commission-proposed directives based on Article 13 of the Amsterdam Treaty.

Page (1998) has also sought to measure the EU's impact on British government. He did so through a systematic analysis between 1987 and 1997 of Statutory Instruments (SIs), which are the most common form of implementing EU legislation (see Table 8.1).

Agriculture and trade/industry are clearly the most Europeanized ministries in the sense that large amounts of the legislation for which they are responsible emanate from Brussels. This is hardly surprising given the importance of the CAP and single market. Yet the table also shows that fewer than one in six SIs could be attributed to the EU and that even in the most Europeanized area of agriculture move than half of legislation was national. Page's findings suggest that general arguments about Europeanization and globalization need to be treated with some caution. Page (1998: 809) also argues that his data could suggest that rather than seeing the EU as an interlocked multi-level polity, it may actually more closely resemble a 'separate authority' federal model (Scharpf, 1994) with separate spheres of authority and activity with the result that: 'The interaction between levels of government in many non-routine policy processes might be one of interpenetration and multilevel bargaining, but we cannot assume that this multi-level model runs very deep into the grain of policy-making in Britain'.

When changes have occurred to the Whitehall process as a result of European integration, they are characterized by Bulmer and Burch (1998) as slow and accretive. The following changes can be detected.

Responses to growing complexity

As the complexity of EU tasks grows then there has been a tendency to devolve these tasks to specialist networks composed of officials from relevant departments with the effect that the Treasury will deal with the technicalities of economics and financial policy while the DTI will concern itself with the single market, DEFRA with agriculture and fisheries, and so on.

Territorial tensions

Devolution since 1997 has altered the political equation. Even before devolution, Scotland had been more purposeful in its dealings with the EU.

Table 8.1 European influence on Statutory Instruments 1987–97 (by ministry/ministry grouping)

Ministry	% European	No. of SIs
Agriculture	51.3	1,378
Northern Ireland*	39.5	577
DTI	28.6	1,053
Scottish Office	26.7	2,579
Defence	26.5	166
Welsh Office	23.6	2,587
Transport	21.0	1,086
Treasury	14.5	2,325
Employment	14.4	514
Health/social security	13.6	2,022
Education	9.1	701
Environment	7.9	1,335
Home Office	7.9	810
Other	18.4	234
All	15.8	17,367

* During the period of Direct Rule most legislation in Northern Ireland took the form of statutory rules that are not included in the database leading to a high figure for technical reasons.

Source: Reproduced from Page (1998: 806).

Since devolution there has been more scope for 'territorial tensions' within the British polity, which are considered more fully in the chapter's next section.

Scrutiny and accountability

Mechanisms for parliamentary scrutiny have been established with the Select Committee for European legislation in the House of Commons and the EU Select Committee of the House of Lords. The Commons tends to sift proposed legislation while the House of Lords undertakes more detailed inquiries into particular issues. Since 1980 it has been established practice that no minister will enter into an agreement in the Council of Ministers if the proposed measure has not been scrutinized in the House of Commons. EU documents are sent to the relevant committee within 48 hours of receipt, and within 10 days a document outlining the government's position is sent by the relevant minister to the committee. In addition debates will be held on the floor of the House and

MPs can ask ministers oral or written questions. Patterns of scrutiny and accountability have been criticized because the volume of EU legislation makes it difficult to keep a close check on developments. Moreover, the EU's move into matters of 'high politics', such as CFSP and JHA – which are prone to secrecy at national level anyway – has been seen as exacerbating problems of oversight and control.

The iron fist of the Treasury

There has been particular concern to keep a close check on EU expenditure in response to both the growing size of the EU budget and Britain's net contribution to it. The Treasury has developed sophisticated financial control measures known as EUROPES that require compensatory cuts in domestic spending for extra EU spending. The reason for this approach is the Treasury view that UK receipts from the EU budget are reimbursement for contributions made rather than fresh funding. The result is that responsible departments must pick up a significant proportion of the costs of EU projects set against their own budget. One effect of this has been that the UK government will often take a very tough line in financial negotiations and resist new budget lines because of the constraining logic of domestic public expenditure procedures led by the Treasury (Bulmer and Burch, 1998: 619). This led to conflict over EU regional development expenditure because the Commission insisted on 'additionality', by which was meant that EU funding would be matched by funding from member state governments. This insistence on additionality conflicted with the logic of EUROPES and encountered Treasury resistance. The result was that the Commission suspended RECHAR funding aimed at the regeneration of former coal mining areas. Eventually agreement was reached although, according to Bache (1998), the Treasury held its ground by making changes to the accounting mechanisms but not the end result.

The firm hand of the Treasury can also be detected in economic and financial policy. This has become particularly apparent as the Labour government agonized about whether or not to join the Euro-zone. As will be discussed more fully below, the Treasury has the final say on membership because of the 'five economic tests'. Chancellor Brown was keen to keep a tight grip on EMU and shift discussion to bilateral forums with the Prime Minister. There were also tensions between the Treasury and other government departments during the first Labour term, most notably because of the more positive pro-Euro line taken by Robin

Cook as Foreign Secretary and Peter Mandelson during his brief stint at the DTI.

Closer analysis of the Treasury's role provides affirmation of the ways in which understandings of the EU can differ across Whitehall in line with departmental histories and interests. Dyson (2000) identifies the 'limited Europeanisation' of the Treasury and suggests a number of reasons for this. First, EMU and the process of economic convergence was not an external source of policy change for the UK as it was for countries such as France and Italy. The UK has undergone economic changes since the 1980s that did not require the external discipline of EMU. Second, Dyson identifies both a lingering Euroscepticism among Treasury mandarins, plus the powerful role of economic beliefs within the Treasury that have tended to have a strong Atlantic rather than European component. Third, scepticism about EMU was reinforced by the ERM ejection in September 1992, which consolidated the view that 'credibility is made at home' (Dyson, 2000: 902). Finally, the position of the City of London as a global financial centre has been central to the UK's position on EMU. The UK has resisted measures such as tax harmonization on income earned from savings that could jeopardize the City's role. In addition to this, it is easier to detect US rather than European influences within the Treasury. Gordon Brown is known for his good contacts with leading US economists (Naughtie, 2001) while many of his closest advisers were educated at elite US universities. That said, this affinity tends to be with US Democrats and not with Republicans.

The result was that EMU was viewed as a set of external constraints on the UK economy while Treasury officials had not routinely been exposed to EU socialization effects and had not 'internalized' EU norms. The result of these two factors is that the 'five tests' revealed 'a conditional and instrumental view of participation ... linked to a Treasury agenda of exporting British ideas about structural economic reform to goods, labour and capital markets. The Euro-zone was to be "Anglicized" rather than Britain "Europeanized"' (Dyson, 2000: 899). The case of the Treasury illustrates once again how European integration has had important effects on central government, but that these effects have been consistent with the formal, informal and cultural logics of Whitehall.

The accretion of know-how

The institutional knowledge and know-how at Whitehall's command has steadily developed over the years. Officials have access to over 70 sets of guidance notes that detail the proper manner for dealing with EU business. In addition, departments may also issue their own notes which supplement these. These notes are not codified in any official statute or directive, but it is well-established that matters such as correspondence with the European Commission which has implications for other departments will also be copied to that department.

Whitehall career paths

Finally, growing numbers of British officials have EU work experience: for instance, a period of time in UKRep or as a 'detached national expert' within the Commission is seen as part of the career development cycle for high-fliers.

Sub-national government

A key element of the multi-level thesis is the development of sub-national levels of governance. Any discussion of sub-national government in the UK is complicated by the fact that the United Kingdom of Great Britain and Northern Ireland is a multi-national state and that 'British' national identity is a problematic concept. England, Scotland, Wales and (more problematically) Northern Ireland are more than 'regions' but less than independent states.

This articulation between the UK as a multi-national state and multi-level governance has become particularly evident since 1997 when devolution saw the establishment of a Scottish Parliament and a Welsh Assembly. The shape of devolution has differed. Scotland has a Parliament with primary legislative and tax-varying powers while the Welsh Assembly possesses neither of these powers. Since 1997 England has been carved into nine regions with Regional Development Agencies, Regional Assemblies and Regional Government Offices, but still lacks a regional tier of government. Plans announced by the Deputy Prime Minister, John Prescott, at the end of 2002 also mooted the creation of a regional tier of government in the UK, although whether Parliament or the people in these regions will accept this remains to be seen.

In their analysis of developments in England, Burch and Gomez (2002) identify what they characterize as an elite-driven 'new regionalism' that reflects a strategic readjustment on the part of regional tiers of government to new opportunity structures provided by the EU. They see this as being particularly driven by the EU's structural funds targeted at regional economic development and, in the case of England, as not being reflective of deep-seated regional identities.

This differs from Scotland and Wales where there was evidence in the 1990s (more so in Scotland than in Wales) of a desire for devolved government. The claims for devolved power were strongly domestic and rooted in resentment at Thatcherism's strong English characteristics, but the new opportunities offered by Europe also played a part in arguments for devolved power. This was because a united Europe and the development of a 'Europe of the regions' offered a sustainable future to smaller nations and regions that would exert more influence within a united Europe than they could if they sought go-it-alone independence.

The situation in Northern Ireland has been rather different and rather complex. Northern Ireland is in receipt of Objective One funding for the EU's least economically developed regions. The EU also launched a Programme for Peace and Reconciliation in Northern Ireland and the Border Region of Ireland (2000–4) known as the 'PEACE II' Programme. The attempts to establish mechanisms for power sharing between the leading political parties have been riven by difficulties and prone to suspension. European integration appears decidedly peripheral to any resolution of this particular deep-seated conflict.

In this consideration of regionalism and multiple levels, as in the previous section's analysis of Whitehall and central government, it is important to introduce some caveats. It has already been shown how the domestic political and institutional context can filter the effects of European integration. This allows us to avoid over-exaggerated accounts of Europeanization that apply the concept too broadly and in a way that strips it of meaning. Three points can be emphasized with respect to European integration and sub-national government in Britain. First, devolution and regionalism in Britain have been more strongly driven by a domestic agenda of constitutional change than they have by EU developments. 'Europe' has become a clear part of the opportunity structure for sub-national tiers of government, but has not determined the success or failure of arguments for devolved power. Second, the extent to which the sub-national dimension is additional to or bypasses Whitehall is unclear. Central government maintains a tight grip on EU policy and is particularly concerned to monitor the EU budget and financing system. It seems possible to say that even in the contemporary era of devolved power Whitehall retains a gatekeeper role with regards to the EU that is redolent of its role in a unitary state rather than the more complex inter-governmental relations within a federal system. Third, the regional tier of government has developed quite rapidly, but there is still no clear and defined view of what role these tiers will play in the formulation of EU policy. Devolution in the UK accords with fairly long-established UK processes of incremental change and, as such, leaves many loose ends untied. One of these loose ends is the question of the links between regional tiers and the EU. As Hazell (2003: 1) says: 'devolution has not reached a steady state and the dynamics continue to unfold'. Some of the associated 'territorial tensions', as Mitchell (2002) puts it, will be analysed below.

Access to resources has played an important part in stimulating sub-national mobilizations. In particular, the growth and development of the EU's structural funds for regional economic development has been highly influential in the development of the 'third level' of European governance and the inculcation of what Jeffrey (2000) calls 'sub-national mobilization'. This sub-national mobilization has four main elements. First of all, there is direct regional involvement in EU decision-making through the Committee of the Regions and other mechanisms for consultation and dialogue. Federal states such as Austria, Belgium and Germany also send representatives of their regions to the Council for matters that affect their competencies. Second, there has been increased EU level activity by sub-national government which can, for instance, take the form of the creation of European committees or the appointment of European officers. 'Europe' has become institutionalized as a responsibility at sub-national level with greater attention paid to the opportunities on offer. Third, the development of co-operation between EU regions can either be within national units or between them. Perhaps because of their relatively isolated geographical position, regions within the UK have been slower to respond to the opportunities for cross-regional link-ups than other parts of Europe where land borders lead to more obvious links between regions. That said, Kent and Nord-Pas-de-Calais have developed links (Holliday and Vickerman, 1990), as too has East Sussex with Haute-Normandie and Picardy. Finally, there is also the development by regional governments of lobbying activities directed at EU institutions. By 2002 all nine English regions had offices in Brussels, compared to 1994 when only two did. Scotland and Wales are also well represented. One result of this sub-national mobilization has been the creation of a culture of 'mutual dependence' in the sense that the EU needs the regions for the disbursement of funds and the development of regional regeneration strategies, while regions need Europe because it provides a new 'opportunity space' for them (Burch and Gomez, 2002: 768).

The EU's structural funds have grown considerably as a proportion of the EU budget since the late 1980s. These structural funds have been a source of controversy, as we saw earlier in this chapter when the Treasury desire to keep a tight grip on expenditure conflicted with the Commission's 'additionality' principle. In 1998 they accounted for around 12.5 per cent of the total budget. By 2002 they accounted for more than 35 per cent of the EU budget. The funds are targeted at various objectives: Objective One is the main financial effort and is targeted at the least favoured regions defined as those with a GNP per capita of less than 75 per cent of the Union average. Cornwall, the Isles of Scilly, the Scottish Highlands and Islands, Merseyside, Northern Ireland, South Yorkshire and West Wales and the Valleys have all been in receipt of Objective One funding in the 2000–6 budget round. Objective Two focuses on regions facing difficulties such as the decline of industrial or service sectors or the problems of the fishing industry. Interreg III funds inter-regional co-operation, while Urban II offers support for the sustainable development of urban areas. Table 8.2 shows the disbursement of this funding between 1994 and 2006 in the nine English regions.

A key issue on the agenda is the development of a regional tier of government in England. One of the reasons that this came on to the agenda was in response to the devolution of power to Scotland and Wales. This would consolidate the development of trends that have been evident since the 1990s and the emergence of 'the new English regionalism' linked by Burch and Gomez (2002) to seven factors. First, there is a

Table 8.2   Structural Fund allocations to English regions 1994–9, 2000–6

Region	Structural fund allocations	
	1994–9 (Euros, million)	2000–6 (Euros, million)
Eastern	79	156
East Midlands	329	376
Greater London	216	260
North East	758	717
North West	1,806	2,141
South East	83	36
South West	341	688
West Midlands	959	854
Yorkshire and Humberside	823	1,690
Total	5,394	6,918

Source: Data from Burch and Gomez (2002: 700 and 774).

changed mentality at regional level which has seen less moaning about central government and a greater determination to promote the interests of sub-national government. Second, the immediate aims of this mobilization were economic and linked to economic regeneration. They were thus inspired by the single market programme and by the development of the structural funds. Third, this mobilization developed within the regions rather than being inculcated from London. In this sense it was an authentic, albeit elite-driven, expression of regional interests rather than top-down Whitehall paternalism. Fourth, this mobilization was directed towards Brussels as much as it was towards London. Fifth, it was based on partnership between the private and public sectors. Sixth, it has not been based on any particular popular expression or demand for regional government. The North West, for instance, has been to the fore in these developments, but the idea of a North West region is deeply problematic because no such thing has existed before and there have been tensions between the major urban centres of Greater Manchester and Merseyside, as well as between rural and urban interests (Burch and Holliday, 1993). Perhaps in the South West and North East more convincing arguments can be made about regional identity (often defined as distance from London correlated strongly with neglect). Finally, and in contrast to the situations in Scotland and Wales, these regional responses can best be understood as a pragmatic response to changed opportunities rather than as deeper-seated expressions of identity.

There remains scope for tension as these new regional structures unfold. One reason for this is the rather fundamental problem that underlies the debate about regional governance in Britain: namely, the UK government has favoured 'a more flexible approach to economic development' with 'ambivalence, if not antipathy, towards regional plans and regional development structures' (Boland, 1999: 212). The result, as Boland puts it, is the development of a 'contested multi-level polity' with a battle for the direction of policy and access to/control over resources. The case of Merseyside illustrates these points.

Merseyside was in receipt between 1993 and 1999 of around £1.6 billion of regional development assistance because of its designation as an 'Objective One' region with GNP per capita less than 75 per cent of the EU average and in particular need of regeneration. Funding on this scale was bound to cause some tensions. Four can be identified. First, there was a technical debate about central government contributions, which reflects the Treasury's desire to keep a tight grip on EU expenditure given that it sees much of the money flowing from Brussels as reimbursement for contributions made rather than fresh money.

Second, there was criticism of power asymmetries as new regional net-works tended to favour those with knowledge and expertise of EU pro-cedures. There has also been criticism from some Merseyside MPs of a lack of accountability and the absence of 'social partners', such as trade unions, from key networks. Third, as Boland (2000: 217) puts it, the huge amounts of money sent local groups into a 'feeding frenzy as they scrabbled away among themselves for a share of the spoils'. Boland wrote of the application of 'the law of the jungle' with 'the dominant actors able to use their strength and power to obtain the lion's share of EC funding while others are left to pick upon the scraps left behind'. Finally, the bigger question remains. After the first tranche of Objective One funding had been spent there was little sign of improvement in key economic and social indicators. Merseyside continued to lose population while high levels of economic informality (also known as 'the black economy') pointed to major challenges ahead for economic regeneration of the region.

A number of unanswered questions remain in any analysis of sub-national government in the British multi-national state because of the incremental development of the devolution programme and the territorial tensions that arise. The big question, as Mitchell (2002) sees it, is whether devolution has helped resolve some of the problems of territorial politics in Britain or whether it has undermined coherent government through further territorialization. As things stand, Mitchell (2002: 762) sees that 'asymmetrical devolution created asymmetrical problems with asymmet-rical preparation'. Moreover, while the transition to European integration by central government was fairly smooth and closely co-ordinated, any transformation to a Europe of the regions is likely to raise all kinds of boundary, responsibility and co-ordination problems. This is because the 'ongoing Whitehall process' has the durability to remain an ongoing Whitehall process, while the 'ongoing devolution process' is more of a venture into the constitutional unknown.

Conclusions

This chapter has explored the effects of European integration on the British polity. It has examined the ways in which Britain has organized for Europe and the ways in which the organization of the British polity has been affected by European integration. Over time, the EU has become a 'thicker' institutional constraint with effects that are noticeable across central government and at sub-national level too. Over time, these competencies and intensive interactions with the EU institutions and other member states have meant that 'Europe' has become more deeply constitutive of the identities and interests of domestic political actors. At the same time, these effects are not uniform. Thus the lens provided by the domestic political and institutional context has filtered the effects of European integration. For instance, adaptation by central government has been strongly influenced by existing and well-established patterns within Whitehall and by different departmental histories and interests. While European integration has clearly had important effects on central government, the co-ordination of responses to these effects have tended to be in line with the established Whitehall ethos. This can lead to varying patterns of adaptation across Whitehall with some policy areas such as agriculture and trade extensively Europeanized, while others such as the Home Office have less direct contact with the EU (although this is changing as the EU deals with crime, policing and border controls). The key role of the Treasury in the debate about EMU was also highlighted. If and when the UK does join the Euro then the Treasury is likely to undergo a far more intense process of EU socialization than it has previously experienced.

In contrast, the development of sub-national government in the UK has been a process for which there are not well-established historical precedents and templates from which responses can be drawn. Britain has undergone significant changes because of the devolution of power introduced by the Labour government after 1997. European integration has also played a part in the development of sub-national government. The expansion in structural funding offered new opportunities for the regions. European integration also strengthened claims from Britain's sub-state nations for greater autonomy because they could point to other small-sized units that were viable actors in a united Europe. Devolution has, however, created some uncertainties, blurred responsibilities and led to some territorial tensions. While the EU has created new 'opportunity spaces' for sub-national mobilization, the more precise institutional parameters of these 'spaces' remain to be clearly specified because devolution remains an institutional novelty in the UK.

9

British Party Politics and the Rise of Euroscepticism

Introduction

European integration has been both a divisive and explosive issue in British party politics, yet, paradoxically, the intensity of elite level debates about European integration within the political parties and in Parliament has not been matched by a similar fascination about European integration and its implications amongst the general public. This chapter focuses on these elite level debates within the political parties and in Parliament. The next chapter then extends the discussion to explore public attitudes to Europe and the media representation of Europe to further highlight this disjunction between the media representation of Europe and the apparent lack of shared intensity amongst the greater part of the general public.

Neither of the two main national parties has adopted a consistent stance on European integration. Labour was divided during the 1970s and 1980s when the majority of the party's MPs and rank and file members opposed Common Market membership and sought withdrawal. The EC was seen as a capitalist club that offered little to working people and would confound the aspirations of a socialist Labour government. Tony Blair entered the House of Commons in 1983 on the basis of a Labour Party manifesto that called for British withdrawal from the EU. Labour's 'modernization' since 1984 has coincided with increased enthusiasm for European integration. This enthusiasm was one component that symbolized Party change and the move towards the political centre ground. The Liberal Democrats have been consistently the most pro-EU of the main national parties. Ironically, the pro-EU Liberal Democrats profited strongly at the polls from the rise of Conservative Euroscepticism.

The oscillations in position of the two main parties make fascinating viewing and tell us as much, if not more, about changes in British politics as they do about European integration. In 1975 the new leader of the Conservative Party, Margaret Thatcher, could rightly claim that the Conservatives were the more pro-European of the two main parties. The integration consequences of the 1986 Single European Act (SEA) induced the development of a free market nationalist critique of European integration that has fuelled right-wing Euroscepticism within the Conservative Party since the 1990s. The Maastricht Treaty, the deeply damaging ERM exit in September 1992, and disputes about the Euro all fed Conservative conflicts over European integration Euro-wars in the 1990s and contributed to the Party's landslide general election defeats in 1997 and 2001 (Geddes and Tonge, 1997, 2002).

This chapter examines the ways in which the texture of debate in British party politics about Europe has shifted since accession and explores the new political constellations that have emerged on the pro-European and Eurosceptic sides. The main arguments are set out below:

1   Divisions about Europe have tended to be within rather than between the main parties and it has been difficult for Eurosceptic forces to unite across the party divide and to coalesce into powerful anti-integration groups.

2   Debates about European integration in Britain can tell us far more about British politics than they do about the EU. A lot can be learnt about the ideological shifts in the Conservative and Labour parties, changed ideas about the role of the state and the market, and the relative importance of Parliament in public life. The EU tends to lurk in the background as a much maligned and often misunderstood external constraint on the activities of the British political class.

3   Labour's 'modernization' involved renouncing opposition to the EC/EU and adopting a far more positive stance towards European integration, but in ways that involve a 'third way' reappraisal of both Britain's place in the global economy and the main strands of European social democratic thought.

4   Conservative debates about European integration acquired a more ideological character in the 1990s. When understood in ideological terms these intra-party disputes became far more difficult to resolve through normal pragmatic methods of party management because convictions ran deep and could transcend party loyalties.

5   Parliament has been the key arena for debates about Britain's place in Europe with an occasional spillover into broader public discussion

such as during the 1975 referendum campaign. Indeed, a strategically important victory for the Eurosceptics was to flush the debate on the Euro into the open and make any decision on whether the UK adopts the single currency subject to a referendum. This move away from Parliament reduces the power of the party managers and renders the outcome more uncertain.

6 The size of the majority of the governing party has been a key variable. In the 1970s the situation in the House of Commons was finely balanced between Labour and the Conservatives. In the mid-1980s, large Conservative majorities marginalized opponents of the SEA. In the 1990s the knife-edge majority of John Major's government between 1992 and 1997 provided ample scope for exploitation by Eurosceptic Conservative MPs who fought what amounted to a guerrilla war from the backbenches. While not exactly energizing the masses, the Maastricht Treaty did impel a broader public debate about Europe and prompted the profusion of extra-parliamentary anti-EU groups (mainly on the right of the political spectrum) with whom Parliamentary rebels were able to make common cause.

Arguing about Europe

Debates about Europe have tended to focus on two themes nested within a broader discussion of Britain's place in the world and the impact of 'globalization' on the sovereign authority of the nation state. The first is the slippery concept of sovereignty, and the second is the relation between socio-economic policies pursued in Britain and those pursued in other member states.

The essential elasticity of the theory and practice of national sovereignty is demonstrated by the fact that the term can be used to both support ('pooling') and oppose integration ('surrendering'). Pro-Europeans contend that sovereignty is not a static concept to be jealously guarded; rather, it is matter of using this state power and authority in the best possible way to secure advantages for the British people. This 'non-zero-sum' perspective contrasts with a Eurosceptical zero-sum understanding of national sovereignty: you either have it or you do not.

Eurosceptic arguments focus on the negative implications of European integration for their particular understanding of national sovereignty, of Britain's place in the world, and an idea of self-government linked to the nation state and 'its people'. From this perspective,

European integration denudes 'the people' of their ability to decide who decides, so to speak, and thus mounts a significant challenge to the nation state as the basic, legitimate unit of international politics and to the core principles of the uncodified British constitution, particularly parliamentary sovereignty. European integration poses this threat by granting increased power to decision-makers in EU institutions that can over-ride decisions made at national level.

Linked to this discussion of sovereignty are questions about the relation of the unwritten British constitution to the emergent EU constitution, the legal principles that under-pin it, and the role, powers and autonomous authority of EU institutions. There is much suspicion on the Eurosceptic side towards EU institutions and the perceived federalizing agenda of, in particular, the European Commission and European Court of Justice as agents of integration by stealth.

These debates can play out rather differently in different parts of the UK. Conservative Euroscepticism has been seen as an expression of a form of English nationalism the lineage of which can be traced to Enoch Powell, but which also found expression among 'Thatcher's children' (the generation of Conservative MPs that entered Parliament in the 1980s and 1990s). The key difference was that Powell combined dislike of European integration with an equal dislike for the USA. Thatcher was Ronald Reagan's ideological soul mate and fellow Cold War warrior; she had no time for anti-Americanism.

The Englishness of Thatcher's vision of Britain and Europe also merits attention. Debates about sovereignty, independence, autonomy and national interest can mean rather different things when viewed from Cardiff, Edinburgh or Belfast. This becomes increasingly relevant in the Conservatives' downfall that involved a retreat to their electoral bastions of southern England and the process of asymmetrical devolution initiated by Labour since 1997. There is now a stronger regional dimension to British politics, as explored in the previous chapter.

As well as these concerns about sovereignty, there are vital strategic questions linked to the relation between the UK's socio-economic model and the approaches evident at EU level and in other member states. To what extent is the organization of the British economy, labour market and welfare state compatible with those in other EU member states? The terms of the debate about the socio-economic implications of European integration have shifted quite considerably since the 1970s when left-wing opponents of European integration denounced the EC as a 'capitalist club' that offered little to working people. More than this, they thought that the EC could threaten the ability of any future Labour government to attain its objectives, which included state control of industry as outlined in Labour's 'Alternative Economic Strategy' of 1983. During the 1970s, the Conservatives were far more amenable to economic integration because it was seen as good for business, although there was some lingering concern on the Conservative side that the EC was protectionist and confounded the UK's long-standing interest in global free trade.

The terms of the socio-economic debate about Europe changed in the wake of the SEA when ambitious plans for EMU and a greater social policy role for the EC/EU were hatched. By the 1990s, Conservative Eurosceptics were condemning the EU for trying to re-impose social and economic regulations that had been removed by the Thatcher governments through the 'the back door'. Meanwhile, there was a growing tendency among opponents of Thatcherite social and economic policy to espouse the virtues of the 'Rhineland model' of German capitalism as opposed to the harsher world of Thatcherite deregulation, although this ardour has diminished as the German economy limped into the twenty-first century. Nevertheless, at the time, adherence to a successful (in the 1990s at least) European model such as that provided by German consensus capitalism offered intellectual ballast to a modernizing Labour Party. By the late 1980s, erstwhile Labour Party and trade union opponents of European integration seemed to have been converted to the merits of a 'European social model' if only because this allowed Labour to distinguish themselves from the Conservatives. Meanwhile the trade unions could see a path to influence at EC level that was denied them at national level.

That said, New Labour in power have been keen to pursue an economic reform agenda at the EU level which matches well-established UK policy priorities but does not always draw enthusiasm from other member states: liberalization and deregulation do not always prompt support from those concerned that their jobs and welfare state provisions (which are seen as protecting them and their families) may be on the line in a more liberal, deregulated and global economy. New Labour's attempts to find EU allies in the quest for market liberalization has led to alliances being forged with right-wing governments in Italy and Spain rather than with social democratic governments, which one could assume to be more natural allies.

As the pace of European integration quickened from the mid-1980s with single market integration and EMU, questions about the compatibility of the UK socio-economic model and that in other EU member states became more important. For instance, would it be in Britain's longer-term interests to become ever more closely linked to the EU by joining the Euro and participating in common economic policies? Such dilemmas are particularly evident in the debate about EMU. The answers have ranged from John Major's 'wait and see' to Tony Blair's 'prepare and decide'. Neither of these stances, couched in equivocation, doubt and pragmatic calculations, provides a particularly firm footing for a serious debate about EMU.

This chapter now moves on to explore three key periods in the chequered history of Britain's relations with the EU. First, we examine UK accession and renegotiation in the 1970s. Second, the origins and effects in the 1980s and 1990s of Conservative Euroscepticism are explored. Third, the EU's role in Labour's modernization and the dilemmas that have confronted New Labour in power, particularly EMU, are assessed.

For and against Europe in the 1960s and 1970s

Conservative opponents of European integration were largely excluded from the party mainstream in the 1960s, 1970s and for much of the 1980s. Conservative 'anti-marketeers' in the 1970s, such as Teddy Taylor, gave up ministerial careers to pursue from the backbenches their dislike for European economic and political integration. Only after Thatcher's 1988 Bruges speech and the Maastricht Treaty ratification saga was 'Euroscepticism' legitimated as a mainstream school of thought within the Party. Labour has followed a different trajectory. Divisions over Europe were evident at the highest levels of the Party through the 1960s and 1970s. Only after Labour's crushing 1983 election defeat were anti-EC/EU views pushed to the Party's margins as it undertook root and branch 'modernization'.

Between the election of Edward Heath's Conservative government in 1970 and the referendum on the Labour government's renegotiated membership terms in June 1975 a debate about Britain's place in the EC spilled over from Parliament into wider public debate, culminating in Britain's first ever national referendum. The June 1975 referendum on the membership terms renegotiated by the Labour government after their 1974 return to power resulted in a resounding victory for the 'yes' campaign, but the issue was far from resolved. The legacy of the 1975 referendum was an intensification of anti-EC sentiment within the governing Labour Party which helped plunge the party into civil war after its 1979 election defeat.

EC membership was largely an elite concern in the 1960s and 1970s. The general public was not enthusiastic about joining the Common

Market, but these opinions were neither strongly held nor deeply felt. In Parliament, however, the staking out of battle lines between pro- and anti-accession forces can be detected since the early 1960s with strong feelings on both sides.

The size of the governing party's majority has important effects on the potential for anti-EC opposition to make an impact. In the late 1960s and early 1970s Labour and the Conservatives were closely matched and majorities in the House of Commons were narrow. For instance, when Edward Heath proposed to take Britain into the EC his Commons majority was a mere 30, while a leading Conservative opponent of EC membership, Neil Marten, estimated that there were between 70 and 80 opponents on the Conservative benches (Forster, 2002b: 33). It was cross-party support from 69 Labour backbenchers (including Roy Jenkins, Roy Hattersley and the future Party leader, John Smith) that secured Britain's EC membership.

Although there were anti-EC groups in both the main parties they found it difficult to coalesce into a credible and cohesive force. Instead, there tended to be groupings within the parties that did not readily form alliances across the party divide. The organizations within the Conservative Party which expressed this anti-EC sentiment were the Anti-Common Market League, founded in 1961, and the 1970 Group, founded as a right-wing dining club that had close links to Enoch Powell (Forster, 2002b: 35). Enoch Powell was a key figure in the development of Conservative Euroscepticism and to him can be attributed a right-wing, free market and nationalist critique of European integration (Gamble, 1998: 18). Powell had been sacked from the Shadow Cabinet in April 1968 following inflammatory comments about immigration and immigrants. Labour MPs were unlikely to have much sympathy for Powell's right-wing brand of anti-EC thought. Powell's influence rapidly diminished when he left the Conservative Party and called for a Labour vote in the February and October 1974 general election because Labour offered a referendum on accession. Powell's philosophical legacy (without the anti-Americanism) had more profound effects on the Conservative Party with latter-day sceptics – such as the former Conservative cabinet minister, John Redwood – aspiring to the Powellite mantle (Williams, 1998).

The support in 1972 of 69 Labour MPs for EC accession reflected divisions within the Labour Party. Although there were prominent pro-EC voices, the majority of the Party opposed EC membership. This opposition was evident at all levels of the party: the cabinet, the parliamentary party, the rank and file membership, and the trade union movement. The main anti-EC grouping within the Labour Party was the Labour Safeguards Committee, founded in 1967, which became the Labour Committee for Safeguards on the Common Market (Forster, 2002b: 35). Prominent left-wing groups such as Tribune were also hostile to EC membership. Anti-EC sentiment encompassed most strands of thought within the party from the left to the right. Leading figures of the day, such as Tony Benn, Barbara Castle, Douglas Jay and Peter Shore, were advocates of staying out. The scope for division is illustrated by the fact that other senior figures, such as Roy Jenkins and Shirley Williams, argued for membership. As Forster (2002b: 35) notes: 'The Labour Party was therefore more anti-market than the Conservative Party, but it was also more divided at every level of the parliamentary party, on the frontbench as well as the backbenches.' The leading trade unions also opposed EC membership, which meant that the powerful trade union block vote within the Labour Party was firmly aligned with the anti-EC camp (Robins, 1979).

The question for opponents of the Common Market was whether organizations could be established that tapped into anti-EC sentiment in both the Conservative and Labour parties and could form the basis for a strong cross-party anti-EC coalition. This was likely to be difficult given party loyalties and the major political differences between right- and left-wing opponents of European integration such as Enoch Powell and Tony Benn. There were some attempts to establish broader anti-EC coalitions through the two main anti-accession organizations: the Keep Britain Out (KBO) movement established in 1962, and the Common Market Safeguards Campaign (CMSC), created in 1970. The KBO campaign sought a broad anti-EC movement beyond the parliamentary arena, but was hindered by the diversity of its membership, which included right-wing Conservative MPs and left-wing Labour MPs who found it difficult to work together. The CMSC was divided because some of its members wanted to open negotiations and then judge the terms available, while others were opposed outright to membership.

On the pro-EC side, the British Council of the European Movement (BCEM) experienced no such divisions because it was unequivocally pro-membership (Butler and Kitzinger, 1976; King, 1977; Forster, 2002b: 37). There are some parallels here with the contemporary anti-Euro campaign, which suggest some potential for stresses and strains during a referendum campaign. Groups such as New Europe and Business for Sterling are anti-Euro but support continued EU membership, while others (such as the UK Independence Party and the Democracy Movement) want withdrawal from the EU.

As Prime Minister between 1974 and 1976, Harold Wilson's main concern was party management. The background conditions were not good. A weak economy and poor industrial relations blighted his government. Wilson also appreciated the simmering opposition to European integration within his Party. Although Wilson had made an application for membership in 1967, he was more than happy when Labour returned to opposition to use the EC as a stick with which he could beat Heath's Conservative government. Wilson claimed not to be opposed to membership *per se,* but to oppose the terms of entry as negotiated by Heath. Wilson then called for a renegotiation and a referendum on the renegotiated terms. This referendum pledge moved Enoch Powell to desert the Conservative Party and call for a Labour vote in the 1974 general elections.

Short-term advantages for Wilson were outweighed by longer-term losses. An early indication of the European issue's potential to fracture the Labour Party was provided following Shadow Cabinet agreement in 1972 that a referendum would be held on Britain's EC membership. This prompted the resignation of the Deputy Leader, Roy Jenkins, who was not prepared to stand this affront to his pro-European sensibilities, particularly as its motives seemed grounded in the low politics of party advantage. Wilson was keen to ensure that when a referendum campaign was held it did not lead to further outbreaks of feuding within his government. The potential for it to do so was clear. Within the Cabinet, the renegotiated terms were agreed by 16 votes to seven in March 1975. The opponents were Tony Benn, Barbara Castle, Michael Foot, William Ross, Peter Shore, John Silkin and Eric Varley (Forster, 2002b: 56). Divisions were even more pronounced within the Parliamentary Labour Party with 145 voting against the terms, only 137 voting in favour and 33 abstaining. A Labour Party special conference in March 1975 saw 3.9 million votes cast against membership compared to 1.7 million in favour. There was parliamentary as well as rank and file hostility to the EC. The support of Conservative MPs saw the renegotiated terms through the Commons. Wilson permitted an 'agreement to disagree' during the referendum campaign. This allowed cabinet ministers to follow their consciences during the referendum campaign so long as they did not appear on platforms in opposition to each other. There was, though, serious trouble in store for Labour. Wilson could attempt to 'manage' these issues, but could not suppress them. As economic and political problems piled up from the mid-1970s onwards, the Labour Party became increasingly anti-EC.

The 1975 referendum was the first time that the issue of Britain's place in Europe was opened to a broader public debate. This was something of a novelty because debates about European integration had tended to be framed in technical language that did little to enthuse the electorate. During the 1975 referendum campaign a successful pro-EC campaign managed to harness a cross-party group of leading centrist politicians with broad public appeal. Their argument was that the EC offered practical economic and political advantages to Britain which far outweighed any loss of sovereignty. The anti-EC campaign had significantly less funding, lacked media support and was led by a motley collection of politicians from the left- and right-wing fringes. They argued that the terms of membership were disadvantageous and would lead to higher prices, and that EC membership was a threat to self-government.

The referendum campaign was organized by two umbrella organizations. The Britain in Europe (BIE) campaign mobilized on the pro-EC side, while the National Referendum Campaign (NRC) led the anti-EC movement. The Britain in Europe campaign had a number of advantages: it was composed of leading centrist politicians such as Edward Heath and Roy Jenkins, while the NRC was composed of politicians such as Tony Benn and Enoch Powell who came from opposite ends of the political spectrum. The BIE campaign also enjoyed considerable financial advantages and strong support from the main national newspapers. The BIE campaign managed to raise around £1.5 million while the NRC mustered around £250,000 (King, 1977) and earned the ringing endorsement of Fleet Street. The BIE campaign also possessed a clear and unambiguous argument: membership was in Britain's interests. The NRC campaign was less focused on a single coherent theme. Some of its campaigners opposed the membership terms but did not rule out membership, while others were deeply opposed to European integration. Those who opposed the terms quickly got submerged in mind-numbing detail, while those who were outright opponents of membership were portrayed as extremists (Forster, 2002b).

Even though enthusiasm for EC membership did not run deep these views were not strongly held and shifted during the course of a campaign as pro-EC arguments were made by relatively popular politicians expounding a simple, clear message (Butler and Kitzinger, 1976; King, 1977). With their financial advantages, media backing and government support the result was a not wholly unsurprising victory for the 'yes' campaign, with a 67.2 per cent 'yes' vote on a 64.5 per cent turnout.

The referendum did not put the issue to rest. In fact, the campaign provided some opening shots in what was to become a damaging and divisive period in Labour's history, marked by a growing distance between the party leadership and the rank and file. There was disappointment that manifesto commitments had not been pursued in government. This prompted calls for internal party democratization which would give activists more control over Labour MPs. A left-wing critique of Labour in power began to emerge. This involved a radical reappraisal of economic and social policies and the development by 1983 of Labour's Alternative Economic Strategy, which contained a full-blooded commitment to Socialism. Labour's move to the left also led to a hardening of opposition to European integration. The Treaty of Rome and the constraints that it would impose on member state governments were incompatible with the kind of programme that Labour proposed to develop. Withdrawal from the EC became official party policy and was endorsed by 5 million votes to 2 million votes at a special Party conference convened in October 1980. This prompted the 'gang of four' ex-ministers (Roy Jenkins, David Owen, Bill Rodgers and Shirley Williams) and a gaggle of MPs to leave the party and found the Social Democratic Party, which soon struck up an alliance with the Liberals.

Following the calamitous electoral defeat in 1983 the question was not so much whether Labour could win power, but whether it could survive. This problem faced the party leader elected in the wake of the 1983 debacle, Neil Kinnock. Kinnock had been a staunch and eloquent left-wing opponent of the EC throughout the 1970s. He was now to begin a personal and political odyssey that would see him advocate the 'modernization' of the Labour Party, endorse positive engagement with the EC, and conclude with him moving to Brussels to become a European Commissioner (Westlake 2001).

Almost as soon as Kinnock became party leader the commitment to outright withdrawal was watered down to a commitment to withdraw if satisfactory renegotiated terms could not be secured. By the 1989 European Parliament elections, Labour was advocating active engagement with the EC at a time when Conservative Euroscepticism was beginning to emerge in the wake of Margaret Thatcher's seminal Bruges speech. Labour would, however, need to climb an electoral mountain if they were to regain power. They were considerably aided in this task by the Euro-war that broke out in the Conservative Party during the 1990s and that helped shatter the party's electoral credibility.

Conservative Euroscepticism

In the 1970s Conservative support for the EC was based on a pragmatic and instrumental acceptance of the potential benefits that EC membership could bring. Enthusiasm for European integration did not run deep. Support could dry up if these benefits were seen to cease. Conservative support for European integration was thus based on a rather narrow trade-based idea of European integration that was unlikely to be adaptable to the ambitious programmes for economic and political integration which were launched in the 1980s.

At the root of these difficulties has been a tension within the Conservative Party about Britain's place in the international economy. Baker, Gamble and Ludlam (1994) liken Conservative splits during the 1990s to two other deeply divisive events in the Party's history: the repeal of the Corn Laws in the 1840s and tariff reform in the first years of the twentieth century. Both consigned the Party to long periods in opposition. Thatcher's successor John Major was unable to navigate these serious challenges both to his party and his leadership with the result that Maastricht was 'the most serious parliamentary defeat suffered by a Conservative government in the twentieth century' (Baker, Gamble and Ludlam, 1994: 57; see also Baker, Gamble and Ludlam, 1993a, 1993b).

The motives of Eurosceptic Conservative opponents of Maastricht were various. However, it has been argued that during the 1990s a new strain of Conservative Eurosceptic thought emerged. This new strand of thought has been labelled as 'hyperglobalist' by Baker, Gamble and Ludlam (2002) in the sense that it sought to square the Thatcherite circle through the pursuit of neo-liberal objectives of openness, deregulation and privatization in a global economy, but with nation states remaining the pre-eminent units of international politics. This marks an attempt to evince an alternative political economy that involves a particular understanding of 'globalization' and of Britain's place in the world economy. This theme in Eurosceptic thinking will be explored more fully when the main strands of Eurosceptic thought within the Conservative Party are explored.

In case the impression be given that Euroscepticism was rife within the Conservative Party during the 1980s it is useful to provide a little context. Between 1979 and 1984, relations between Margaret Thatcher's governments and the EC were overshadowed by the dispute over the Britain's budget contributions. Once this had been resolved in 1984, the single market project elicited far greater enthusiasm from Conservatives about forms of European economic integration that mirrored domestic economic policies. The Thatcher decade saw the pursuit at national level of the neo-liberal doctrines of openness, flexibility and competition and some attempt to translate these themes into EC policy-making

(Baker, Gamble and Ludlam, 2002: 400). Buller (2000) argues that Conservatives saw the single market programme as possessing the potential to embed at EC level a programme of economic changes similar in content to those introduced in Britain. Liberalization and deregulation would be elevated to a European level and a return to government interventionism would become well nigh impossible. Thatcherism could be 'exported' to Europe and entrenched as a dominant ideology. The growth, development and virulence of Conservative Eurosceptic opposition can then be related to the steady realization that this Thatcherite vision was not widely accepted by other EC member states.

European integration after the SEA fundamentally exposed the limitations of this minimalistic Conservative view of European integration. The SEA of 1986 heralded both a major transfer of sovereignty to the EC with single market integration and significant institutional reforms (such as increased use of QMV in the Council of Ministers). The Conservative governments of the 1980s were prepared to accept economic integration, but were unprepared to countenance the much deeper economic and political integration that the SEA was seen as presaging. As Forster (2002b: 66) puts it: 'The SEA therefore raised the stakes and changed the nature of the game.' For Thatcher's Conservative governments, the single market was an end in itself. For other member states and the Delors-led European Commission, it was a means to an end. This unhappy state of affairs was to be the source of Conservative Euro-wars as Thatcherites railed against what they saw as the unwelcome spillover effects of the SEA. The practical benefits of a free-trade Europe were threatened by deeper economic and political integration which challenged the core Conservative idea that 'democracy and legitimacy are located in the nation state, which is the basic unit of all legitimate democratic politics' (Baker, Gamble and Ludlam, 2002: 402).

Despite its important implications, there was curtailed parliamentary debate about the SEA and a small number of opponents. There were 43 votes against ratification at the bill's third reading, but the Conservatives enjoyed a large majority plus the support of the Liberals and Social Democrats. There was no cross-party anti-European integration organization that would bring anti-EC campaigners together across the Party divide.

The 1980s have been characterized by Anthony Forster (2002b: 66) as a period during which there were few opportunities for debates about European integration. For instance, the 1984 and 1989 European Parliament elections were dominated by domestic concerns, although Margaret Thatcher's highly negative 1989 campaign (based on the slogan 'Don't live on a diet of Brussels') led to Labour becoming the largest British party in the European Parliament and prompted some Conservative MPs to question her leadership. There were also some important developments beneath the surface; as Forster observes, the 1980s was a period during which Eurosceptic tactics began to evolve with close scrutiny of EC measures, a developing technical expertise and a committed readiness to fight a war of attrition.

Who were these Eurosceptics and in what did they believe? Hugo Young (1999) identified five strands of Eurosceptic thought during the 1980s that were to meld in the crucible of opposition to Maastricht and EMU in the 1990s:

1 *Irreconcilables* such as John Biffen and Teddy Taylor who were long-standing opponents of European integration and its entire doings. Taylor's opposition was voiced from the backbenches; Biffen's was licensed within government, although Thatcher's press secretary was moved to describe him as a 'semi-detached' member of her government.

2 *Constitutionalists* such as Bill Cash, James Cran and Richard Shepherd, who were particularly concerned about parliamentary sovereignty.

3 *Free marketers* such as Michael Spicer and Nicholas Budgen, who were ardent Thatcherites and who became disillusioned by what they saw as an interventionist EC that threatened Thatcherite policies. A cadre of young Thatcherites – including Michael Forsyth, Neil Hamilton, Peter Lilley, Michael Portillo, Edward Leigh, Francis Maude and John Redwood – entered the House of Commons after 1979 and were to organize within the No Turning Back Group. All were to become government ministers.

4 *Nationalists* such as John Carlisle, Tony Marlow and Nicholas Winterton.

5 *'Wets'* (a term used in Thatcherite parlance to refer to those on the left of the party) such as Peter Tapsell, who opposed what they saw as EC protectionism.

Baker, Gamble and Ludlam (2002) supplement these classifications with a 'hyperglobalist' strand of Conservative Euroscepticism that developed during the 1990s and constituted an attempt to envisage an alternative political economy for the UK outside the EU (see also Gamble, 1998). In its extreme form, hyperglobalization would be difficult to accept for any national political party because it would imply the redundancy of the nation state in the face of capital mobility in a global economy. Could the Conservatives reconcile their vision of politics within which the nation state is central with 'globalization'? Baker, Gamble and Ludlam (2002) argue that a particular notion of globalization has been articulated within Conservative Euroscepticism. This posits a vision of Britain as a sovereign state with a low tax, low spending, deregulated and privatized economy. The result is that 'The national policy-making constraints of globalization are welcomed because they rule out the kind of social democratic and socialist measures which are viewed as incompatible with British national identity, forcing the government to set the people free whatever its ideological predilections' (Baker, Gamble and Ludlam, 2002: 409; see also Portillo, 1998). The language of 'no alternative' and 'no turning back' that was central to Thatcherite thinking in the 1980s ascends to a global plain. In this context, the EU and its member states are portrayed as high spending, high tax, over-regulated and uncompetitive encumbrances on the UK's ability to compete in a global economy. If the EU continues to pursue this path then Conservative 'hyperglobalists' would call either for a renegotiation of Britain's terms of membership (the party's 2001 election stance), or might even head towards the exit.

In no other EU member state is such a strand of 'globalist' Eurosceptic thinking evident. The affinity of such thinkers is most clearly with the USA. As Baker, Gamble and Ludlam (2002: 423) put it: 'No other political elite or political elite has the same kind of material links, or the same kind of ideological attachment to the United States as do the British Conservatives, and New Labour would arguably come second in such a comparison'. Following this argument through, *The Daily Telegraph* has argued that Britain could even renounce the irredeemable EU and throw in its lot with the USA and the North American Free Trade Area.

The Maastricht rebellion

These strands of Eurosceptic thought were to coalesce into the most sustained parliamentary rebellion of the twentieth century. When tracing the historical lineage of modern Euroscepticism then pride of place needs to be given to Margaret Thatcher's Bruges speech of September 1988. This speech legitimized Euroscepticism, provoked a debate within the Conservative Party about Britain's place in the global and international economy, provided an intellectual justification for Euroscepticism, and

> **Box 9.1**   **Extract from Margaret Thatcher's speech at the College of Europe, Bruges, 20 September 1988**
>
> My first guiding principle is this: willing and active co-operation between independent sovereign states is the best way to build a successful European Community. To try to suppress nationhood and concentrate power at the centre of a European conglomerate would be highly damaging and would jeopardise the objectives we seek to achieve. Europe will be stronger precisely because it has France as France, Spain as Spain, Britain as Britain, each with its own customs, traditions and identity. It would be folly to try to fit them into some sort of identikit European personality.
>
> **Founding fathers:** Some of the founding fathers of the Community thought that the United States of America might be its model. But the whole history of America is quite different from Europe. People went there to get away from the intolerance and constraints of life in Europe. They sought liberty and opportunity; and their strong sense of purpose has over two centuries, helped create a new unity and pride in being American – just as our pride lies in being British or Belgian or Dutch or German. I am the first to say that on many great issues the countries of Europe should try to speak with a single voice. I want to see us work more closely on the things we can do better together than alone. Europe is stronger when we do so, whether it be in trade, in defence, or in our relations with the rest of the world.
>
> **A European super-state:** But working more closely together does not require power to be centralised in Brussels or decisions to be taken by an appointed bureaucracy. We have not successfully rolled back the frontiers of the state in Britain, only to see them reimposed at a European level, with a European superstate exercising a new dominance from Brussels. Certainly we want to see Europe more united and with a greater sense of common purpose. But it must be in a way which preserves the different traditions, parliamentary powers and sense of national pride in one's own country; for these have been the source of Europe's vitality through the centuries.
>
> **Utopia never comes:** If we cannot reform those Community policies which are patently wrong or ineffective and which are rightly causing public disquiet, then we shall not get the public's support for the Community's future development. What we need now is to take decisions on the next steps forward rather than let ourselves be distracted by Utopian goals. Utopia never comes, because we know we should not like it if it did. Let Europe be a family of nations, understanding each other better appreciating each other more, doing more together but relishing our national identity no less than our common European endeavour. Let us have a Europe which plays its full part in the wider world, which looks outward not inward, and which preserves that Atlantic Community – that Europe on both sides of the Atlantic – which is our noblest inheritance and our greatest strength.

impelled the organization of anti-EC groups both within and outside the Conservative Party.

Thatcher's Bruges speech recycled some old Gaullist themes with a Powellite twist (see Box 9.1). The Bruges Speech understood the EC in Gaullist terms as an association of states whose core purpose was to strengthen the sovereignty of the member states. She opposed what she saw as integration by stealth driven by the Commission rather than integration that was the conscious choice of the member states. She was also suspicious of the ability of other member states to dress up the pursuit of their national interest as being in the European interest. As she put in her memoirs, 'I had by now heard about as much of the European ideal as I could take' (Thatcher, 1993: 473). Thatcher sought to deflect criticism that she was anti-European by arguing that she was actually pro-European, but that she favoured a different vision of Europe based on loser intergovernmental ties. She alluded to a wider Europe that included Budapest and Warsaw as well as London, Paris and Bonn. At the core of her speech was a statement of her mounting objection to an emergent EC socio-economic model in which she famously stated that she had not 'rolled back' the frontiers of the state in the UK only to see new controls imposed from the EC.

The Rubicon had been crossed. Following Thatcher's Bruges speech a loose organization was formed centred on the Bruges Group, which had strong financial support from Sir James Goldsmith, the former British Airways boss, Lord King, and the hotel magnate, Lord Forte. Eurosceptic arguments also began to find a home in right-wing newspapers, particularly *The Daily Telegraph* and *The Times*. The strands of the argument were as follows (H. Young, 1999; Forster, 2002b):

1 The alleged insincerity of other member states that expressed commitment to single market integration but reneged on core free market principles.
2 Basic institutional incompatibilities between British legal, political, social and economic institutions and those of other member states.
3 The EU was seen as moving in the direction of over-regulation and social democratic interventionism. The UK, in contrast, could position itself as a low tax, low regulated economy on the edge of Europe.
4 The spillover effects of the SEA were unacceptable, particularly the plans for social policy integration and EMU, as well as the role of supranational institutions in driving this process which grossly infringed on the authority and autonomy of the British executive to pursue British national interests.

5   The autonomy of supranational institutions such as the European
     Commission and the European Court of Justice posed a real threat to
     British national sovereignty. Interestingly, despite the fact that
     neo-functionalist theorizing with its idea that the Commission could
     be a driving force had fallen into abeyance in the 1970s, it was resus-
     citated in grand style by the British Eurosceptic press who lambasted
     Delors and his sinister plots. The apotheosis was *The Sun*'s 'Up
     Yours Delors' front page headline of 1 November 1990 that urged its
     readers to tell the 'filthy French' to 'frog off'.
6   Nationalism, xenophobia and an obsession with the Second World
     War. For instance, Thatcher's notorious seminar on Germany and the
     Germans (Urban, 1996). Nicholas Ridley was sacked from the
     cabinet following an interview with *The Spectator* magazine in which
     he described European integration as 'a German racket designed to
     take over the whole of Europe'. *The Spectator* used the opportunity
     to portray Chancellor Kohl with a Hitler-style moustache on its front
     page. The Euro '96 football tournament prompted similar nationalist
     and xenophobic eruptions targeted at Spain and Germany.

The significance of Thatcher's downfall and Major's Maastricht negotiations were fivefold. First, a lingering resentment simmered within the
Party caused by the manner of Thatcher's departure (a 'Conservative
coup' as Alan Watkins, 1991, put it). Second, Euroscepticism had been
given an intellectual justification, the origins of which lay with core
Thatcherite tenets which the EU in its post-Maastricht guise was deemed
to threaten. Third, the intellectual justification for Euroscepticism
brought together previously disparate groups within the Party, impelled
the formation of extra-parliamentary anti-EU groups, drew funding from
leading business people, and found an echo in the opinion columns of
right-wing newspapers. Fourth, John Major may have been the desig-
nated heir, but was an unknown quantity as Prime Minister. He had risen
without trace in the sense that he had quickly become a government
whip and then government minister following his election to Parliament
in 1979. If he had views on Europe, then these were unclear. He was,
though, happy to give the impression during the 1990 leadership contest
that he was the carrier of the Thatcherite flame (and Thatcher to give the
impression that she would be 'a good back seat driver', as she put it). If
anything Major's track record indicated pragmatism rather than the sort
of hardline opposition to European integration that was beginning to
acquire a foothold within his Party. Eurosceptic disappointment with
Major fuelled notions of 'sell out' and 'betrayal'. Finally and crucially,

Major possessed a parliamentary majority of only 21 after his 1992 election victory. This diminished as the government lurched from crisis to crisis, from by-election defeat to by-election defeat, and from defection to defection (the pro-EU Liberal Democrats were the principal beneficiaries of these, by the way).

The anti-Maastricht rebellion was an intra-Conservative conflict. Labour Eurosceptics did not make common cause with Conservative Eurosceptics, although the Labour whips were happy to plot defeats for Major's government with hard-line anti-Maastricht opponents. There were generational differences at work here too. The Conservative Eurosceptics were Thatcher's children. The future belonged to them, or so they thought. Labour Eurosceptics were older, nearing the end of their political careers, and easily picked off by the modernizers. If Labour and Conservative Eurosceptics had been able to find common cause then, given Major's small majority, it would have been difficult to ratify the Treaty. It was, however, hard for Labour's Eurosceptics (many of whom saw themselves being on the left of the Party) to make common cause with the Conservative brand of right-wing, Thatcherite Euroscepticism.

The Maastricht ratification saga

While basking in election victory in the spring of 1992 the Major government could not possibly have foreseen the scale and extent of the difficulties that would be experienced during the Maastricht ratification that would lead to the collapse of the Conservative party as an electoral force. Clearly there was opposition to Maastricht, but party management and party loyalty should prevail, or so party managers thought. They were dramatically, calamitously and ruinously wrong. One reason why they were wrong was the series of blows that struck the EU and British government in 1992. These delayed the Treaty and emboldened the Eurosceptics.

The first blow occurred on 2 June 1992 when the Danes rejected the Maastricht Treaty by a narrow margin of 51 per cent to 49 per cent. Despite the narrow margin, rejection was rejection and the Treaty required ratification in all member states. The ratification process was suspended. Perhaps if Major had pushed ahead at this time then many of the later difficulties could have been avoided. The delay gave the Eurosceptics a vital ingredient in any war of attrition: time. In the wake of the Danish 'no' Michael Spicer established the Fresh Start Group (FSG). The FSG collected 84 signatures for an Early Day Motion calling for the Maastricht Treaty to fall and for the negotiations to be re-opened. Even though this was an unlikely scenario, there was now some belief among the Eurosceptics that the tide of European integration could be halted, perhaps even turned back. Many Tory MPs strode Canute-like to the water's edge.

September 1992 was to be another month of woe for Major's government with serious long-term implications for Conservative credibility. In France the *petit oui* (another 51 per cent–49 per cent narrow squeak, albeit this time in favour of the Treaty) in Mitterrand's referendum indicated the lack of public enthusiasm for the Treaty (as well as the declining popularity of the Mitterrand government: referendums are imperfect devices, it should be recalled). Worse was to come. On 16 September 1992 sterling was ejected from the ERM. During a day of frantic market activity and government chaos (during which interest rates were increased to 15 per cent at one point) the Conservatives' reputation for economic competence was shattered (Stephens, 1996: ch. 10). They may not have been the 'nice' party, but the public saw them as the party that knew how to manage the finances. Now with the threat of repossession looming over mortgage-holders, this reputation for economic competence was lost. As billions of pounds were drained from the nation's reserves, Conservative claims to be effective stewards of the national economy became fanciful (Wickham Jones, 1997).

Despite being a bleak day for the country, the ERM crisis was another boon for the Eurosceptics. Following his May 1993 departure from the government, the Chancellor of the Exchequer who presided over the ERM ejection, Norman Lamont, went so far as to claim that 'golden Wednesday' might be a better term because the British economy was freed from the unwelcome shackles of EU economic rules. In fact the golden opportunities were those provided to the Conservatives' opponents who fed off the Tories' fratricidal Euro-war and the economic crisis management that saw the supposedly tax-cutting Conservative Party preside over tax hikes. Yet, in the peculiarly insular world of Conservative Party politics in the early 1990s, there were those who believed – wrongly on all counts as it turned out – that the European issue mattered deeply to British people, that opposition to European integration could reconnect the Conservative Party with the electorate, and that the tide of events was flowing in their direction with the effect that the Maastricht Treaty could be stopped. But, put simply, the issue mattered to too few people. Those to whom it mattered were probably Conservatives anyway. Maastricht became a synonym for tedium while rebellions, in-fighting and sleaze were the public representation of the Conservative Party (Cowley, 1997).

This relative lack of public interest mattered little to the growing number of Eurosceptics within the ranks of Conservative MPs. They enjoyed financial support from wealthy patrons. They were militant in their opposition to Maastricht, and this militancy could over-ride their Party loyalty. They had a formidable modus operandi based on a command of detail that bordered on the obsessive and far exceeded that of their opponents. Eurosceptics who had absorbed every paragraph and sub-clause took as a shocking indictment Kenneth Clarke's admission that he had not even read the Maastricht Treaty, while doubtless a copy nestled on the bedside table of every good Eurosceptic.

The FSG developed a new form of opposition to European integration with its members harbouring deep dislike of the EU and their own Party leadership while also being prepared to liase with Labour whips to defeat the Maastricht bill. FSG members tabled more than 500 amendments to the ratification bill, proposed 100 new clauses and abstained on 1,515 occasions (Forster, 2002b: 87). The belief that the Maastricht Treaty could be stopped in its tracks set the 'unwhippable in pursuit of the unratifiable' (Baker, Gamble and Ludlam, 1994: 38). An incipient transnationalization of this anti-Maastricht protest occurred when Tory Eurosceptics sought common cause with their colleagues in Denmark, but they had little in common and anti-Maastricht opposition remained grounded in national politics.

While ostensibly about Britain's place in Europe, the Maastricht ratification process was also a Conservative Party identity crisis. European issues were refracted through the lens of national politics and national institutions and can tell us as much (if not more) about this politics and these institutions than they do about the EU.

Political life within the Conservative Party became tumultuous and chaotic as the 1990s progressed (see, for instance, Gorman, 1993; Williams, 1998; Gardiner, 1999; Walters, 2001, for some insight into the poisonous world of Conservative Party politics in the 1990s). The Party's conferences became redolent of Labour's hate-fests of the 1980s. They were great entertainment for the viewing public but disastrous for a Party that aspired to re-election. At the 1992 Party conference Norman Tebbit led the opposition to Maastricht and elicited huge support from the party faithful in a speech that alluded to the treachery of the Party leadership. The ranks of the Eurosceptics had also been replenished by the 1992 general election, which brought hard-line Maastricht rebels such as Iain Duncan Smith and Bernard Jenkin into Parliament.

Major had a slim parliamentary majority and a divided and fractious parliamentary party, the Eurosceptic wing of which was well-organized, committed and determined to do all it could to ditch the Treaty. The opt-outs from the Social Chapter and the third stage of EMU that Major had negotiated at Maastricht did little to help his position in the Commons. In fact, the opt-outs were used by Labour to oppose the ratification bill on the grounds that they should be re-inserted. Yet the opt-outs also did little to appease Conservative Eurosceptic ultras that wanted to see the whole Treaty defeated irrespective of opt-out clauses which they saw as largely meaningless. Consequently, the government's small majority ensured repeated embarrassment due to the persistent strength of the rebellion and the willingness of the two main opposition parties to support amendments that were pro-Maastricht (including the Social Chapter) but destroyed the government's semi-detached position (Baker, Gamble and Ludlam, 1994: 38). The ratification process was an unmitigated nightmare for Major's Conservative government. The government slumped to by-election defeats in Christchurch and Newbury and lost 500 seats in the May 1993 local council elections.

Meanwhile the ratification bill limped through Parliament for over a year. There were 70 parliamentary votes and 61 debates. By the third reading in May 1993 there were 41 Conservative rebels and five abstentions (Baker, Gamble and Ludlam, 1994). The bill was only passed in July 1993 when the government chose the 'nuclear option' and made the issue a matter of confidence in the government. All but one Tory MP (the absentee being Rupert Allason, the member for Torbay) supported the government. The bill was carried, but the blood spilt within the Conservative Party during the ratification process had inflicted terminal damage. It was impossible to pretend that Euroscepticism was the preserve of a few backbench fanatics. There were Eurosceptics at all levels of the government. Even so, Europhiles such as Kenneth Clarke and Michael Heseltine were a small but powerful minority. Within the cabinet were those such as John Redwood, Michael Portillo and Peter Lilley who had been members of the No Turning Back Group. Their views were probably more reflective of Party sentiment, but they were seen as troublemakers by Major and his pro-European colleagues.

In the 1970s Edward Heath had kept the harder-line opponents of British membership of the EC out of his cabinet. By the 1990s the presence of prominent Eurosceptics within Major's cabinet prompted one of the most famous off-guard moments in British politics. At the end of a television interview on 23 July 1993, the day on which his government had just secured a vote of confidence, Major thought that the microphone had been switched off. It had not. What he had to say illustrated the scale of his problems and his inability to deal with them:

> The real problem is only a tiny majority. Don't overlook that I could do all these clever decisive things which people wanted me to do – but I would have split the Conservative Party into smithereens. And you would have said I acted like a ham-fisted leader. Just think it through from my perspective. You are the Prime Minister with a majority of 18, a party that is harking back to a golden age that never was, and is now invented. You have three right-wing members of the cabinet who actually resign. What happens in the parliamentary party? ... I could bring in other people. But where do you think most of the poison is coming from? From the dispossessed and the never possessed. You think of ex-ministers who are going round causing all sorts of trouble. We don't want another three more of the bastards out there. (cited in Baker, Gamble and Ludlam, 1994: 37)

The aspersions on legitimacy were directed at Lilley, Portillo and Redwood, although the more fanatical and determined Conservative Eurosceptics adopted the term as a badge of honour for the irreconcilables (Gorman, 1993). Maastricht did not end the in-fighting. Instead, attention turned to EMU and other instances of the Major government's 'betrayal, complacency, lack of attention to detail and complicity' (Forster, 2002b: 93).

There were to be two more set-piece confrontations that were landmarks on the Party's path to opposition. The first occurred in November 1994 when eight Conservative MPs (Nicholas Budgen, Michael Cartiss, Christopher Gill, Teresa Gorman, Tony Marlow, Richard Shepherd, Sir Teddy Taylor and John Wilkinson) defied a three-line whip to oppose the European Community (Finance) Bill. The whipless eight were then joined by Sir Richard Body, who combined Euroscepticism with opposition to what he saw as draconian tactics by the party whips. For a few brief months the rebels became important, if never quite serious, political figures who revelled in 'the adrenalin of the camera and the allure of the lens' (Williams, 1998: 72). Scarcely a television debate could be held without these champions of Euroscepticism advertising the deep divisions within the Conservative Party. Even when the rebels were readmitted to the Party fold in April 1995 they were able to boast that they had not been forced to repudiate their views (Williams, 1998: 77).

The second landmark was John Major's resignation on 22 June 1995 from the Party leadership. In a bid to test the Eurosceptics' mettle, Major invited a challenge to his leadership. The more obvious Eurosceptic challenger, Michael Portillo, wavered while the Secretary of State for Wales, John Redwood, decided to stand. Redwood's campaign did not get off to the best of starts when the brightly garbed whipless rebels provided the backdrop to the press conference launching his campaign. As Redwood's own special adviser noted: 'The impression was that of a coup launched by a group of dissident Latin-American colonels who had just taken over the local airport and cancelled all flights' (Williams, 1998: 105). Apparent eccentricity belied the seriousness of Redwood's challenge, the threat it posed to Major's leadership, and the dedicated group of Eurosceptics (such as future Party leader, Iain Duncan Smith) who supported it. Major needed to secure a simple majority of the 329 MPs eligible to vote, and he also needed to be 15 per cent ahead of his challenger. However, simply to win was not enough; Major needed a convincing margin of victory. By the time of the election, it had been established – following furious briefings and counter-briefings from each side – that a vote against Major by 100 MPs would seriously undermine his leadership. On Tuesday, 4 July 1995, 218 MPs voted for Major, 89 for Redwood, and 22 either abstained or spoilt their ballot papers. Fewer than 100 MPs had voted for Major's challenger, but 111 – one-third of the parliamentary party – had failed to endorse his leadership. As soon as the results were announced and in a well-planned media-management operation, Major loyalists appeared on television screens and radio stations to pronounce upon the Prime Minister's resounding triumph. But the victory was pyrrhic because 'Major's summer contest had institutionalized conflict within the Party' (Williams, 1998: 121).

What did the Eurosceptics achieve? Above all, it could be argued that the divisions that were exposed were central to the Conservative's 1997 and 2001 election defeats. There were other consequences. First, persistent anti-EU campaigning forced Major to convince his Chancellor, Kenneth Clarke, that British Euro membership would need to be conditional on a referendum. Labour too made a commitment to a referendum in the run-up to the 1997 general election in order to avoid being outflanked on this issue. Second, constraints were imposed on Major's government because the scale of rebellion made it clear that no further measures could be brought before Parliament that would increase the EU's role. Third, Major's government ceded to the Eurosceptics a greater voice in policy-making, although Major continued to bounce between the pro-European and Eurosceptic wings of the Party. Fourth, the election in 2001 as party leader of one of the most inveterate Maastricht rebels, Iain Duncan Smith, showed how the Eurosceptic wing had captured what remained of the Party. Fifth, Conservative Eurosceptics linked their campaigning to like-minded and often wealthy extra-parliamentary organizations. Eurosceptic think tanks were created, such as the European Foundation run by Bill Cash and the European Reform Group run by Michael Spicer. In the aftermath of his defeat in the leadership election John Redwood established Conservative 2000 to advance his particular brand of Conservatism. In addition to this there were campaigning organizations within the Conservative Party and beyond such as the Campaign for UK Conservatism, the League of Concerned Conservatives, and Conservatives Against a Federal Europe.

There were also groups pushing for a referendum on Maastricht. The Maastricht Referendum Campaign organized a phone-in in which it managed to elicit 94 per cent support from respondents for their demand for a referendum. The multi-millionaire financier, Sir James Goldsmith, who used his personal fortune to advance his own views on European integration, took up this challenge. Goldsmith's Referendum Party ran candidates in the 1997 general election against any MPs that refused to pledge their support for a referendum which would not be on EMU but on the question of whether Britain should stay in the EU. The Referendum Party contested 547 seats and garnered 810,778 votes, which, when the £20 million spent by Goldsmith on the Party is taken into account, works out at £24.67 a vote (Geddes, 1997). The UK Independence Party (UKIP) was overshadowed by Goldsmith's dramatic entry on to the British political scene. Goldsmith's Party failed to win a single seat, but did contribute to the removal of some Conservative MPs, most famously in Putney where Goldsmith himself stood against David Mellor and contributed to Labour's victory.

Europe in the 1997 general election

The European issue was not a salient concern at the 1997 general election. Even the very limited scope for 'clear blue water' to be opened between Labour and the Conservatives was swiftly neutralized by Labour which was eager to adopt a similar unyielding stance on core sovereign concerns. Blair even felt moved (or at least Alastair Campbell, his press officer, did) to pen an article for *The Sun* in which he proclaimed his 'love for the £'.

Labour's 1997 general election manifesto called for 'an alliance of independent nations choosing to co-operate to achieve the goals they cannot achieve alone. We oppose a federal European superstate.' This language did not differ markedly from that in the Conservative manifesto. On the issue of EMU, both Labour and the Conservatives pledged to hold a referendum. Labour also promised to uphold the national veto on taxation, defence and security, immigration, the budget and changes to the Treaty. The main difference between the two parties was on their stance to the Social Chapter. Labour said that they would sign up. To counter accusations of being insufficiently patriotic Labour used a British bulldog – often an emblem of the far right – in one of their Party Election Broadcasts. The Conservatives retaliated with an election poster showing a miniature Tony Blair sitting on Chancellor Kohl's knee, with the implication that senior EU statesmen would bamboozle the naive Blair.

The salient concerns in 1997 were, however, not the EU; instead, they were the divisions, incompetence and sleaze that were seen to characterize the Conservative Party (Cowley, 1997). The electorate appeared to make no judgement about the stances of MPs as they voted both Eurosceptics (such as Michael Portillo) and pro-EU Conservative MPs (such as Edwina Currie) out of the House of Commons. The result was the election of a New Labour government with a more positive approach to the EU, albeit with some reservations about the Euro.

Europe in the 2001 general election

The 2001 general election was noticeable for William Hague's attempts to make European integration a key issue and to festoon his campaign with the motif 'save the pound'. Never before had a national campaign by an aspiring party of government veered so close to single-issue politics. Hague sought to open 'clear blue water' between the Conservatives and Labour on European integration because this was one issue on which voters seemed to prefer the more sceptical stance of the Conservatives to that of Labour (although there was an element of contradiction here because Blair was vastly more popular as a potential Prime Minister – and thus Britain's representative in Europe – than Hague, whose personal ratings in the polls were resolutely negative).

Four reasons have been identified for the Conservatives' 2001 embrace of Euroscepticism as a key campaign theme (Geddes, 2002: 145). First, since 1997 pro-EU voices such as Michael Heseltine and Kenneth Clarke had been marginalized. Second, Hague and his advisers – after an early flirtation with a more inclusive version of Conservatism – saw a series of core issues on which they might stand some chance of eroding Labour's dominant position (Europe was one, asylum and tax cuts were the others). Third, there was a lingering bitterness within the Party surrounding Thatcher's removal from office in 1990. The disputes in the 1990s were in many ways a battle for the Party's soul. Fourth, Eurosceptics dominated the parliamentary Conservative Party.

Clear blue water was indeed opened in 2001. The Conservatives advanced a vision of a 'network Europe' with states coming together in areas of mutual benefit. States could opt into or out of those parts of the *acquis* that they favoured. The Euro was ruled out for the lifetime of two Parliaments, while any further extension of competencies to the EU would be opposed. 'In Europe, not run by Europe' was Hague's campaign theme. This minimal vision of the EU would be reinforced by the creation of powers reserved for the British state and therefore forbidden from becoming EU competencies. Such a policy would raise serious questions about Britain's continued membership of the EU because the UK government would be placed in a position of almost perpetual opposition to other member states. In a speech made on 4 March 2001, Hague alluded to Britain as a 'foreign land' with a second-term Labour government and called for cross-party support in what he portrayed as a last-ditch defence of the British nation state (Hague, 2001).

Labour's stance, as was discussed in Chapter 5, reflected some core underlying themes that have informed elite attitudes to European integration: a preference for intergovernmentalism, rejection of federalism and the maintenance of strong ties with the USA. Labour's support for the Euro would depend on the five economic tests being met.

The Liberal Democrats supported transfers of sovereignty to the EU when in the national interest, and were more positive about the Euro (although with a referendum as the basis for entry). Yet their manifesto also revealed an underlying conceptualization of the EU as an association of sovereign states that is distinct from the kind of unionist style federalism that informs the thinking of their sister parties in other member states. The Liberal Democrats tend to see a 'lower case' federalism focused on the local level rather than connected to any grand plan for an upper case Federal Europe. Moreover, Liberal Democratic support for European integration is tempered by some on-the-ground realities with a Party membership with strong Eurosceptic inclinations. This has been seen as a central aspect of the Liberal Democrats' 'dual identity' with some distance between the Party in Westminster and the

Party membership (Fieldhouse, McAllister and Russell, forthcoming). A study of Liberal Democrat members found them to be 'scarcely more pro-European than the electorate as a whole' (Bennie, Curtice and Rudig, 1996: 141). Furthermore, Liberal Democrat support is at its strongest in the south west of England and parts of rural Wales and Scotland where agriculture and fishing interests are strong and which, as a result, do not tend to be hotbeds of pro-EU sentiment.

The result in 2001 was famously another landslide victory for New Labour. The Conservative campaign failed because Hague was not popular and because his core themes, such as European integration, mattered to too few people, and those to whom it mattered would probably vote Conservative (or UKIP) anyway. The key election issue was the state of Britain's public services. The Conservatives had almost nothing to say on this issue.

New Labour and European integration

Chapter 5 surveyed New Labour's engagement with the EU and argued that significant continuities can be detected. In such terms, the party's position has conceptual and strategic components, while much also hinges on the key relationship at the heart of New Labour between Blair and Gordon Brown.

In conceptual terms, the majority of Labour MPs have moved since the 1980s to a position that is supportive of economic and political integration. The great fissure over Europe that existed in the late 1970s and early 1980s has dissipated, perhaps to be replaced in the aftermath of the second Iraq war with divisions over the USA. Even if there were very much Eurosceptic opposition to the EU within the Labour Party then it would be difficult for it to make its voice heard, given the Party's crushing parliamentary majorities after the 1997 and 2001 general elections. Most Labour MPs seem to have embraced what Baker, Gamble and Ludlam (2002: 413–15) characterize as 'open regionalism', involving acceptance of major changes in the global economy that diminish the sovereign authority of states and which mean that 'traditional goals of national economic management are now best pursued at the collective level of the EU, rather than left to the nation state alone'.

To this conceptual re-orientation can be added strategic calculation. This introduces a complication into the analysis because of the necessary interaction between this support for 'pooling' sovereignty and the core concerns of the new Labour government. New Labour were elected in 1997 and re-elected in 2001 to make good their promises to deliver high quality public services. At the 2001 election, health, education and law and order were the top three salient concerns at the 2001 general election, while European integration was outside the top ten in twelfth place. Despite William Hague's attempts to make Europe a key issue and to 'save the pound', voters were influenced by concerns such as the standards of schools and hospitals that had a far more direct effect on their lives.

It is, however, worth noting that while New Labour may appear to be in a dominant position following two crushing landslide victories, their share of the vote was a little over 40 per cent while turnout slipped to a worryingly low 59 per cent at the 2001 general election (Fielding, 2002a, 2002b). New Labour's coalition is surprisingly fragile, based as it is on an appeal to 'middle England'. It is unlikely that any journey to 'the heart of Europe' will be made if 'middle England' is not felt to be ready to accompany New Labour on this expedition, or if it jeopardizes the attainment of public service objectives that are central to the success or failure of New Labour.

The third factor is the question of New Labour's leading personalities, particularly the relationship between Blair and Brown and their coteries of advisers (Naughtie, 2001). New Labour in power with their crushing majority have helped expose the myth of parliamentary sovereignty, the weakness of cabinet government and the potential for concentrated power around key governmental figures. Scarcely a week goes by without stories emerging of divisions between Tony Blair and Gordon Brown (the TeeBeeGeeBees, as these divisions have been called). No one seems to quite know the exact positions of these two figures or how things will resolve themselves. It seems that Blair sees it as part of his mission as Prime Minister to make Britain a leading player within the EU. Brown, on the other hand, is a €-sceptic in the sense that he is not convinced either conceptually or strategically that adoption of the single currency is right for either Britain or New Labour. Brown's position has been strengthened by the departure from office of pro-Euro cabinet ministers such as Robin Cook, Peter Mandelson and Stephen Byers. Brown's April 2003 budget statement added grist to the €-sceptic mill when the UK was consistently compared favourably with a poorer performing, sluggish, low growth Euro-zone economy. The extent to which these positions reflect the reality of debate within government was revealed when the negative assessment of the five economic tests was made in June 2003.

A key question in contemporary British politics is thus whether or not the Euro should replace sterling. In conceptual terms, it would seem that there are still obstacles within the Labour Party to this step being taken. The view that European integration can create the conditions for sustaining key elements of the social democratic project has been widely accepted (even though the relationship between New Labour and European social democracy is rather more ambiguous). In strategic terms, there are more grounds for equivocation because New Labour was re-elected to make good their public service promises, and it is on this that they will be judged. The debate about the Euro also exposes the concentration of power and the key power relationship within the Blair government and the tensions that can run across it. Moreover, any decision on the Euro will depend on a referendum. This takes the issue beyond the domain of party management and increases the levels of uncertainty and risk. As will be seen in the following chapter, there are no good grounds for supposing that the British people are enthusiastic about deeper European integration or the adoption of the Euro.

Conclusions

European integration has possessed the potential to strike at the heart of British politics. In the 1990s European integration was a cause of serious divisions within the Conservative Party that not only contributed to its 1997 and 2001 election defeats, but also led to questions being asked about whether it can ever recover. Analysis of British party politics and European integration since the 1970s shows that divisions over European integration have tended to be within rather than between the main parties, and that the size of the governing party's parliamentary majority has been a key factor in the scope for Eurosceptic opposition to be effective. Moreover, since the late 1980s it has been possible to detect relatively coherent strands of Eurosceptic thought within the Conservative Party that have been reflected in an extra-parliamentary campaign groups and leading national newspapers. The fissile party politics of European integration imposed real constraints on the EU policy of the Major government and have induced caution and nervousness on the part of New Labour. A key reason for this is the perceived extent of public scepticism about European integration and the apparent absence of Europeanized collective identities in the UK; or, put another way, people in the UK neither seem to see themselves as, nor to feel, particularly European. The next chapter explores these public attitudes to European integration more closely and also assesses the impact of media representations of Europe on these attitudes.

10

Public Attitudes and Media Representation

Introduction

This chapter explores public attitudes in Britain towards European integration and media representation of Europe. The chapter will show that British public attitudes towards the EU appear to be structured by a self-declared lack of knowledge of the EU, and when opinions are held they appear to be based on cost-benefit calculations of the advantages and disadvantages of membership; neither collective identities nor methods of political communication in the UK seem particularly Europeanized. Compared to other member states public perceptions of the benefits of EU membership by British citizens appear to be more negative.

The power of the press?

The view that media representations of Europe can have negative effects on public perceptions of European integration has been voiced from the highest level. Tony Blair reacted in exasperated fashion in November 1998 to the hostile coverage in Eurosceptical newspapers to proposals for a European Rapid Reaction Force: 'I'm used to the British media being hostile on Europe, but I hope that the public will be given the facts' (Horrie, 2000). In a speech made in Gent, Belgium, in February 2000 he again expressed frustration:

> If people tell you that the argument for Europe has been lost in Britain, they are wrong. Of course our position is made more difficult by our media. One part has abandoned all sense of objectivity and is essentially hostile to the European Union. The other part is supine in the face of that hostility. Take the example of last year's financial negotiations at Berlin. Europe is always at its most hard-headed when it comes to paying for it.

But by making our case persuasively, we protected Britain's rebate and got a very good deal on structural funds. Yet that got a fraction of the media attention that attended the failure by France to lift the ban on British beef, even though the financial consequences for Britain were more far-reaching. Another example is Vodafone-Mannesman. For weeks, our media had been telling us that this was the test of reform, and that Europe would flunk it. That politicians, rather than shareholders, would decide. When the deal went through, the British media barely commented on its enormous implications. (Blair, 2000)

What effects does this media coverage have? Since the 1990s newspapers owned by Rupert Murdoch and Conrad Black have taken a strongly anti-EU line, while politicians have seemed fearful of press influence and eager to court the approval of newspaper barons. Philip Stephens (2001: 67) has argued that the national press, 'weaned on the confrontations of the Thatcher/Major years, is undoubtedly hostile to an approach which sees Europe as a partner rather than an enemy', while Peter Riddell (1998: 112) claimed that 'the shift in the press during the 1990s probably had a cumulative impact on influencing public attitudes, particularly during the absence of a clear lead from politicians'.

Does an unrelentingly negative diet of Brussels lead to a negative view of the EU from Britain? Regular EU-wide opinion polls in the Eurobarometer series show British people to be relatively unenthusiastic about European integration. In addition, Britain is the self-declared 'don't know' capital of the EU with low levels of public knowledge of the EU and its workings. Simon Hix (1999) has argued that this problems extends beyond Britain's borders to an EU-wide 'information deficit' when it comes to knowledge of the EU. This seems to be particularly pronounced in Britain, where there also seems to be an 'interest deficit' too. Moreover, most British citizens have little direct exposure to the EU. Most people will use the context of domestic politics to acquire information about the EU (Gavin, 2000). Assessment of public opinion and media representation of Europe allows consideration of the ways in which the EU and European integration is represented to British people, the inter-play between public opinion and media representation, and the extent to which collective identities in the UK have been 'Europeanized'.

United Kingdom public attitudes towards European integration

The Eurobarometer opinion polls provide regular snapshots of public attitudes across the EU. Table 10.1 shows that in 2002 British respondents

Table 10.1 Responses in the United Kingdom to a series of key European Union issues compared to the European Union average

	Membership a good thing	Benefit from membership	Support for the Euro	Support for common foreign policy	Support for common defence and security policy	Trust in the European Commission	Support for EU constitution
UK	31	30	28	38	49	31	49
EU15	55	50	63	67	73	53	65

The questions posed were as follows:

1 Generally speaking do you think that (your country's) membership of the EU is a good thing, neither good nor bad, a bad thing?
2 Taking everything into consideration, would you say that (your country) has on balance benefited or not from being a member of the EU?
3 What is your opinion on each of the following statements: Please tell me for each statement, whether you are for it or against it: A European Monetary Union with one single currency?....
4 What is your opinion on each of the following statements: Please tell me for each statement, whether you are for it or against it: One common foreign policy among the member states of the EU, towards other countries....
5 What is your opinion on each of the following statements: Please tell me for each statement, whether you are for it or against it: A common defence and security policy among EU member states....
6 And for each of the following institutions, please tell me if you tend to trust it or tend not to trust it? The European Commission...
7 Do you think that the EU should or should not have a Constitution?

Source: Data from *Eurobarometer Standard Report* (Autumn 2002).

were less likely than respondents in other EU member states to see EU membership as a good thing, to think that EU membership had been advantageous to them personally, to support the Euro, to support common foreign, defence and security policies, to trust the Commission and to support an EU constitution. Regular surveys also show that the level of 'don't knows' in response to questions about the EU far exceeds that in other member states. To rephrase William Hague's 2001 Conservative party election slogan: 'in Europe, not particularly interested in Europe' would seem to be the message.

Figure 10.1 provides evidence of self-declared levels of knowledge of the EU in all member states where 10 corresponds with 'knowing a great deal' and 1 with 'no knowledge at all'. UK respondents declared that they knew less about the EU than respondents in any other member state, reflecting both an 'information deficit' and an 'interest deficit'.

At the 1992, 1997 and 2001 general elections European integration was not a highly salient concern for the electorate (Geddes, 1997, 2002). The traditional concerns of national general elections – management of the economy, law and order, health care and employment – were to the fore. European integration was, however, an issue that had noticeable and strong effects on the main political parties, as was seen in Chapter 9. This provides us with the sense of a disjunction between the ability of the European issue to engender deep controversy at elite level, but without seeming to be a matter of intense concern to the population more generally. As the *Daily Express* wrote at the time of the 1997 general election campaign, Europe is the issue that makes the parties swoon and the voters yawn.

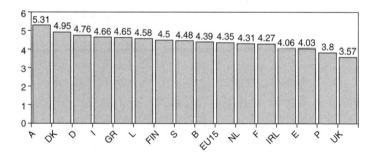

Figure 10.1   Self-declared knowledge of the European Union (1 = no knowledge at all, 10 = know a great deal)

Source: Reproduced from *Eurobarometer Standard Report* (Spring 2002).

The most significant change of recent years is perhaps more subtle. European integration and understandings of it by MPs, party members, supporters and the general public have become part of the strategic environment within which national politicians operate (Hix, 1999, ch. 6). Moreover, since the 1990s and the Maastricht ratification saga, popular opposition to Maastricht has been 'uncorked', as Franklin, Marsh and McLaren (1994) put it. National political leaders cannot rely on passive acceptance of European integration; the 'permissive consensus has been shattered', as Hix (1999: 140) averred. The case for European integration has to be made to a British public that appears not to have widely accepted the more idealistic arguments for a united Europe and seems more likely to make material cost/benefit evaluations of membership.

What then does the evidence suggest about these cost/benefit assessments? The Spring 2002 Eurobarometer poll showed UK respondents to be sceptical about the advantages that European integration had brought. Only a tiny majority thought that the country had benefited (36 per cent of UK respondents) compared to the 35 per cent that thought it had not. Indeed, as Figure 10.2 shows, a correlation can be established between those UK respondents who support EU membership and those who think that their country has benefited from EU membership.

Support in the UK for European integration has been lower than that in most other member states, although the 'national interest' is far from monolithic in the multi-national British state where there is more

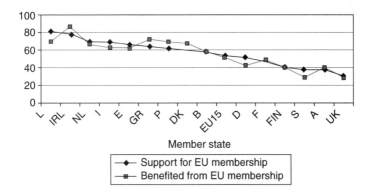

Figure 10.2   Correlation between support for European Union membership and perceptions of benefiting from European Union membership (%)

Source: Data from *Eurobarometer Standard Report* (Spring 2002).

support for European integration in Scotland and Wales. Northern Ireland has been less enthusiastic. Ulster was actually the only part of the UK to vote 'no' in the 1975 referendum. There was a steep increase in support at the time of the 1975 referendum when a powerful pro-EC campaign was mobilized with strong backing from a cross-party alliance of mainstream politicians plus most national newspapers, although support soon dipped back to pre-referendum levels. Support surged again towards the end of the 1980s as there was a concerted effort by the government to sell the benefits of single market integration. It is interesting to note the effects of powerful government and media backing for European integration in the mid-1970s and late 1980s. Since the early 1990s, however, the ERM crisis, the resurgence of Euroscepticism, the Maastricht ratification saga, and an increasingly hostile and negative press coverage could all be argued to have played a part in diminished enthusiasm for European integration.

Using Easton's (1965) classification, this public support for European integration can be said to have two components. First there is an *affective* dimension based on ideological or non-material identification with European integration. There is also a *utilitarian* dimension based on individual cost-benefit calculations. The affective dimension can be linked to Inglehart's work on the rise of post-materialism in advanced industrial democracies, particularly amongst younger generations, which would mean that material prosperity would stimulate increased interest in non-material issues and, in turn, this would increase support for European integration. Gabel (1998) has identified since the 1990s the increased importance of utilitarian measures influencing public support for European integration. This requires a more hard-headed case to be made. Politicians cannot rely on lofty appeals to European ideals, but must seek to ground their arguments for more European integration in the practical benefits that it could bring.

How can this case be made? Obviously various media outlets newspapers, radio, television and the Internet play a key role in providing information about European integration. Their role can become particularly important when so few members of the public have direct experience of the EU. European integration is not an issue like health care, education or crime of which people are likely to have direct first hand experience; rather it is an issue from which, as Neil Gavin (2000: 356) puts it, they are 'one stage removed'. The chapter's next section explores these potential media effects in more detail and goes beyond the 'information deficit' to analyse the ways in which media representation of European integration can affect public attitudes.

Media representation of Europe

The question of the extent to which the media influence public opinion has been one of the more pressing concerns in contemporary British political studies (for example, Franklin, 1994; Anderson and Weymouth, 1998). In this section, two questions are addressed: from which sources do British people get their information about the EU, and what effects do these sources then have on their attitudes towards Europe?

Table 10.2   Main sources of information on the European Union

	UK	EU15 Average
Daily newspapers	36	44
Other newspapers/magazines	11	20
Television	47	65
Radio	23	31
Internet	13	14
Books, brochures and information leaflets	11	10
Discussion with relatives, friends and colleagues	14	21

Source: Data from *Eurobarometer Standard Report* (Spring 2002).

People in the UK use a wide range of sources of information to gather information about the EU, as shown by Eurobarometer evidence. What is also striking is that when asked from where they got their information about the EU, 37 per cent of UK respondents said that they did not look for information on the EU, compared to a 21 per cent EU uninterested average. Those who responded gave television and daily newspapers as their main sources of information, although the Internet is becoming more widely used. Respondents were also asked which of these sources of information they preferred. Television was the preferred medium for information about the EU, as Tables 10.2 and 10.3 show.

Table 10.3   Preferred sources of information about the European Union

	UK	EU15 Average
Television	53	61
Daily newspapers	39	39
Radio	23	29
Short leaflet	23	18
Detailed brochure	21	19
Internet	18	14

Source: Data from *Eurobarometer Standard Report* (Spring 2002).

Table 10.4   Trust in the media

	Press	Radio	Television
UK	20	59	58
EU15 Average	44	61	55

Source: Data from *Eurobarometer Standard Report* (Spring 2002).

Respondents were also asked which forms of media they trusted. The evidence from Table 10.4 is quite striking. UK respondents' levels of trust in television and radio were on a par with those in other member states (slightly higher for television and slightly lower for radio), but the level of trust in the press was less than half (20 per cent) the average level of trust in newspapers across the EU (44 per cent), as Table 10.4 shows.

Despite these low levels of public trust in newspapers, the press has been the focus of one of the most sustained analyses of media representation of the EU and European integration (Anderson and Weymouth, 1998). Of particular interest have been the ways in which various newspapers represent the EU. Table 10.5 shows the average daily readership in December 2002 of the UK's national daily newspapers while also indicating in broad terms the stances of the various newspapers on European integration.

Eurosceptic newspapers have a powerful presence in the tabloid, mid-market and quality sections of the daily newspaper market. *The Sun* has adopted a distinct, populist anti-EU line that has given rise to some memorable front pages. These include the 'Up Yours Delors' in November 1990 directed at the Commission President, Jacques Delors, the proclamation of the 'The Cattle of Britain' in March 1996 when the EU imposed a ban on British beef, and in June 1998 it asked whether Tony Blair was the 'most dangerous man in Britain' for his apparent desire to persuade Britain to replace sterling with the Euro. During the Euro '96 football tournament held in the UK the *Daily Mirror* indulged in some wild xenophobic ranting against both the Spanish and the Germans (most notably their 'Achtung Surrender' headline invoking memories of the two world wars when England played a game of football against Germany).

Not everything is as clear-cut as it may first appear, however. When the Euro was launched in January 2002, *The Sun* in Britain announced 'the dawn of a new €rror' while across the Irish Sea in pro-EU Ireland *The Sun* proclaimed 'the dawn of a new €ra' (Black, 2002). Quality

Table 10.5   National newspaper total daily circulation and stance on European integration, December 2002

	Total daily circulation	Broad stance on European integration
National Morning Popular		
Daily Mirror	2,031,596	Pro-EU
Daily Record	525,148	Pro-EU
Daily Star	819,232	Pro-EU
The Sun	3,447,300	Eurosceptic
National Morning Mid-Market		
Daily Express	967,020	Pro-EU
The Daily Mail	2,401,393	Eurosceptic
National Morning Quality		
The Daily Telegraph	943,635	Eurosceptic
Financial Times	473,588	Pro-EU
The Guardian	394,277	Pro-EU
The Independent	218,710	Pro-EU
The Scotsman	73,151	Pro-EU
The Times	678,508	Eurosceptic

Source: Circulation data from Audit Bureau of Circulation, December 2002.

newspapers such as *The Daily Telegraph* and *The Times* have made particularly important contributions to the development of Eurosceptic thought on the right wing of British politics and provided space for columnists eager to develop these new strands of Conservative thought.

Interest in the press stems from their clear importance to the daily life of the nation, an increased fascination bordering on obsession in the UK with political communication, media management and 'spin doctors', and a sociological interest in the role that newspapers can play in national identity formation. The 'we-feeling' that newspaper reading can invoke was memorably put by Benedict Anderson (1991: 35) when he observed that:

> The significance of the mass ceremony is paradoxical. It is performed in silent privacy in the lair of the skull. Yet each communicant is well aware that the ceremony is being replicated simultaneously by thousands (or millions) of others of whose existence he is confident, yet of whose identity he has not the slightest notion.

Billig (1995) has argued that everyday representations of 'we', 'us' and 'them' communicated on a daily basis by newspapers contribute to what he calls 'banal nationalism'. National newspapers can help develop and sustain national communities. Brookes (1999: 248) argued that one of the key attributes of a national press is the representation of 'the nation as the natural political and cultural unit'. To support this observation, Brookes analyses the BSE and foot and mouth crises to show that both had an 'us' versus 'them' element in the sense that incidents such as the March 1996 EU ban on British beef were turned into arguments about whether EU membership was in Britain's interests because other EU member states were allegedly engaged in dirty tricks to hide the extent of the problems in their own farming sectors while seeking to take advantage of British problems.

Anderson and Weymouth (1998) survey both the pro- and anti-European press to argue that the British press has become more hostile to the EU; that the heavy hand of proprietorial influence has been very influential in the development of these anti-EU lines; and that the EU has contributed to the problem through its own 'great public relations disasters', as Chapter 6 in Anderson and Weymouth's book is entitled. Neil Gavin (2001: 308) criticizes the approach of Anderson and Weymouth who, he argues, implicitly maintain that there are lots of positive stories about the EU, but the press ignore these and focus only on the negative. Some examples of this apparently negative reporting would include an undue focus on the corruption allegations levelled at the Commission in the late 1990s and the Commission's resignation in March 1999, as well as continued focus on the 'democratic deficit' and the threat to national sovereignty and national identity posed by European integration. Gavin argues that many of these stories also correspond with newspaper calculations about stories that are newsworthy. It may well be 'negative' to focus on allegations of corruption levelled at the Commission and these stories may well have been sensationalized, but it is also the case that there were serious allegations made against the Commission that merited attention. Moreover, and this may be one of the more problematic issues for the EU, much of what it does is grey, technical and intangible or difficult to represent in a snappy tabloid-style headline. As Gavin (2001: 309) tellingly puts it, the headlines 'Still no war after fifty years' or 'Europe has brought us peace and prosperity that we might not otherwise have had' are unlikely, while 'Beef war with France, again' is newsworthy and likely to satisfy the sensationalist agenda of the tabloid newspapers that dominate the UK daily market.

Research evidence suggests that the effects of newspapers on public attitudes are questionable, however. Readers may control for political

Table 10.6   Percentage of people paying attention
to news on the European Union

	A lot	A little	None
UK	16	41	41
EU15 Average	20	49	30

Source: Data from *Eurobarometer Standard Report*
(Spring 2002).

bias when reading a newspaper, may select a newspaper because it
accords with their political views, may select a newspaper for entertainment value rather than political analysis, or may well not trust their
newspaper as a source of impartial advice. Evidence points to only limited press effects on public attitudes towards politics and politicians
(Norris *et al.*, 1999). Tables 10.2, 10.3 and 10.4 also demonstrated that
people were more likely to use, prefer and trust television as a source of
information about the EU, which makes it pertinent to ask what effects
television coverage has on public attitudes towards the EU given that
this is the preferred and most trusted of sources.

A threefold distinction can be used when thinking about how these
effects could be assessed (Gavin, 2000: 356–7). First, television can play
an 'agenda-setting' role in the sense that it 'directs the gaze' of the public towards newsworthy issues. Second, there can be 'priming' effects
that go beyond agenda-setting and arise from the ways in which news
coverage can affect public perceptions of the salience of a particular
issue. Finally, there can be 'media dependency' effects when a lack of
direct experience increases the public's reliance on the media. Gavin
(2000: 357) suggests that this media dependency is particularly important because few British people are likely to have direct experience of
the EU and are likely to rely on 'one stage removed' news coverage.

Eurobarometer research suggests that people in the UK are slightly
less inclined to pay attention to news about Europe, which falls into line
with the 'don't know, don't care, not interested' part of British public
attitudes towards the EU, as Table 10.6 shows.

Gavin's (2000) study of media influences on public attitudes towards
the EU focuses on economic news on television (BBC and Independent
Television News) because it is well established that economic news has
important effects on political attitudes while television is a preferred and
relatively well-trusted medium. His research suggests that television
coverage of economic news 'is an unlikely platform for the development
in the UK of European solidarity or identity'. He reaches this conclusion

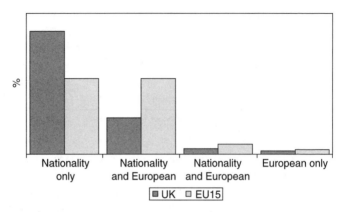

Figure 10.3   Feelings of European and national identity

Source: Data from *Eurobarometer Standard Report* (Spring 2002).

by demonstrating that EU stories on British television news often centre on intra-EU squabbles and conflicts rather than 'Europe versus the world' stories that could inculcate 'we-feeling' among Europeans. Few stories were found that emphasized the civic entitlements that European integration could bring. In such terms, television news reinforces zero-sum ideas of national sovereignty with EU member states arguing across a range of issues in line with their well-established national preferences. The result is that in terms of 'agenda-setting' and 'priming', the public's gaze is not directed towards material benefits of membership and, in terms of 'media dependency' effects, there is little scope for the development of an awareness of rights and entitlements as part of an integrated Europe. The EU is typically represented as 'clashes, disputes and zero-sum games' (although it could be argued that British politics is similarly represented).

These findings are reflected in Figure 10.3, which shows the answers given in the UK in comparison with the EU15 average when people were asked to define their own political identity in either 'national' or 'European' terms. British people appeared to hold a strong 'zero-sum' understanding of national identity (71 per cent responded 'nationality only'), with less perception of the kinds of shared or multiple identities that appear to exist in other EU member states (where on average 44 per cent felt a sense of both national and European identity).

In addition to analysis of the EU coverage in the British press, there has also been criticism of the ways in which the EU engages with journalists. There have been tensions between journalists and EU officials, allegations of ineffective media management and a lack of newsworthy stories. Gavin (2000: 300) argues that 'the image problems faced by the EU are not just a reflection of newspaper proprietor hostility, but stem from more deeply seated difficulties that revolve around the structure of EU institutions and the absence of an integrated, pro-active and professionalised public relations machinery'.

There were some post-Maastricht efforts to sharpen up EU media management skills (Tumber, 1995) but Gavin (2001: 300) identifies the need for developments in four areas. First, proactive liaison between EU officials and the media with more attempts to shape the agenda rather than reacting with clarification, rebuttals or denials to already reported stories. Second, better planning of communication with co-ordination between the various EU institutions and the units within them. Third, communications professionals with the trust of journalists placed close to the executive (although within the EU's 'dual executive' it is not clear what this would mean). Fourth, more effort made to speak with 'one voice'.

The EU does, however, face the rather basic problem that many of the day-to-day issues that it deals with are technical matters which do not lend themselves to the snappy press release. Moreover, the Commission and other institutions do not reflect the Whitehall ethos of co-ordination and information sharing. They accord more closely with coalitional styles in other EU member states where there can be competing interests within and between institutions that make any attempt to speak with one voice rather problematic. In addition to this, there may also be 'cultural' differences between the British press that may revolve around understandings of reporting as either tenacious, vigorous and robust or intrusive, misleading and disrespectful. In addition to these points, it is also worth noting that the EU can be a useful lightning rod when things go wrong. Member states may be quite happy to offload responsibility to Brussels for unpopular measures and let the 'Brussels bureaucrats' take the blame, even though national governments are likely to have been closely involved with decisions. Finally, we can also consider the US influences on British political communication, media management and public relations. The analysis of political communication and the techniques of media management that has been adopted in the UK looks to the USA rather than to Europe. New Labour, for instance, were eager students of President Clinton's political communication techniques and did not look to other EU member states for lessons. While the British media and British political communication appears not to be particularly Europeanized, the EU has not been noticeably 'Anglicized' either.

Conclusions

This chapter's analysis of British public attitudes towards the EU has shown that the British public combine scepticism about Europe with high self-declared levels of lack of knowledge about the EU and its workings. ' "Don't know", "don't understand" and "don't trust" would appear to be the mantra when looking at the EU' (CEC, 2002c: 24). The UK also has powerful Eurosceptic voices in the press and much EU coverage has been strongly negative. Research suggests that direct effects of press coverage on public attitudes are limited. Effects might be subtler if they reinforced understandings of the 'naturalness' of the 'imagined national community', and also reinforced zero-sum understandings of national identity.

Television is the preferred and most trusted source of information about the EU. Studies of television coverage of European economic news suggest that coverage tends to reinforce the idea of European integration as a zero-sum game, perhaps reflecting the UK's own 'winner takes all' political system. Such coverage is not likely to be fertile ground for the development of 'we-feeling' that is important to the construction of European identity.

In the UK neither public opinion nor the media industries appear to be particularly Europeanized. People in Britain appear not to feel particularly European or to identify strongly with the EU while the structures of the UK's media industries, political communication and public relations seem Americanized rather than Europeanized. At the same time, EU institutional structures appear unlikely to lend themselves too easily to the forms of political communication that have become prevalent in the UK since the 1990s.

11

Conclusions: The European Union and British Politics Assessed

Introduction

No account of political change in Britain can ignore the ways in which European integration works its way into the nooks and crannies of British political life. For more than 30 years 'Europe' has become institutionalized as a core concern of the British state with important effects on political actors, the strategic environment within which they operate, and the various elements that need to be accounted for when political change in Britain is assessed. This book has sought to account for these effects, for the changes that European integration has brought about in British politics, and has endeavoured to weigh these developments alongside other causes of change.

The analysis has centred on Britain's *conditional* and *differential* engagement with European integration. The roots of this conditional and differential engagement were traced to decisions made about Britain's place in Europe and the world after the Second World War. Decisions made at this time have had important structuring effects on political outcomes ever since because they ordered the strategic environment within which politicians have operated. To return to the historical institutional analogy used in Chapter 2, choices made after the Second World War can be likened to a tree from which have grown over the last 50 years three strong branches of Britain's European policy. Even though the EU has developed considerably since the 1950s while the British state has undergone major changes, they still remain identifiable aspects of the contemporary British approach. The first branch is a preference for intergovernmentalism rather than supranationalism, combined with a dislike of federal solutions and a self-consciously pragmatic distrust of grand designs aimed at Europe's *finalité*. The second branch is in the realm of the international political economy and marked by a preference for global free trade, which has brought with it since the 1980s a consistent support for market liberalization that unites Conservative and Labour governments. The third branch is the continued emphasis placed on the Atlantic alliance as a core British interest. This tree and its three strong branches have been consistent elements of Britain's European policy.

The book then developed its analysis of Britain's conditional and differential engagement by distinguishing between two analytical themes that each explored the ways in which Britain has participated in the EU and the ways in which the EU has then impacted on British politics. First, a *Britain in Europe* theme assessed Britain's role in European integration through analysis of relationships with developing processes of integration since the 1950s with other member states and with EU institutions. This involved thinking about the ways in which national policy preferences in the UK have been pursued at European level since the 1940s. Second, a *Europe in Britain* theme allowed examination of the 'Europeanization' of British politics and the ways in which European integration has been absorbed as a concern in domestic politics and the effects on laws, institutions, policies and collective identities. A number of questions were raised in the book's first chapter, to which we now return.

What factors have motivated British policy towards the European Union?

The underlying issues here are the continuities and changes in British relations with Europe during more than 30 years of membership. Have there been major variations in British relations with the EU, or can strong continuities be detected? It has been argued that there are strong core elements – the three branches referred to in the previous section – that continue to have important structuring effects on British relations with the EU. Preferences for intergovernmentalism, market liberalization and Atlanticism can frustrate any attempt by British governments to locate themselves at the heart of Europe because any such move could compromise these underlying preferences that have been central to the British state's perception of itself and its place in the world during the post-war period.

New Labour in power provides a good test of the continued resonance of these branches of Britain's European policy. Beneath Blair's genuine pro-EU beliefs and his call for 'constructive engagement' rest a series of well-engrained national preferences that are not so readily moulded into a policy stance that facilitates any move to the heart of Europe. The three strong branches of British European policy mean that it has been difficult to characterize Britain's commitment to Europe as amounting to full-hearted consent. There is too much equivocation, too much doubt about where Britain's interests lie, and too much deep-rooted reluctance (bordering sometimes on scepticism) for the aspiration for 'ever closer union' to be an objective that lies close to the heart of many in Britain's political elite or general public.

Have British governments possessed the capacity to turn preferences into European Union priorities?

Given that equivocation and doubt have characterized British relations with the EU then this does not appear to provide a propitious setting for the translation of British preferences into EU priorities. Indeed, the three branches of British European policy have proved difficult to accommo-date by core EU member states since at least the 1960s. If we look at the scope, direction, form and content of European integration since the mid-1980s then the development of forms of deeper integration and a shift into areas of high politics can be detected that did not necessarily coincide with British interests expressed in the run-up to these negotia-tions, but that require British accommodation with their central objec-tives once they are adopted and implemented. Moreover, there has also been an integrative dynamic led by other member states and supported by key EU institutions (such as the Commission and Court of Justice) that has sometimes aroused suspicion in the UK, particularly in the Eurosceptic right who fear a secret federalizing agenda and are willing to proclaim the bad faith of EU partners.

A core test of whether Britain can turn preferences into EU priorities (i.e, upload its domestic agenda) will be proposals for European economic reform (and, linked to this, membership of the Euro). The UK has sought to upload preferences for market liberalization into a pan-EU agenda of economic reform. It has become increasingly clear as the Euro debate has developed that the perceived capacity of the British government to make and win arguments about its vision of economic reform and modernization in Europe is central to wholehearted engagement with the EU's defining feature, the single currency and EMU.

Have British governments been particularly effective players of the European Union game?

The evidence accumulated over more than 30 years of British membership is that Britain has not always been a particularly effective player of the EU game. At the most basic level, the UK has spent nearly half of its time as an EU member in dispute with other member states (renegotiation in the 1970s, the budget in the early 1980s, the Maastricht saga and Conservative Euroscepticism in the 1990s). One reason for this is that membership in the 1970s was not based on wholehearted conversion to the merits of supranational European integration. Another is that the 'EU game' requires rather different skills from those required in the winner takes all UK system. The EU centres on coalition building, compromise, deal making and the search for consensus. Not surprisingly these were anathema to Margaret Thatcher, the arch conviction politician. As it became ever more clear that other EU leaders did not share her convictions (and neither, it must be said, did key members of her own government) her distaste for the EC grew concomitantly.

Moreover, the capacity to win arguments at EU level can depend on the maintenance of a stable domestic coalition. Between 1988 and 1997, UK governments were wracked by divisions over Europe, which made the development of a consistent EU policy well nigh impossible. The Major government was predictably unpredictable to its EU partners while peering anxiously over its shoulder at the turmoil within the Conservative parliamentary party. This was not the strongest position to be in while engaged in complex intergovernmental negotiations. Tony Blair was able to heal some of these fractured relations, not least because his crushing parliamentary majority marginalized the small number of Eurosceptic voices in his parliamentary party. Yet Blair's dilemma is that while he has been able to make the case for Britain in Europe (although the war in Iraq fractured some relationships), he has not been able to make the case for Europe in Britain. Even as the most instinctively pro-European Prime Minister since Edward Heath (although the competition is not exactly tough) there has been a noticeable reluctance to advance the pro-European cause, particularly the case for the Euro. It is here that the book's analysis switched to the Europe in Britain theme and assessed the ways in which European integration has been incorporated as a core concern in British politics.

What impact has European integration had on the organization of the British political system?

The intra-state dimension of Europeanization is the issue at stake when exploring the effects of European integration on the organization of the British political system. Rather than simply absorbing European integration's effects and prompting uni-directional change driven by European integration, it was argued that the British political system (like those in other member states) will refract these effects in accordance with the standard operating practices and animating ideas of the domestic process. It is necessary to distinguish Europe's effects on the British political system from other sources of political change. The EU's impact on Whitehall, Westminster and devolved government were all explored and various explanations for change explored. It was shown that a well-established Whitehall ethos was the template on which the adaptation of British central government to European integration was based and that, despite the substantial changes which European integration has brought with it, this Whitehall ethos based on co-ordination, collective responsibility and information sharing remains strong, supplemented by an emphasis on effective transposition into UK law of agreed policies. Europe's impact on devolved government since 1997 was set against the impetus from a domestic constitutional reform agenda driven in the main by domestic politics, although the EU's structural funds have created new political opportunities for regional and sub-national government and contributed to their post-1997 flowering. There has been no well-established template from which regional and sub-national governmental responses to European integration could draw because these were new issues for the British state. This causes some tensions between the EU's multiple levels and the UK's asymmetrical process of devolution. Important questions remain unresolved about the role and function of these sub-national tiers of government in Britain's EU policy.

Some of the most tumultuous EU-related events have occurred in the legislative arena. The main divisions over Europe have occurred within rather than between the main parties. Anti-European integration sentiment has evolved from the anti-marketeers of the 1960s and 1970s into a distinct brand of (mainly) right-wing and Conservative Euroscepticism since the 1990s. Although the issues of Maastricht and the Euro have engaged the political class rather more than they did the general public, arguments about Europe were flushed out into the open and Eurosceptics (supported by key sections of the press) developed a powerful critique of the EU. The key drivers of this Euroscepticism were the EU's move into areas of high politics (EMU and the Maastricht Treaty, in particular) in the late 1980s and early 1990s, coupled with the small parliamentary majority of John Major's Conservative government between 1992 and 1997.

To what extent do British policy priorities and the organization of the British economy and welfare state fit with those in other member states and with an emerging European Union model?

The question of the Europeanization of British politics does, of course, extend beyond the arena of Whitehall and Westminster. It also touches upon core socio-economic priorities. A series of core EU policy issues were explored, and a varied pattern of adaptation and change was found, although it was also seen that Britain's late membership meant that key policy priorities were established in the UK's absence and were not necessarily to the UK's advantage. This was then the basis for wrangling as the UK sought a better deal from other member states (with their own interests tied up with these policy choices) which were not always disposed to accommodate UK demands. Underlying these policy debates has been a branch of UK European policy that prefers free trade and market liberalization. The UK economy has become more closely linked with the EU since accession, although this has not necessarily generated demands for 'more Europe' in the way that straightforward transactional approaches might suggest. Rather, there remains a perception that the UK socio-economic approach is different even in the face of greater concentration of economic activity within the EU. These developments motivated the desire of the Thatcher governments to raise economic liberalization to a European level through the single market programme and, more recently, New Labour's links between British participation in the Euro and economic reform that mirrors UK emphasis on liberalization and labour market flexibility (and look to the US as an example of good practice). This 'Anglo-Saxon' approach seems as likely to engender suspicion as it does support in other member states, while illustrating New Labour's move away from mainstream social democratic thinking.

In what directions have public attitudes towards the European Union developed and what part has the mass media played in shaping these views?

Public opinion data shows Britain to be the 'don't know, not interested and don't trust' capital of the EU. These attitudes and the factors under-pinning them were the subject of Chapter 10, which examined public opinion and the media representation of Europe. It was shown that while it is difficult to make straightforward links between press coverage and public opinion, coverage of the EU has become particularly negative since the early 1990s. It was shown that media representation of Europe in the UK (particularly television and newspaper coverage) are unlikely to support the development of 'we-feeling' often seen as necessary for the development of European identity. The result is that collective identities in the UK do not appear to be particularly Europeanized and there is little space for Europe, while UK forms of political communication are Americanized rather than Europeanized. Indeed, it is not clear what a European form of political communication would involve given the diverse national models and the often rather technical (and thus difficult to represent) core purposes of the EU.

In search of a critical juncture

The arguments developed in this book have explored the ways in which there has been a historical institutional patterning of Britain's relations with the EU. Reluctance, awkwardness and semi-detachment have been based on the three well-established branches of policy. The effects of historical choices on the interests and identities of political actors are fairly well-entrenched components of the strategic environment within which they operate. In such circumstances, it can be easier to explain institutional persistence than it is to account for political change.

In the light of these circumstances, what predictions can be made about future engagement with the EU and its core projects? Of these core projects, the Euro stands out as particularly important. Trying to detect the UK government's approach is akin to advanced forms of Kremlinology as subtle shifts in positions are spun in the national newspapers and inside sources provide accounts of the attitudes of the two key players (Brown and Blair). While the criteria for accession are economic, the real decision is intensely political and will be a defining moment in the history of New Labour in power. Whether or not the decision is taken in the lifetime of the Parliament elected in 2001 to have a referendum on the Euro remains an open question.

There is, however, a deeper issue. The UK has spent much of the last 30 years running to catch up with the other member states. The cognitive readjustment that EU membership requires has been filtered through a domestic context and underlying EU preferences that have militated against active and full-hearted participation in key EU ventures. The result is that the debate about Britain and the Euro is another example of the difficulty that the British political class has found in adjusting to European integration. As one adjustment occurs then the pace of economic and political integration means that others are required (the Convention, reforms of institutions, the impact of enlargement all loom on the horizon too). Thus whether Britain replaces the pound with the Euro is the current manifestation of a deeper, underlying trend in relations between British politics and European integration. These centre on the three core elements of Britain's European policy (intergovernmentalism, market liberalization, Atlanticism), which have not always rested well with the EU's core purposes. If we accept that Britain's future lies with the EU (and no British government since accession has thought otherwise) then either Europe becomes more British, or Britain needs to become more European. Either way, Europe will remain a core dilemma at the heart of British politics that forces us to think about the underlying, organizing principles of the British political system and their expression in current debates about Britain's place in the world.

Bibliography

Anderson, B. (1991) *Imagined Communities: Reflections on the Origin and Spread of Nationalism* (London: Verso).

Anderson, P. and Weymouth, A. (1998) *Insulting the Public? The British Press and the European Union* (London: Longman).

Aspinwall, M. (2000) 'Structuring Europe: Powersharing Institutions and British Preferences on European Integration', *Political Studies*, 48 (3), 415–42.

Aspinwall, M. (2003) 'Britain and Europe: Some Alternative Economic Tests', *Political Quarterly*, 74 (2), 146–57.

Bache, I. (1998) *The Politics of European Union Regional Policy: Multi-Level Governance or Flexible Gate-Keeping* (Sheffield: Sheffield Academic Press).

Baker, D. (2002) 'Britain and Europe: More Blood on the Euro Carpet', *Parliamentary Affairs*, 55 (2), 317–30.

Baker, D., Gamble, A. and Ludlam, S. (1993a) '1846...1906...1996? Conservative Splits and European Integration', *Political Quarterly*, 64 (2), 420–35.

Baker, D., Gamble, A. and Ludlam, S. (1993b) 'Whips or Scorpions? The Maastricht Vote and the Conservative Party', *Parliamentary Affairs*, 46 (2), 151–66.

Baker, D., Gamble, A. and Ludlam, S. (1994) 'The Parliamentary Siege of Maastricht 1993: Conservative Divisions and British Ratification', *Parliamentary Affairs*, 47 (1), 37–59.

Baker, D., Gamble, A. and Ludlam, S. (2002) 'Sovereign Nations and Global Markets: Modern British Conservatism and Hyperglobalism', *British Journal of Politics and International Relations*, 4 (3), 399–428.

Balls, E. (2002) 'Why the Five Economic Tests', The Cairncross Lecture, St Peters College, Oxford, 4 December 2002.

Bauman, Z. (2002) *Society Under Siege* (Cambridge: Polity).

Beloff, M. (1970) *The Intellectual in Politics and Other Essays* (London: Weidenfeld & Nicolson).

Bennie, L., Curtice, J. and Rudig, W. (1995) 'Liberal, Social Democrat or Liberal Democrat? Political identity and British centre party politics', in D. Broughton *et al.* (eds), *British Elections and Parties Yearbook 1994* (London: Frank Cass).

Billig, M. (1995) *Banal Nationalism* (London: Sage).

Black, I. (2002) 'How The Sun Cast a Two-Faced Shadow on the Euro-Zone', *The Guardian*, 8 January.

Blair, T. (2000) 'Speech at Ghent City Hall', 20 February 2000.

Blair, T. (2003) 'Speech at the Foreign Office Conference', 7 January 2003, http://www.number10.gov.uk/output/Page1765.asp

Boland, M. (1999) 'Urban Governance and Economic Development: A Critique of Merseyside and Objective One Status', *European Urban and Regional Studies*, 7 (3), 211–22.

Börzel, T. (2002) 'Member State Reponses to Europeanization', *Journal of Common Market Studies*, 40 (2), 193–214.

Bosco, A. (ed.) (1991) *The Federal Idea: The History of Federalism from the Enlightenment to 1945* (London: Lothian Foundation Press).

Brookes, M. (1999) 'Newspapers and National Identity: The BSE/CJD Crisis and the British Press', *Media, Culture and Society*, 21 (2), 247–63.

Buchan, D. (1993) *Europe: The Strange Superpower* (Aldershot: Dartmouth).

Bull, H. (1979) *The Anarchical Society: A Study of Order in World Politics* (London: Macmillan).

Buller, J. (2000) *National Statecraft and European Integration: The Conservative Government and the European Union 1979–97* (London: Pinter).

Bulmer, S. (1983) 'Domestic politics and European Community decision-making', *Journal of Common Market Studies*, 21 (4), 349–63.

Bulmer, S. and Burch, M. (1998) 'Organizing for Europe: The British State and the European Union', *Public Administration*, 76 (4), 601–28.

Bulmer, S. and Wessels, W. (1987) *The European Council: Decision-Making in European Politics* (London: Macmillan).

Bulpitt, J. (1996) 'Federalism', in I. McLean (ed.), *The Oxford Concise Dictionary of Politics* (Oxford: Oxford University Press).

Burch, M. and Gomez, R. (2002) 'The English Regions and the European Union', *Regional Studies*, 36 (7), 767–78.

Burch, M. and Holliday, I. (1993) 'Institutional Emergence: The Case of the North West Region of England', *Regional Politics & Policy*, 3 (2), 29–50.

Burch, M. and Holliday, I. (1996) *The British Cabinet System* (London: Prentice Hall).

Burgess, M. (1986) *Federalism and Federation in Western Europe* (London: Croon Helm).

Butler, D. and Kitzinger, U. (1976) *The 1975 Referendum* (London: Macmillan).

Camilleri, J. and Falk, J. (1992) *The End of Sovereignty· The Politics of a Shrinking and Fragmenting World* (Aldershot: Edward Elgar).

Camps, M. (1964) *Britain and the European Community 1955–63* (London: Oxford University Press).

Caporaso, J. (1996) 'The EU and Forms of State: Westphalian, Regulatory or Post-Modern?, *Journal of Common Market Studies*, 34 (1), 29–52.

Capotori, F. (1983) 'Supranational Organizations', in R. Bernhardt (ed.), *Encyclopaedia of Public International Law* (Elsevier: Amsterdam).

CIE (1999a) *First Report on Allegations Regarding Fraud, Mismanagement and Nepotism in the European Commission*, http://www.europarl.eu.int/experts/default_en.htm

CIE (1999b) *Second Report on Reform of the Commission: Analysis of Current Practice and Proposals for Tackling Mismanagement, Irregularities and Fraud*, http://www.europarl.eu.int/experts/default_en.htm

Cini, M. (1996) *The European Commission: Leadership, Organisation and Culture in the EU Administration* (Manchester: Manchester University Press).

Clift, B. (2001) 'New Labour's Third Way and European Social Democracy', in M. Smith and S. Ludlam, *New Labour in Power* (London: Macmillan, now Palgrave Macmillan).

Cohen, B. (1998) *The Geography of Money* (Ithaca, NY: Cornell University Press).

Colley, L. (1992) *Britons: Forging the Nation* (New Haven, CT: Yale University Press).

CEC (2002a) The EU Economy 2002 Review (Brussels: OOPEC). CEC (2002b) *Mid Term Review of the Common Agricultural Policy,* COM(2002) 394 final.

CEC (2002c) *Eurobarometer: Public Opinion in the European Union* (Brussels: Directorate General Press and Communication).

Committee for the Study of Economic and Monetary Union (1989) *Report on Economic and Monetary Union in the European Community* (Luxembourg: Office for the Official Publication of the European Communite).

Cowley, P. (1997) 'The Conservative Party: Decline and Fall', in A. Geddes and J. Tonge (eds), *Labour's Landslide: The 1992 British General Election* (Manchester: Manchester University Press).

Cram, L. (1994) 'The European Commission as a Multi-Organisation: Social Policy and IT Policy in the EU', *Journal of European Public Policy*, 1 (2), 195–217.

Cram, L. (2000) 'The Commission', in L. Cram, D. Dinan and N. Nugent, *Developments in the EU* (London: Macmillan).

Curry, D. (2002) *Farming and Food: A Sustainable Future* (London: Cabinet Office).

Duchêne, F. (1994) *Jean Monnet: The First Statesman of Interdependence* (New York: Norton).

Dyson, K. (2000) 'Europeanization, Whitehall Culture and the Treasury as Institutional Veto Player: A Constructivist Approach to Economic and Monetary Union', *Public Administration*, 78 (4), 897–914.

Easton, D. (1965) *A Framework for Political Analysis* (Englewood Cliffs, NJ: Prentice Hall).

Edwards, G. (1993) 'Britain and Europe', in J. Story (ed.), *The New Europe: Politics, Economy and Government Since 1945* (Oxford: Basil Blackwell).

Ellison, J. (2000) *Threatening Europe: Britain and the Creation of the European Community 1955–58* (London: Macmillan).

Fairbrass, J. and Jordan, A. (2001) 'European Union environmental policy and the UK government: a passive observer or a strategic manager?', *Environmental Politics*, 10 (2), 1–21.

Fella, S. (2002) *New Labour and the European Union: Political Strategy, Policy Transition and the Amsterdam Treaty Negotiations* (Aldershot: Ashgate).

Fieldhouse, E., McAllister, I. and Russell, A. (2004) *Neither Left Nor Right but Forward: The Electoral Politics of the Liberal Democrats* (Manchester: Manchester University Press).

Fielding, S. (2002a) *The Labour Party: Continuity and Change in the Making of New Labour* (Basingstoke: Palgrave Macmillan).

Fielding, S. (2002b) 'No-one Else to Vote For? Labour's Campaign', in A. Geddes and J. Tonge (eds), *Labour's Second Landslide: The 2002 British General Election* (Manchester: Manchester University Press).

Forster, A. (2002a) 'Anti-Europeans, Anti-Marketeers and Eurosceptics: The Evolution and Influence of Labour and Conservative Opposition to Europe', *Political Quarterly*, 73 (3), 299–308.

Forster, A. (2002b) *Euroscepticism in Contemporary British Politics: Opposition to Europe in the British Conservative and Labour Parties Since 1945* (London: Routledge).

Forsyth, M. (1986) *Unions of States: The Theory and Practice of Confederation* (Leicester: Leicester University Press).

Franklin, B. (1994) *Packaging Politics: Political Communication in Britain's Media Democracy* (London: Edward Arnold).

Franklin, M., Marsh, M. and McLaren, L. (1994) 'Uncorking the Bottle: Popular Opposition to European Unification in the Wake of Maastricht', *Journal of Common Market Studies*, 32 (4), 455–72.

Gabel, M. (1998) *Interests and Integration: Market Liberalization, Public Opinion and European Integration* (Ann Arbor, MI: University of Michigan Press).

Gamble, A. (1988) *The Free Economy and the Strong State: The Politics of Thatcherism* (London: Macmillan).

Gamble, A. (1998) 'The European Issue in British Politics', in D. Baker and D. Seawright (eds), *Britain For and Against Europe. British Politics and the Question of European Integration* (Oxford: Clarendon Press).

Gamble, A. (2003) *Between Europe and America: The Future of British Politics* (Basingstoke: Palgrave Macmillan).

Gamble, A. and Kelly, G. (2000) 'The British Labour Party and Monetary Union', *West European Politics*, 23 (1), 1–25.

Gardiner, G. (1999) *A Bastard's Tale: The Political Memoirs of George Gardiner* (London: Aurum).

Garton Ash, T. (2001) 'Is Britain European?', *International Affairs*, 77 (1), 1–14.

Gavin, N. (2000) 'Imagining Europe: Political Identity and British Television Coverage of the European Economy', *British Journal of Politics and International Relations*, 2 (3), 352–73.

Gavin, N. (2001) 'British Journalists in the Spotlight: Europe and Media Research', *Journalism*, 2 (3), 299–314.

Geddes, A. (1997) 'Europe: Major's Nemesis', in A. Geddes and J. Tonge (eds), *Labour's Landslide: The 1997 British General Election* (Manchester: Manchester University Press).

Geddes, A. (2000) *Immigration and European Integration: Towards Fortress Europe?* (Manchester: Manchester University Press).

Geddes, A. (2002) 'In Europe, not interested in Europe', in A. Geddes and J. Tonge (eds), *Labour's Second Landslide: The British General Election 2001* (Manchester: Manchester University Press).

Geddes, A. (2003) *The Politics of Migration and Immigration in Europe* (London: Sage).

Geddes, A. and Guiraudon, V. (2004) 'The emergence of an EU policy paradigm amidst competing national models: Britain, France and EU anti-discrimination policy', *West European Politics*, 26 (4).

Geddes, A. and Tonge, J. (1997) *Labour's Landslide: The 1997 British General Election* (Manchester: Manchester University Press).

Geddes, A. and Tonge, J. (2002) *Labour's Second Landslide: The 2002 British General Election* (Manchester: Manchester University Press).

George, S. (ed.) (1992) *Britain and the European Community: The Politics of Semi-Detachment* (Oxford: Oxford University Press).

George, S. (1998) *An Awkward Partner: Britain in the European: Britain in the European Community*, 3rd edn (Oxford: Oxford University Press).

Geyer, R. (2000) *Exploring European Social Policy* (Oxford: Basil Blackwell).

Golub, J. (1996) 'British sovereignty and the development of EC environmental policy', *Environmental Politics*, 5 (4), 700–28.

Gorman, T. (1993) *The Bastards: Dirty Tricks and the Challenge to Europe* (London: Pan Books).

Gowland, D. A. and Turner, A. (2000) *Reluctant Europeans: Britain and European Integration 1945–1998* (Harlow: Longman).

Grant, W. (1997) *The Common Agricultural Policy* (London: Macmillan).

Green Cowles, M., Caporaso, J. and Risse, T. (eds) (2000) *Transforming Europe: Europeanization and Domestic Change* (Ithaca, NY: Cornell University Press).

Haas, E. (1958) *The Uniting of Europe: Political, Economic and Social Forces* (Standford, CA: Stanford University Press).

Haas, E. (1971) 'The Study of Regional Integration: Reflections on the Joy and Anguish of Pre-Theorizing', in L. Lindberg and S. Scheingold (eds), *European Integration: Theory and Research* (Englewood Cliffs, NJ: Prentice Hall).

Hague, W. (2001) Speech to the Conservative Party Spring Forum', Harrogate, 4 March 2001.

Harris, R. (ed.) (1997) *The Collected Speeches of Margaret Thatcher* (London: Harper Collins).

Hay, C. and Rosamond, B. (2002) 'Globalization, European Integration and the Discursive Construction of Economic Imperatives', *Journal of European Public Policy*, 9 (2), 147–67.

Hayes-Renshaw, F. (1999) 'The European Council and the Council of Ministers', in L. Cram, D. Dinan and N. Nugent (eds), *Developments in the European Union* (London: Macmillan).

Hayes-Renshaw, F. and Wallace, H. (1997) *The Council of Ministers* (London: Macmillan).

Hazell, R. (2003) 'Introduction: The Dynamism of Devolution in its Third Year', in R. Hazell (ed.), *The State of the Nations 2003: The Third Year of Devolution in the United Kingdom* (London: Imprint Academic).

Heath, E. (1998) *The Course of My Life: My Autobiography* (London: Hodder & Stoughton).

Heffernan, R. (2002) 'Beyond Euro-scepticism: Explaining the Europeanisation of the Labour Party Since 1983', *Political Quarterly*, 72 (2), 180–9.

HM Government (1984) 'Europe: The Future', *Journal of Common Market Studies*, 23 (1), 74–81.

HM Treasury (2001) *European Economic Reform: Meeting the Challenge* (London: HM Treasury).

HM Treasury (2002) *European Community Finances: Statement on the 2002 EU Budget and Measures to Counter Fraud and Mismanagement* (London: HM Treasury).

Hirst, P. and Thompson, G. (1996) *Globalization in Question: The International Economy and the Possibilities of Governance* (Cambridge: Polity Press).

Hix, S. (1999) *The Political System of the European Union* (London: Macmillan).

Hix, S. (2000) 'Britain, the EU and the Euro', in P. Dunleavy, A. Gamble, I. Holliday and G. Peele (eds), *Developments in British Politics 6* (London: Macmillan, now Palgrave Macmillan).

Hobsbawm, E. and Ranger, T. (1983) *The Invention of Tradition* (Cambridge: Cambridge University Press).

Hoffmann, S. (1966) 'Obstinate or Obsolete: The Fate of the Nation State and the Case of Western Europe', *Daedalus*, 95, 892–908.

Holliday, I. (2000) 'Is the British State Hollowing Out?', *Political Quarterly*, 71 (2), 167–76.

Holliday, I. and Vickerman, R. (1990) 'The Channel Tunnel and Regional Development: Policy Responses in Britain and France', *Regional Studies*, 24 (5), 455–66.

Hooghe, L. (1997) 'Serving "Europe": Political Orientation of Senior Commission Officials', *European Integration On-Line Papers*, http://eiop.or.at/eiop/texte/1997–008a.htm

Hooghe, L. (1999) 'Images of Europe: Orientations to European Integration among Senior Officials of the Commission', *British Journal of Political Science*, 29 (3), 345–67.

Hooghe, L. (2001) *The European Commission and the Integration of Europe: Images of Governance* (Cambridge: Cambridge University Press).

Horrie, C. (2000) Method in Blair's tabloid outburst', BBC News On-Line, 24 November 2000, http://news.bbc.co.uk/1/hi/uk/1037551.stm

Howe, G. (1995) *Conflict of Loyalty* (London: Pan).

Howorth, J. (2000) *European Integration and Defence: The Ultimate Challenge* (Paris: Institute for Security Studies, West European Union).

Hughes, K. and Smith, E. (1998) 'New Labour, New Europe?', *International Affairs*, 74 (1), 93–103.

Jacobs, F., Corbett, R. and Shackleton, M. (2000) *The European Parliament* (London: John Harper).

Jeffrey, C. (2000) 'Sub-National Mobilization and European Integration: Does It Make Any Difference?', *Journal of Common Market Studies*, 38 (1), 1–23.

Jenkins, R. (1991) *A Life at the Centre* (London: Macmillan).

Jessop, R. (1994) 'Post-Fordism and the State', in A. Amin (ed.), *Post-Fordism* (Oxford: Basil Blackwell).

Jordan, A. (2000) *The Europeanisation of UK Environmental Policy 1970–2000: A Departmental Perspective*, School of Environmental Science Working Paper No. 11/00, University of East Anglia.

Jordan, A. and Fairbrass, J. (2001) 'European Union environmental policy after the Nice summit', *Environmental Politics*, 10 (4), 109–14.

Kagan, R. (2002) 'Power and Weakness', *Policy Review*, http://www.policyrview.org/JUN02/kagan.html

Kaiser, W. (1996) *Using Europe, Abusing the Europeans: Britain and European Integration 1945–63* (New York: St Martins Press).

Kaufman, G. (1980) *How to be a Minister* (London: Sidgwick & Jackson).

Keegan, W. (2003) 'Who wants to go down in history?', *The Observer*, 5 January 2003.

Keohane, R. and Hoffmann, S. (eds) (1991) *The New European Community: Decision-Making and Institutional Change* (Boulder, CO: Westview).

King, A. (1977) *Britain Says Yes. The 1975 Referendum on the Common Market* (Washington, DC: American Enterprise Institute).

Koopmans, T. (1992) 'Federalism: The Wrong Debate', Guest Editorial, *Common Market Law Review*, 29 (6), 1,047–52.

Laffan, B. (1992) *Integration and Co-operation in Europe* (London: Routledge).

Laffan, B. (1997) *The Finances of the European Union* (London: Macmillan).

Lambert, J. and Hoskyns, C. (2000) 'How Democratic is the European Parliament', in C. Hoskyns and M. Newman (eds), *Democratizing the European Union: Issues for the Twenty First Century* (Manchester: Manchester University Press).

Lamont, N. (1997) *In Office* (London: Warner Books).

Lenschow, A. (ed.) (2001) *Environmental Policy Integration: Greening Sectoral Policies in Europe* (London: Earthscan).

Leonard, M. (2000) *Britain™: Renewing Our Identity* (London: Demos).

Levi, M. (1997) 'A model, a method and a map: rational choice in comparative and historical analysis', in M. Lichbach and A. Zuckerman (eds) *Comparative Politics: Rationality, Culture and Structure* (Cambridge: Cambridge University Press), pp.19–41.

Lowe, P. and Ward, S. (eds) (1998) *British Environmental Policy and Europe* (London: Routledge).

Ludlam, S. (1998) 'The Cauldron: Conservative Parliamentarians and European Integration', in D. Baker and D. Seawright (eds), *Britain For and Against Europe: British Politics and the Question of European Integration* (Oxford: Clarendon Press).

Majone, G. (1996) *Regulating Europe* (London: Routledge).

Major, J. (1999) *John Major: The Autobiography* (London: HarperCollins).

Manners, I. (2002) 'Normative Power Europe: A Contradiction in Terms', *Journal of Common Market Studies*, 40 (2), 235–58.

Marsh, D., Richards, D. and Smith, M. (2001) *Changing Patterns of Governance in the UK: Reinventing Whitehall?* (Basingstoke: Palgrave).

Metcalfe, L. (2000) 'Reforming the Commission', *Journal of Common Market Studies*, 38 (5), 817–41.

Milward, A. (1992) *The European Rescue of the Nation State* (London: Routledge).

Mitchell, J. (2002) 'England and the Centre', *Regional Studies,* 36 (7), 757–65.

Mitrany, D. (1943) *A Working Peace System* (London: Royal Institute for International Affairs).

Moravcsik, A. (1994) *Why the European Union Strengthens the State: Domestic Politics and International Co-operation*, Harvard Centre for European Studies Working Paper series No. 52, http://www.ces.fas.harvard.edu/working_papers/Moravcsik52.pdf

Morgan, K. (1997) *Callaghan: A Life* (Oxford: Oxford University Press).

Naughtie, J. (2001) *The Rivals: The Intimate Story of a Political Marriage* (London: Fourth Estate).

Norris, P., Curtice, J., Sanders, D., Scammell, M. and Semetko, H. (1999) *On Message: Communicating the Campaign* (London: Sage).

Nugent, N. (1999) *The Government and Politics of the European Union* (London: Macmillan).

Page, E. (1997) *People Who Run Europe* (Oxford: Clarendon Press).

Page, E. (1998) 'The Impact of European Legislation on British Public Policy Making: A Research Note', *Public Administration*, 76 (4), 803–9.

Page, E. and Wouters, L. (1995) 'The Europeanization of the National Bureaucracies', in J. Pierre (ed.), *Bureaucracy in the Modern State: An Introduction to Comparative Public Administration* (Aldershot: Edward Elgar).

Page, E. and Wright, V. (eds) (1999) *Bureaucratic Elites in Western European States: A Comparative Analysis of Top Officials* (Oxford: Oxford University Press).

Pentland, C. (1973) *International Theory and European Integration* (London: Faber & Faber).

Pierson, P. (1998) 'The path of European integration: a historical institutionalist analysis', in W. Sandholtz and A. Stone Sweet (eds), *European Integration and Supranational Governance* (Oxford: Oxford University Press).

Pierson, P. (2000) 'Increasing returns, path dependency and the study of politics', *American Political Science Review*, 94 (2), 251–67.

Pinder, J. (1968) 'Positive Integration and Negative Integration: Some Problems of Economic Union in the EEC', *The World Today*, 24 (3), 88–110.

Pollack, M. (1999) 'Delegation, Agency and Agenda-Setting in the Treaty of Amsterdam', *European Integration On-Line Papers*, http://eiop.or.at/eiop/texte/1999-006.htm

Portillo, M. (1998) *Democratic Values and the Currency* (London: Institute for Economic Affairs).

Prodi, R. (2000) *Speech to the European Parliament*, www.europa.eu.int/comm/external_relations/news/02_00/speech_00_41.htm

Radaelli, C. (1999) *Technocracy in the European Union* (London: Longman).

Radaelli, C. (2000) *Whither Europeanization: Concept Stretching and Substantive Change*, European Integration Online Papers, 4 (8), http://eiop.or.at/eiop/texte/2000-008a.htm

Reif, K. and Schmitt, H. (1980) 'Nine National Second Order Elections: A Systematic Framework for the Analysis of European Elections Results', *European Journal of Political Research*, 8 (1), 3–44.

Rhodes, R. (1994) 'The Hollowing Out of the State: The Changing Nature of Public Service in Britain', *Political Quarterly*, 15 (1), 138–51.

Rhodes, R. (1997) *Understanding Governance: Policy Networks, Governance, Reflexivity and Accountability* (Buckingham: Open University Press).

Richardson, J. (1996) *European Union Power and Policy-Making* (London: Routledge).

Riddell, P. (1998) 'EMU and the Press', in A. Duff (ed.), *Understanding the Euro* (London: The Federal Trust).

Risse, T. (2001) 'A European Identity? Europeanization and the Evolution of Nation-State Identities', in M. Green Cowles, J. Caporaso and T. Risse (eds), *Transforming Europe: Europeanization and Domestic Change* (Ithaca, NY: Cornell University Press).

Robins, L. (1979) *The Reluctant Party: Labour and the EC 1961–75* (Ormskirk: G.W. & A. Hesketh).

Rosamond, B. (1998) 'The Integration of Labour? British Trade Union Attitudes to European Integration', in D. Baker and D. Seawright (eds), *Britain For and Against Europe: British Politics and the Question of European Integration* (Oxford: Clarendon Press).

Rosamond, B. (2000) *Theories of European Integration* (London: Macmillan).
Rosamond, B. (2003) *Globalization and the European Union* (Basingstoke: Palgrave Macmillan).
Sandholtz, W. and Stone Sweet, A. (1998) *European Integration and Supranational Governance* (Oxford: Oxford University Press).
Scharpf, F. (1994) *Community and Autonomy: Multi-Level Policy-Making in the European Union* (Florence: European University Institute).
Schmitter, P. (1996) 'Examining the Present Euro-Polity with the Help of Past Theories', in G. Marks, F. Scharpf, P. Schmitter and W. Streeck (eds), *Governance in the European Union* (London: Sage).
Seldon, A. (1997) *John Major: A Political Life* (London: Weidenfeld & Nicolson).
Soames, C. (1972) 'Whitehall into Europe', *Public Administration*, 50 (2), 271–90.
Stephens, P. (1996) *Politics and the Pound: The Conservatives Struggle with Sterling* (London: Macmillan).
Stephens, P. (2001) 'Blair and Europe', *Political Quarterly*, 72 (1), 67–75.
Stevens, A. (2002) *Europeanization and the Administration of the EU*, Queen's Papers on Europeanization, No. 4/2002.
Stevens, A. and Stevens, H. (2000) *Brussels Bureaucrats: The Administration of the European Union* (London: Macmillan).
Stone Sweet, A. and Sandholtz, W. (1998) 'Integration, supranational governance, and the institutionalization of the European polity', in W. Sandholtz and A. Stone Sweet (eds), *European Integration and Supranational Governance* (Oxford: Oxford University Press).
Story, J. (ed), (1993) *The New Europe: Politics, Economy and Government Since 1945* (Oxford: Basil Blackwell).
Taylor, P. (1994) 'Functionalism: The Approach of David Mitrany', in A.J.R. Groom and P. Taylor (eds), *Frameworks for International Co-operation* (London: Pinter).
Thatcher, M. (1993) *The Downing Street Years* (London: HarperCollins).
Tilly, C. (ed.) (1975) *The Formation of National States in Western Europe* (Princeton, NJ: Princeton University Press).
Tugendhat, C. (1986) *Making Sense of Europe* (London: Viking).
Tumber, H. (1995) 'Marketing Maastricht: The EU and News Management', *Media, Culture and Society*, 17 (3), 511–19.
Tyson, A. (2001) 'The negotiation of the European Community Directive on racial discrimination', *European Journal of Migration Law*, 3 (2), 111–229.
Urban, G. (1996) *Diplomacy and Disillusion at the Court of Margaret Thatcher: An Insider's View* (London: I.B. Tauris).
Usherwood, S. (2002) 'Opposition to the European Union in the UK: The Dilemma of Public Opinion and Party Management', *Government and Opposition*, 37 (2), 211–30.
Virilio, P. (2001) *Virilio Live: Selected Interviews with Paul Virilio* (edited by J. Armitage) (Cambridge: Polity).
Wall, S. (2002) 'Insider Interview', *Global Thinking,* Spring 2002 (London: Foreign Policy Centre).
Wallace, H. (1997) 'At Odds with Europe', *Political Studies*, 45 (4), 677–88.
Wallace, H. and Wallace, W. (1973) 'The impact of Community membership on the British machinery of government', *Journal of Common Market Studies*, 11 (4), 243–62.

Wallace, W. (1986) 'What Price Interdependence? Sovereignty and Interdependence In British Politics', *International Affairs*, 62 (3), 357–69.

Wallace, W. (1990) 'Introduction: The Dynamics of European Integration', in W. Wallace (ed.) (London: Pinter/Royal Institute for International Affairs).

Wallace, W. (1991) 'Foreign Policy and National Identity in the United Kingdom', *International Affairs*, 67 (2), 65–80.

Walters, S. (2001) *Tory Wars: The Conservatives in Crisis* (London: Politicos).

Waltz, K. (1979) *Theory of International Politics* (New York: McGraw-Hill).

Warleigh, A. (2003) *Democracy and the European Union: Theory, Practice and Reform* (London: Sage).

Watkins, A. (1991) *A Conservative Coup: The Fall of Margaret Thatcher* (London: Duckworth).

Weigall, D and Stirk, P. (eds) (1992) *The Origins and Development of the European Community* (Leicester: Leicester University Press).

Westlake, M. (1999) *The Council of the European Union* (London: John Harper).

Westlake, M. (2001) *Kinnock: The Biography* (London: Little, Brown).

Wheare, K. (1963) *Federal Government* (Oxford: Oxford University Press).

Wickham Jones, M. (1997) 'How the Conservatives Lost the Economic Argument', in A. Geddes and J. Tonge (eds), *Labour's Landslide: The 1992 British General Election* (Manchester: Manchester University Press).

Wilks, S. (1996) 'Britain and Europe: An Awkward Partner or an Awkward State?', *Politics*, 16 (3), 159–67.

Williams, H. (1998) *Guilty Men: Conservative Decline and Fall 1992–1997* (London: Aurum Press).

Willis, V. (1982) *Britons in Brussels* (London: Policy Studies Institute).

Young, H. (1989) *One of Us: A Biography of Mrs Thatcher* (London: Macmillan).

Young, H. (1999) *This Blessed Plot: Britain and Europe from Churchill to Blair* (London: Papermac).

Young, J. (1993) *Britain and European Unity* (London: Macmillan).

Index

Index

Santer, J. 98, 99, 103
Schengen Agreement 156
Schreyer, M. 99
Schuman Plan 49–51, 61–2
Schuman, R. 49
Scotland 160, 174–6, 216
Scottish Highlands and Islands 177
Scottish identity 27–8
Scottish Parliament 174
Seattle 25
second order elections 119
September 11 terrorist attacks 115
Serbia-Montenegro 39
service provision model 104
Sharpeville massacre 68
Sheinwald, N. 107
Shepherd, R. 194, 203
Shore, P. 75, 188, 189
Silkin, J. 189
Single European Act 1986 15, 35, 74,
    102, 113, 118, 141, 152, 182, 183,
    185, 193, 197, 216
single market 17, 20, 79–82, 93,
    137–40, 185, 193
Smith, J. 92, 187
Smith, M. 164
Soames, N. 162
social and economic cohesion 81, 130,
    141
Social Chapter 16, 86, 87, 90, 102–3,
    142, 202, 206
Social Charter 141
Social Democratic Party (SDP) 2, 77,
    191, 193
social policy 82, 89, 102–3, 141–2,
    185
Socialist Party (France) 80
Solana, J. 154
Sound and Efficient Management
    Programme 103
South West 178
South Yorkshire 177
sovereignty 11, 27, 31, 38–42, 53, 68,
    77, 183–4
Soviet Union 36, 58–9
Spaak, P.-H. 64
Spain 15, 140, 152, 166, 218
'Special Relationship' 5, 28, 68
Spectator, The 198
Spicer, M. 194, 199, 205

Spillover effects 50–1, 61, 82
St Malo 155
Statewatch 115
Stephens, P. 85–6, 88, 151, 212
Sterling
    devaluation 1967 28, 42
    ejection from ERM 1992 142, 200
Stevens, A. 101, 104
Stevens, H. 101
Stockholm Convention, July 1959 66
Story, J. 58
Strasbourg 60
structural funds 175, 177–8, 180, 229
subsidiarity 44–5, 86
sub-national government 6, 23, 32,
    39, 45
sub-national mobilization 176
Sun, The 198, 205, 218
supranationalism 11, 14–15,
    29, 37–8
supremacy of EU law 122
Sweden 18, 66–7, 116
Switzerland 3, 66

Tapsell, P. 194
taxation 138
Taylor, T 186, 194, 203
Tebbit, N. 201
technocracy 96–7
television news 221–2
Thatcher, M.
    1979–83 government 79
    1983–87 government 79
    attitude to globalization 25
    becomes Conservative leader 77
    Becomes Prime Minister 78
    Berlin summit October 1990 83
    Bruges speech 2, 185, 191, 195–7
    Budget rebate 79
    Council of Ministers 83
    creation of the single market 80–2
    Economic and Monetary
        Union 144–5
    English identity 27, 184
    European Commission 83
    Euroscepticism 82–5
    House of Commons 29–30
    Maastricht Treaty 193–9
    national sovereignty 31
    resignation 2